Shetland's Whalers Remember....

Compiled
by
Gibbie Fraser

Published by Gilbert A Fraser in 2001

Shetland's Whalers Remember....

ISBN 0 9541564

First published by Gilbert A Fraser in 2001

Thanks to all those who gave their stories and photos, Tommy Watt for scanning the photos, J R Nicolson for editing and to G P S Peterson for proof reading.

Printed by Nevisprint Ltd, Fort William

FOREWORD

Antarctic Whaling ceased in 1963 and with it went a way of life for many Shetlanders. Jobs at the whaling were many and varied depending on whether you were on the Island of South Georgia itself or a floating factory ship or a whalecatcher perhaps in sight of the coast of Antarctica at times. It was a long way to go for work but, for many, it was whaling or emigration and in that respect it was very important to the economy of Shetland. Some men overwintered on South Georgia and made as much money as they could in order to set up a business or perhaps buy a fishing boat or some other project. There were dangers in all aspects of the job and sadly some men never returned but, for most of those who did, whaling holds a special place in their memories.

This book is a collection of stories from some of the men who were whalers, some of them from before World War II and I hope it will give the reader an insight into what it was like to be a whaler in that far Southern Ocean amid icebergs, gales and fog all those years ago. The stories range from everyday work to the sadness of burial at sea, things going wrong and breakdowns to relaxation and friendships made that have stood the test of time. Gathering material for this book has been interesting, meeting so many fine men and being welcomed into their homes. I am grateful to them all.

If any reader meets an old whaler, shake his hand, buy him a drink and let him tell you about his experiences in the South Ice. You might hear some of the stories that could never be printed!

DEDICATION

This book is dedicated to all the men from Shetland who went to the Antarctic whaling.

CONTENTS

ALEX PETERSON

The best ship that I was ever on in the Salvesen fleet was the *New Sevilla*. She was a most lovely ship. She was a double decker so when you were between decks you could go from for'ard to aft with your slippers on and never saw a drop of blood or anything and yet up on the top they were working the whales. She was a beautiful ship, she had her bridge amidships and the fore and aft plans. On the aft plan you had the spik kettles and on the fore plan were the bone kettles.

The spik was taken off just like peeling an orange. They set in the knives at the top of the shoulder and just ripped the spik off. They took the carcase for'ard under the saws and they cut it up into blocks small enough to go down the kettle and when the kettles were full they boiled it to get the oil out.

I can't mind how long it took but when they were finally cooked and you opened the door down below on the tank there was nothing left but the bits of crusts like dried up loaf and that was all shovelled over the side. The oil had boiled out of the bones. That would have needed to have been kept but they did not have the machinery aboard her at that time.

We just had the one meat plant aboard the *New Sevilla*. When the new factory ships were built, they had their bridge right up for'ard so that they could get in more machinery to grind up this stuff. The stuff which was dumped from the tanks of the *New Sevilla* would have made lovely bone meal but we had no way to do it so it had to be dumped. The new factories were awkward to work because there was more machinery on them and there was not enough room. I did not fancy them at all. The men who went down after me said it was awfully awkward working them, very cramped up with the machinery.

It would have been 1939 and we had just got the convoy into position when the *New Sevilla* was torpedoed. We were about 10 hours out of Liverpool. There were 48 ships in the convoy and only two made Belfast. The first one to be hit was a tanker and she just disappeared completely. We were screened off because we were drawing an awful lot of water. She was a large ship and was taking all the provisions to South Georgia.

She was well over the plimsoll mark which you were not supposed to do. For two days they had lorried steady nothing but beef and mutton - halves of kye and whole sheep. They put out the cargo net on the pier and the truck would come down with the halves of kye and just set the tipper going and the halves of kye would come rumbling down on to the cargo net. They would draw up the four corners of the net and put in the hook off the factory ship and signal to the crane driver and he lifted it and swung it right up on deck. All that had to be dragged down and put in the store in the fridge - a great big fridge which took days to fill. What meat and stuff went in there. All kinds, tinned stuff as well. All that went to the bottom.

With us drawing such a depth of water the submarine could manage to pick us out and let the other ships chug away. There were two ships on the port side and two on the starboard side, one up ahead and one astern. Of course they were just rusty old tramps which had been around for years, red with rust but everything that could float had to go to sea to carry stuff when the war broke out.

The submarine struck us below the funnel. You felt that there was vibration and then of course the alarm bells went and everyone had to get on their lifebelts and get to hell up on deck. When the submarine put the second one into us, it was right into the engine room and that just finished her completely. It put the engine out of order and she was just lying at the mercy of the sea. There had been no right boat drill and some of the Norwegians got in a bit of a panic. They took the axes which were lying at the lifeboats and chopped the falls and the lifeboat fell into the sea with about 30 aboard her. With the speed that she hit, it just laid her in splinters.

We were thrown in the water. We had lifebelts on but, as luck would have it, the lifeboat had tanks aboard her and she came up on her side so we could get a hold on the lifelines along her side. We hung on there until this ship that was standing by the convoy – she was a new ship only on her second run and had, on both port and starboard sides, great big cargo nets, and as we came drifting down upon her we managed to get hold of the cargo nets and crawl up her side and that was how we were picked up. They stayed around for a long time picking up men. They did not like to stay too long because there was a submarine in the area and because it was dark she could have been lying on the surface.

There were lifeboats and dunnage and Christ knows what and men shouting and going with the tide and all that kind of thing. It was a terrible experience but we got over it. There was just two of the crew lost, the 4th engineer and the carpenter. I had spoken with the carpenter just about half an hour before that. The 4th engineer would likely have got jammed down in the engine room. Willie Winchester and some others stood by to work the lifeboat.

The *New Sevilla* stayed afloat for seven hours and then the engineers decided that they would open the seacocks and run the water for'ard in her. When we had left her the after gun platform was just awash and she was floating nearly perfect. You could see just the huge black bulk of her between you and the skyline. Opening the seacocks did not improve matters because running the sea forward in her made her go down gradually. With the huge weight of cargo which was in her, and her loaded to the scuppers, they had to cut adrift and leave her. There were not enough destroyers and stuff to go around to escort the Merchant Navy.

We went down to South Georgia on the *Coronda*, she was a hell of a ship that. The tanks were all full of coal to take to South Georgia and she was a coal burner herself. She had been in Shetland years earlier when the Olnafirth whaling station was working. If you touched her with the chipping hammer, you could have put it right through her, she was just holding together with rust. Our job was to shovel the coal out of the tanks and then fill up all the bunkers.

During the season I was a labourer – dragging spik, filling kettles and all stuff like that. I was wireman to the flensers for most of my time. It was a very dangerous job because they tried all sorts of gadgets for the spik. It was all right for peerie whales but if it was the big blue whales, the heavy ones, the spik was not easy to come off. What they did was they tried this wooden toggles and they tried wire strops but they could not work because they cut in. They flensed a peerie bit around the nose of the whale and then they made a hole and put in the wire strop and when the pressure came on it, it tore out through the spik so it was no use and then they thought that they would work with chain. The chain was better, it was a braw big bit of chain. We had to put it twice in through the hole and hook into it. They found out that the chain worked the best during the time they were experimenting with this. There was a Norwegian who got killed at this job.

Then of course the spik fell down on the deck and the other boys cut it up into squares with flensing knives and you had meat hooks which you stuck into it and you dragged it along the deck and put it into the kettle. The deck was very slippy and you had to be careful. You had spikes on your heels. They laid a false deck made out of coarse planking over their original deck so that, at the end of the season, the false deck was torn up and dumped and it did not interfere with the main deck at all. If you had not had spikes on your boots you could not have kept your feet at all because it was just like a bottle.

You worked the two shifts, night shift and day shift. Day shift was from 8 to 6 and then the other shift took over. Every shift wanted to have a clean deck when they came on so that they could start afresh. Sometimes it was difficult picking up the flagged whales. We used to put three whales alongside for fenders when supply ships came to us. By the time they had given us fuel oil and taken off our whale oil, the fenders were absolutely stinking. That ones proved most difficult to get aboard. The winches we had were always leaking steam which caused problems at night because you could not see.

Coming on to the end of the season, as the cold weather set in, and with the frost you had to drain the winches every time you used them to stop the water bursting the cylinders. You had to close them up when you started them up again.

When there were no whales we just messed about as there was very little to do. Our shift did nothing at all, we maybe sat in the mess room and played cards, crib or dominoes or darts. Some preferred sleeping. We maybe did a bit of washing down or that for a couple of hours before dinner time. You got an hour for your dinner unless it was an overtime job. You were on overtime all the time you were down there for the jobs you were doing. If it was the season you just got time to go down to the mess room to have your dinner and straight up again. You got two hours overtime every day. If you were working on deck you got an hour for your dinner.

We had a proper concert party of Norwegians, they were good. All their own stuff, an awful lot of music among them, accordions and that. They had all that with them. On the *Sevilla* you took off your boilersuit and all your heavy working gear outside your cabin and put on your slippers and you were never inside your cabin wearing dirty gear. The cabins were lovely. Having been a passenger liner, her portholes were still there and you could open them. She was just alive with rats. They lived well off the whale meat. They would eat anything. They would eat the tatties like mad.

The tatties all came aboard in boxes and they were put down between decks to be handy. They could clean out the box of tatties in no time. There was great sports catching them. We carried our own pigs aboard her. We had a pen up under the whaleback. We had a pig man who looked after them and killed them when they were needed and trussed them up. He knew all about pigs and how to work with them.

A lot of the pigs were put ashore at Leith Harbour and went wild there. They had houses for them but the most of the time they were running around eating anything they could find. The Norwegians liked their pork and their beef. The only thing was that their cooking of beef did not suit me because it was half raw, they just cooked it until it was a bit brownish and when they laid it on the tray and started to cut it the blood just ran out. We decided to split up the mess room ashore, one half for the Norwegians and the other half for the British. The mess boys had 3 tables each to look after. This was in the winter.

There were beams which ran across the tanks and when I was washing the tanks one day I slipped on one and it caught me between the legs and knocked me for six so they had to hoist me out of the bottom of the tank with a chain hoist so that was me out of the game for a while. I was on the *Southern Garden*, she was all right and the *Southern Collins*. Salvesen lost the most of the factory ships in the war, *Salvestria*, *Sourabaya* and *New Sevilla* and some supply ships. The *Salvestria* was mined in the Firth of Forth. They switched off the de-gaussing when she was right above a mine.

On the *New Sevilla* we started to clean her when we left the ice and by the time we got to England, you would hardly have known she was the same ship. The upper structure was all white and she was black on the outside and red below the water line. She fairly showed up the rusty old tramps. Johnnie Moncrieff was the only British boy who was aboard her. Willie Winchester took him down his first time to South Georgia and he got a job as a mess boy.

We called along Aruba and loaded fuel all the times we went down. We used to anchor off in the harbour for it was not deep enough to take her right into the quayside. They floated off the pipeline with peerie barges to put in the fuel - it took a couple of days.

We painted whale boats in the winter and did up the huts and painted them. There were not many Britishers doing the winter at that time, only a handful. You had to put in your name if you wanted to overwinter. It was a cold job on board the whale boats, painting all the time. It was just peerie cabins. We always used brushes – the roller was never introduced to us then.

There was such a godless quantity of rivets on the gun platforms and on the winches and on the deck that it took an endless time with a brush but with the paint sprayer you could do it no problem. On the factory all the flat pieces, the bridge and the bulwarks and all the sides, derricks and samson posts were done by hand. The derricks were lowered right down onto the deck and there were peerie chocks that they rested them in.

After the fishing season they were all cleaned, it was an awful job to clean them with caustic. Dried up blood all over them. It was a hell of a dirty job. If there was any wind at all and it blew in the scuppers, it would blow the mess in over the deck. We had wooden chutes that we lowered over the side and put it over the scuppers and made it fast to the bulwarks and that stopped the spray coming in over.

During the season, everything went down the kettle, guts and the whole lot. There was nothing ever wasted. You squeegeed the deck after every lot of whales. The tongue could give you trouble. Once you got it started you had to run like hell to keep clear of it. If you got caught with a bit of it you could say goodbye. It would force ahead and swirl around the kettle and the blood and mess stood in the heavens. An ordinary blue whale took about 7 hours to cook. If there was still a lot of uncooked stuff in the kettle, they had to shut it down, boil it up again and cook it for another so many hours.

DONALD STEWART SALES

I went down to the whaling in 1939. I married in 1938 when I was 21 years old. My pay was £4.10/- a month when I signed on. I left £4 to the wife so I had 10/- to myself. We went in to Aruba for oil and everybody was wanting to go ashore. We all had to go up for a sub. I said, "I would like £5 of a sub." So he looked up the book and said, "Sales, I don't think you have £5 in the books."

"Oh," I said, "I would have liked £5 to go ashore with". "That's all right," he said, "I'll give you £5."

Anyway, Paddy Bruce and Peter Stewart and some others were there. We were gambling with the few shillings that we had. I won all the money, I don't remember how much it was, a few pounds or something. We went ashore and went into the wine bars. We got a lot of drink, bottles and that, and we were sitting out on the sides of the road drinking and the Police were driving around all the time in their jeeps. They were going around and weighing us up all the time and then the Police came around and picked me up.

They dumped me aboard the Jeep and I wakened up in the jail next day. I was lying in the scupper and there was a big bench and a table and when I looked up there were some black men lying on the bench above me. I got up and started shouting, "I want out of here. My ship will be sailing. I want out of here."

This fellow came with two pistols strapped round him. "What's wrong?" he said.

"My ship will be sailing," I said, "I have to get out of here to go to the ship."

"Where is your ship lying?" he said.

I said, "It's lying down such and such."

"All right," he said, "I'll go down and speak to them." The Secretary from the ship came up and bailed me out.

I was on the *Salvestria* with Capt Jamieson from Sandness and the bosun was Addie Manson, also from Sandness. Work had been going on as usual when I got a telegram from home – "Twin boys born" – that was George and Ellis. Peter Stewart said to me, "Boy, I think if du was to take yon telegram and go up to the bridge and see the Captain, du might get a drink."

I said, "Does du think so? All right. I'll chance it." The 3rd mate was on watch when I came to the lower bridge and he asked, "Where are you going?" I said, "I'm going up to see the Captain to see if I can get a drink from him." "A drink from the Captain? You had better not go up there," he said. But I went up and knocked on the door and he said, "Come in."

Captain Jamieson was sitting there in his room. I said, "I've got a telegram from home and I'm the father of twin boys." So I had to explain to him who I was and that my wife was a sister to Bob Leask, Superintendent Leask in the Leith Office.

"Is that so?" he said, "Oh, I know Bob all right."

I said, "Is there any chance of a drink?"

He went into his peerie cabinet and hauled out a bottle of whisky. "There you are," he said, "that's a dram to go to your cabin and give your mates a drink. But mind to go to your work tomorrow."

But I never got to my work and I missed one watch and Addie Manson came in looking for me. I was lying in my bunk and I said, "I'm not able to turn to, Addie. I'm not coming out today." Capt Jamieson was a very fine man. I also knew his brother Curly who played the fiddle.

That was the *Salvestria*, we were right down as far as the ice barrier. Boy, what a sight, all the icebergs piled up, they had been crushed together. Bonnie blue and green under the water, what a lovely sight. We fished down there for a while and then the pancake ice started to come up to the surface and when it hit the cold air it froze just like pancakes so they called in the catchers to come and break a way out for us. We were in the Weddell Sea and if the catcher could not push a way out for us, they were going to open up the magazines and blast it with ammunition. But the catcher came and broke a way through.

One year with the *Venturer* expedition we fell in with a mass of blue whales. I think I paid off with £500, that was a lot of money at that time. There were so many whales lying behind the ship and we needed so much steam to work them up and cook them that the evaporators were hard pushed to make enough fresh water for steam. It was known as a 'full cook'.

It was 1940 and we joined the *New Sevilla* in Liverpool. We took on stores and were lying outside the locks somewhere when a mate and me decided to go ashore. With the war being on everything was in blackout. We got across the locks and then an air raid started. There was shrapnel falling all around and you could see a bit around you with the light from the fires. My mate jumped over a peerie bridge and I thought I would have to follow him. Thankfully it was shallow water and we took shelter under the bridge. We could have drowned if the water had been deep. We lay in there for six hours until the all-clear went and then went right back on board the ship again.

We sailed and took our place in the convoy. We took up our watches and this meant going up in the barrel and keeping a lookout for submarines. Somebody had taken up a tin to relieve himself in during the watch. When the next fellow went up the tin was overflowing and he happened to kick it over. It poured on to the 4th mate walking down below who shouted, "Hey, are you pissing up there?" "No", he said, "Not me."

The carpenter on board the *New Sevilla* was Tammie Smith from Walls. His job after we sailed was to get shelves put up in the slop chest because everybody was shouting for fags and wanting the slop chest opened. I was down there helping that afternoon and when tea time came I said, "Tammie, I am going away up for my tea now. I might come back after tea time, I'll see." But I did not go back, I had a lie down in the cabin. And that was when we got torpedoed, at 8 o'clock and Tammie was killed down there where the torpedo came in. That's where Tammie lost his life.

I was among the crew who went back aboard the factory and put the men out of the lifeboat aboard other ships. Ten of us were kept aboard and went back aboard and tried to save the ship. We came alongside and the Captain came with a canvas bag and put it down to us in the lifeboat and said, "When you pull off, if you are going to get picked up by a submarine, drop this bag over the side." It must have been all the ship's papers or something.

We went down below and opened up the tanks and tried to take the list off her. We thought we might get her back to port but it was not to be. She began to go down and we had to leave her again. We got on board a tug which landed us back in Greenock. A bus took us from Greenock to Glasgow and there were young boys by the side of the roads who began throwing stones at the bus. They thought we were prisoners of war or something like that. When we got to Leith we were sent to the tailors to get new suits. Everybody got a suit and shirts and it was all paid for by Salvesens. I had nothing but the clothes I stood up in. I'd lost everything when the ship went down. I had been taking down a parcel to my brother, John, because he was doing the winter and that was lost too.

Whaling had strange effects on some people. I've seen men jumping over the side of the ship and into the water on the way down to South Georgia. Once when we were going through the tropics and it was very warm in the cabins and sometime during the night I went up to the mess room to get a cup of coffee. I went to the galley and got a cup of coffee and went into the mess room next door and there was a fellow sitting at the table with his head down. When I came in, he got up and went out the door, stepped onto the capstan outside the door and jumped over the side. From the bridge the mate saw him going and stopped the ship. The siren went off. He took a circle round about but they never saw him again. He was a fellow from Leith. The word went round that he had got bad news from home.

Another time when we were working on board the ship at the ice at mealtimes we used to go through the factory deck to get to the mess room instead of going among the whales on the plan deck. At the after end of the factory deck there were escape hatches which would take you up on to the main deck and then you could get into your accommodation.

There were two of us going aft this day and I was first going up this tunnel. I got a little bit up the ladder when the first that I came on was two feet hanging above my head. I said, "Go down". The man behind me said, "Go down where?" I said, "Go down, there's a man hanging here". "Man", he said, "Don't be silly. Go up". I said, "I can't go up. There's a bloody man hanging here. He's hanged himself." Somebody had hanged himself in the tunnel. He had tied a knot further up the ladder and put the rope around his neck and stepped off. I do not know who he was, I think he was Norwegian.

I was on the *Southern Venturer* when they picked up John Leask. I saw him coming up, we heaved him up in the basket and put him into the hospital. But I never saw him again. The catcher he was on had capsized and had been lost with all hands except John Leask. He came from Burwick near Scalloway.

JOHNNIE JOHNSON

I sailed in the Merchant Navy for a number of years and then after being out east on one of the Ben boats, the *Ben Rinnes*, I came home. My brothers, Christie and Henry, were both going to the whaling so I decided that I would give it a trial too. My first year was the 38/39 season. I got a job on the *Salvestria* and having been an AB in the Merchant Navy, I was put on the wheel. It was a good job. There were four of us on the watch and we had nothing to do but steer and we did an hour each.

We had just slipped the moorings when the second mate came looking for us. He had our names all written down and they were Johnnie Pole, Johnnie Anderson, Johnnie MacKenzie and me so we were known as the 'Johnnie Watch'. Since we were doing nothing but steering the ship, the rest of the time we could please ourselves and when we got into the fine weather we enjoyed lying about the deck. When it started to get a bit colder I decided to grow a beard and I kept that on until we were back in the tropics again.

When the whaling season started I got a job on the after plan driving the big winch and the flensing winches. There were two big winches and they hauled the whales up the chute and then you went on to one of the flensing winches, depending on which side of the whale was up. The wire was made fast to the spik on the whale and you heaved away at it as the flensers cut. When you had done one side the whale had to be turned over and the same thing happened again on the other side. When your winch was not going to be needed for a while, you would go down on the plan deck and haul spik.

There was a Norwegian flenser who did not speak much English and he used to call me 'Seggebus'. I think that meant hairy face or whiskery face or something like that and I called him 'Buster Keating'. I got on well with the Norwegian boys. There was an old Norwegian there too. I think his name was Abraham. He had been at the Olna Whaling Station when he was a boy and he spoke better English than I could. He asked after lots of Shetlanders but I can't remember if I knew any of them. They would all have been older men than me. When it was Abraham's turn to go and haul spik, I would tell him to take my winch and I would go because he was an old man.

At the end of the season the false deck that had been laid for working up the whales on was torn up and thrown over the side and there was an awful lot of cleaning up to do. And then the painting would start. I was again on the wheel so it kept me clear of all the messy jobs. The boys that were chipping and painting would look at us and no doubt felt that we were pretty well off.

One day during the second season we had a whale whose tail had been almost worn away by the pack ice and the whale claw could not grip it properly. It was decided to put a chain strop around it. The plan foreman was Nils, a Norwegian. He got rigged up with ropes and went down to the bottom of the chute to put the chain strop on the tail of the whale. When he had got this done, he had come back up on deck again and the winch started heaving on the claw but with the shape that the whale's tail was in, it did not have a very good grip and when it was about half way up the chute, the chain gave a jerk and a link broke and the whale slid back down into the sea. Nils, after all his struggle, was so upset about it, he took his cap off, threw it on the deck and jumped on it. I couldn't help it, I just roared and laughed. Afterwards, when things had all settled down and we had got another whale up on deck, Nils said to me, "Johnson, you get good laugh at me. But it is all right, I was angry." And it was no wonder he was angry either.

The *Salvestria* had been converted from a passenger ship. Everything had to go down on to a lower deck before it actually went into the kettles so it meant that there had to be more men to handle it. You took the spik off the whale on the aft plan, that was just the fat. Then the carcase of the whale was hauled for'ard and it was cut up there by men known as lemmers. The bones were cut up by a big steam driven saw before being put into the kettles. After the cooking process was finished they opened a door on the side of the kettle at the bottom and the bones and anything that was left over was shovelled out by manpower through a door in the ship's side.

The *Southern Venturer* was a different kind of ship altogether. Her cookers were filled from plan deck level. The residue had to be hauled out with a rake but it went over the side on a conveyor belt so it was a lot easier. When the oil had been cooked out of the spik, it went into what was called a separator. Any grit or impurities were taken out and that left this pure white oil. When it cooled down it was just like lard. Some of the Norwegian boys used to cut bits off and eat it.

To hold the whales at the stern of the factory ship, a wire strop was looped over a bollard. When you went to take the next whale up on deck you had to heave on this strop with a small capstan to get a bit of slack so that you could throw it off the bollard. One day a Norwegian fellow was standing there ready to throw off the strop when the hook on the end of the wire carried away and it came across and struck his leg and broke it. That was about the second whale for the season. A similar thing happened to Charlie Christie but this time they were running a long strip of spik down into the cooker. It started to spin round and round as it went down and Charlie did not manage to get out of the way and it broke his leg.

There was a fellow on the fore plan cutting up some meat. He did not notice that a whale's head was being hauled for'ard and it struck him. With his feet being stuck to the deck by his spiky boots, it knocked him down and his flensing knife nearly took his hand off. The doctors managed to botch him up and he was put on a catcher which took him to South Georgia. He was sent home on the first available transport ship. He was down again after that but his hand never came back to normal. He had to have an easier job after that. The plan deck was a dangerous place to work, there were wires criss-crossing the deck so you had to keep a good look out. After the war I went down to South Georgia again and it was Nils who was my plan foreman again. He remembered me and what job I had been doing.

Another incident that springs to mind happened during my first season. It had been fog and we began to run short of whales to work. I was on day shift and when we turned to in the morning we had only one or two whales to do. When we had worked up the whales, the cleaning started. Nils came to me and asked me to splice some whale tail strops. I said, "I know nothing about splicing wire strops." Nils looked at me and a smile passed over his face and he said, "I don't think you tell me true, Johnson, because you have been on other ships."

Just at that moment Jimmy Peterson from Calliff, who was bosun, arrived. Nils told him what he had been asking me to do and Jimmy said, "Don't try to tell wis a lot of dirt. We ken better than that." So this Norwegian fellow, Mott, and I were sent to splice wires. Mott had been a Merchant seaman too and his job on the factory ship was spik cutter. After that he and I were often put on the job of splicing wires.

I was at the whaling for two years before the war and one year afterwards. The whaling was a good life but after being in the Merchant Service I felt that it was not such a clean job. We were always mucking among blood and such like. On a merchant ship everything was generally very clean except when you maybe had to clean the hold.

PETER POLE

I got a job at the whaling a few weeks after the war started in September 1939. Addie Manson went all around Sandness and many other places throughout Shetland getting as many men as he could to come to the whaling. The Norwegians were frightened to come down owing to the war. There were a few hundred Shetlanders who went down there at that time.

We left Scalloway for Leith in one of the North boats about 3 weeks or so after the war was declared. We had a few days in Leith and joined the *Coronda*. She was loaded with coal for South Georgia. There must have been more than one hundred Shetlanders on her and there were a few Norwegians - more or less the Captains and the Skippers of the whalecatchers and the Mates and gunners. On the way down after we were out of the rough weather, near the Equator, we had to wheel the coal in barrows from the for'ard hold aft to the bunkers because she was a coal burner.

I was a week on the wheeling and the following Monday the Mate came around and asked, "Does anyone want a change?" and I said, "Well, I'll have a change." We all wanted a change. He said, "You can go down the hold and trim." We had nothing to trim, there was no coal when we got down there. It had all been burned over the weekend but they surely had plenty of coal down below to keep the fires going for she did not stop. The steering gear chain broke and it took most of a day to repair it and we were drifting around, no engine going and we could not steer her. They got the chain fixed and got her underway again.

One day in the hold I was supposed to trim coal but as I said there was none to trim. I thought it would be a nice clean day but with tipping down the dry coal and the dust spraying up in the hold, when I came down to have my breakfast, I was as black as any black man ever could be. I sat in the hold for about a week and did no trimming as they never got enough coal down to trim. Eventually we got to South Georgia and I was put in the hold because part of the cargo had to go ashore to keep the fires and heating in the rooms in the huts in South Georgia. I was filling the baskets of coal in the hold.

I had been a few days there and I thought I had done enough in the coal. I went up on deck for a breath of fresh air for there was plenty of that in South Georgia. The bosun was a Norwegian and I said to him, "I want another job." He said to go to Mr Kirkiberg, he wanted man, which was men as he wanted more than one man, but that was how he spoke to you.

I found Mr Kirkiberg and he put me on a job as a kettle emptier - the big tanks where the meat from the whales was put in to be boiled and the oil taken off after all the meat was cooked. There was a line of tanks on a railway with iron trolleys and wagons on them like small carts. They could carry a whole cartload of meat. When the meat was cooked in the tanks you opened the door and raked it out into your wagon. There were three of us in the gang with a wagon each. When we got a full load on we pushed the wagon along the rails to the tip and we had to hook each one together and heave them up into the loft, into what they called the Chamber of Horror. You could not see the men down below for the steam off the hot meat and bones which were all ground and dried and put through a mill. It came out the other end quite a few hundred feet away from where you tipped it and went down and was bagged and weighed into hundred weight sacks and stored up in the very far end of the store called the Guano shed.

I did that job for a day when there were no kettles to empty. There were just three of us in the meat cookery, emptying cookers and three men in the bone cookery where all the bones were cooked. They had more big tanks there and the tanks were about eight feet high and nearly round like a plantie crub in size in the bottom. Some of them could hold half the meat of a whale. You had to go into the tank to clean it out and shovel it into your trolley. When you had finished you would close up the door and then they knew on the top that your tank was empty and they could put in more meat. And that is how the job went on for three months as a kettle emptier. When no whales were caught, there would be no kettles to empty.

One day the Manager and the Chemist went out into the hills and shot some sheep and we had to go and carry them back to the butcher shop. I was with a Norwegian. We had a long pole on our shoulders and we tied the legs of the sheep and carried them back. The only way we could find the shot sheep was where we would see a flock of bonxies. I don't know how many we carried, three or four that day, but by the time we got the last ones there was not much of them left, the bonxies had eaten the most of them but we carried them all to the butcher shop and likely ate the bonxies' leftovers.

Another day when there were no kettles to empty, the nine kettle emptiers out of the bone cookery and three out of the meat cookery went in a whale catcher to the rookery where all the penguins were and gathered eggs for a whole day. We gathered many thousands of eggs and that showed the number of penguins. I know I had quite a few in my pocket that night when we got back to Leith Harbour. It was one of the hardest days I had in South Georgia. The penguins were pecking your legs and you had rubber boots on in a sunny day. It was a hot job carrying the buckets of eggs down to the whale boat and up the hill again among the penguins. The whole day was spent gathering eggs. Anyway, we had a good fry up at night in the room. We had a frying pan on our bogie and we fried penguins' eggs for about an hour, non-stop.

I put my name in for stopping over winter and you got 50% added to your wages. I did not even know that they had put in a big gun up on the side of the hill above the station but I was put down for going on this gun. The gun's crew were all Shetlanders, bar one. Jimmy Harley from Ireland was with me. We worked three watches, two men in each watch. The gun had been all in pieces when they hauled her up the hill and part of her was underground. We had a shed underground and all of the gun was inside except the barrel.

When we got her all put together, we had to fire a shot. We got the motor boat men to take a raft made with barrels out to the far end of the harbour at the entrance into Leith Harbour about a mile away. We all got together and fired this shell. It went over the station down below and smashed all the windows in the buildings but we were only a few yards from the raft so we did a very good aim and if it had been a German ship I think we would have hit her.

Many days when our watch was over we went out. We had bought skis and ski boots – that was a proper hilarity, trying to stand up on the skis. It was a difficult job to do many times. Jimmy Harley and I were out skiing lots of days and we could do pretty well to end up with. We went up the side of Coronda Peak one day. It was frosty and we came down to the valley and up the other side but, not knowing that there was a deep drift of snow in the middle, I crashed into it going at quite a good speed and nearly broke my neck. I went headfirst into the drift. My neck was sore for about two weeks after that. We had many good funs on the skis during the winter time.

Some days were very rough. The gales were well over one hundred miles per hour with severe blizzards. I was told the winter before I was there that there had been more snow. The mess boys carrying the trays of food from the cookhouse had to dig a tunnel under the snow and they could walk to their full height carrying the trays of food into the mess room. The drifts must have been a good few feet high. During the spring of the year when the thaw started, you could hear the cracks of the snow like gun fire. The avalanches came down the side of the mountains and possibly went into the sea. We were told that in Grytviken someone was walking along to the whaling station and he was buried alive in a snowdrift by an avalanche.

When the winter began, I had to join the Falklands Defence Force and I got a .303 Army rifle and a steel helmet and you had to swear on the Bible that you would serve your King and Country. We did not get the Army pay, we were still on our whaling pay. When the season was over I was put on the factory ship, *Svend Foyn* to the South Ice as kettle emptier again, the same job but it was all bones this time on the factory ship. There were three of us on the kettles there for three months. Six weeks on day shift and six weeks on night shift. We had a big Armed Liner which lay near us for the whole three months in case of any German raiders. We were lucky that there were none who came our way. The *Graf Spee* was heading for the Antarctic but she was caught by three British Warships off Montevideo where she had gone to escape. She came out of there and they scuttled her. It was just as well that they did or we might not have been around today.

At the end of the season, the three months, we came back with the factory ship the *Svend Foyn* to Liverpool and discharged our cargo there and paid off in Leith and I was nine days in Leith before I got to Shetland. I had twelve days leave and that was up the day we got to Lerwick and I had to report to the Shipping Office in Lerwick as my leave was up. Anyway, I was home for about a month and then got word to go back to the whaling again, back to Leith and join Salvesen's ship *Saluta* for New York carrying passengers across the Atlantic again to America.

We were three weeks in Brooklyn and then the Argentine ship the *Ernesto Tornquist* was loading stores for South Georgia. A good number of Shetlanders went that same day to Leith Harbour. I went back on the same job as kettle emptier and did the season there again, three months. I started work at 4 o'clock in the morning till 6 o'clock at night. That was two hours overtime. One shilling per hour was the overtime rate. When the season was finished there were five whale catchers made ready to leave South Georgia for Cape Town. Christie Hawick and I were put on one of them; there were two Shetlanders on each boat. Four of them were oil burning boats and one was a coal burner and we had to tow her four or five times. The tow would always break. Thankfully we did not have her on tow in the Roaring Forties. The worst seas that you will see in the world, I think.

We got to Cape Town just a few days after Christmas in 1941. We had a few days in Cape Town. The one I was on, the *Satsa*, and another one left Cape Town for Dar es Salaam right up the east coast of Africa. Lovely weather, calm seas all the way. We had just a few minutes there and then we were packed up and put on board a liner back down the coast of Africa and among the different places we came to was Lourenco Marques and Beira and down to Durban. We joined the *Cameronian* in Durban and went back to Cape Town. She was a big passenger liner and was run by the Navy.

From Cape Town we went to Aruba and Trinidad and put the passengers ashore and took others aboard. From Trinidad to Halifax in Canada where we got two thousand soldiers and airmen aboard, a lot of them were British who had been training in Canada. Another liner was loaded with nurses and we had two small corvettes for escorts. You could not move on the liner for soldiers lying all over the place, many of them sick. They had never seen the sea in their life before. We got safely across to Glasgow and that was the finish of the whaling until the war was over.

SONNY WILLIAMSON

I started the whaling in 1939 and I spent half a season in the tank gang and then there were so many blood poisoned hands on deck that I had to go there for the rest of the season. It was a lot better than working in the tanks. You steamed a tank for maybe 36 hours and it was just roasting hot and they hung drums of caustic in it and you had to go in among the fumes with a hose and wash it out. It was pretty grim that, the worst job I ever did in my life. We came home with the *Salvestria*.

I went out on the *Svend Foyn* in October 1940. We went out via the West Indies and then down to the ice and I think it was in the month of January when the German raider, the *Pingvin*, came down. There were two British factory ships at the ice, the *Southern Empress* and the *Svend Foyn*. The raider came down, took two Norwegian factories, their transport ship and all their catchers. He got them all to France through all the blockades. There was another Norwegian factory down called the *Thorshammer*. She took off for South Georgia when this trouble started and she lay in Stromness and her catchers fished from there for the rest of the season. We were not far away from where this raider found these two Norwegians but we just worked away, always expecting to see the raider approaching.

The Navy sent down an armed cruiser, the *Queen of Bermuda*, but we never knew she was coming and when the Norwegian catchers saw her coming they set off, they thought it was the raider coming back again. This armed cruiser lay near us until the end of the season and then she came up to South Georgia with us. We got water there and then she escorted us all the way to Freetown and then home. That was in 1941.

We were home a while and then we got word to go away again. When we got to Leith, they wanted us to go to New York and join an old Argentine ship called the *Ernesto Tornquist*. There was a bit of a carry on about us going over on a British ship and taking over a neutral one as the Yanks were not in the war at that time. However, it was all sorted out and we had to go to the American Embassy in Edinburgh to get our photos taken and the funny bit about it was that when we were in Salvesen's office and the photos arrived the Clerk there, Palmer they called him, opened the photos and the first one he looked at was Johnnie Manson from Sandness. The Clerk looked at his photo and said, "$50,000 dead or alive," and everybody was just in stitches. Johnnie, who was a peerie bit away did not know what we were laughing about.

We went over to New York and we joined the old *Tornquist* and went down to South Georgia. We did half a season and then the Japs came into the war, that was on 7 December, and the Admiralty started taking away all the catchers for war duties. All of Salvesens ones went to South Africa. To end up with there was nobody left there but myself and one fellow from Hopeman, a Louis MacPherson. We finished up clearing out the catchers and the three catchers that were left were *Busen 6*, *Busen 8* and *Busen 9*. When we left South Georgia the only Britishers left there were Tammy and Willie Laurenson from Bressay, Tammie Johnson from Quarff was the wireless operator and Willie Buchanan from Edinburgh was a mess boy. They made a very lonely sight standing on the waterfront when we were leaving. All they had to blow farewell to us with was the galley whistle, just a toot on it.

Tammy had rigged up a glass house and grew tomatoes there. They were still green when we left in January but they would have been ripened before the end of the season. It must have been a lonely stint for them because Willie came down in 1938 and he went home in 1946 and Tammy was down all the war too. He was in charge of the defence in South Georgia. Falkland Islands Defence Force they called them. Salvesen's men manned the gun in Leith Harbour and the one in Grytviken as well.

We left Grytviken on old Ne'erday 1942, 12 January, and we set off for Cape Town. The old *Busen 6* did not have enough bunkers to take her there so we had to tow her for a couple of days so that it left enough bunkers for her to steam into Cape Town. We were there for two or three days and then we went around to Durban, left her there and came home as passengers. It was fine lying back with nothing to do and being fed like a lord. We fell in with some more of Salvesen's men who had gone up to South Africa before and came home via Durban, Cape Town, Trinidad, Bermuda, Halifax and then home. We landed home in the month of March and we were seven days on the north boat coming up from Aberdeen. We lay most of the time in Orkney, it was freezing cold and there was no grub on board. They ran out of grub and they would not let her go out as there was a bit of a scare on and I mind us eating NAAFI carrots.

On one of the ships there was a great big Norwegian and they called him the "Yule Grice", Neilson was his name. He came waddling there along after the whaling stopped, we were still working on the plan, and it was just a deepness of a mire. He walked straight into it and nearly went out of sight. He made some hole in that mess I am telling you. They dragged him out of there - what a state he was in. The Norwegians thought it a great fun because they did not like him. They said he was a Nazi, I don't know, he might have been.

They took down kye from the Falklands before we left that time and the only way they could handle them was to put them on a barge and tie their feet. They put a noose around their neck and slung them over the side with the derrick. The kye kicked for a while and when they were choked enough they stopped kicking and they were able to tie their hind feet together first and then got them down on the barge and tied their fore feet together and then lashed them on to a ring bolt. They took the barge over to Busen point and cut loose their feet and swam them ashore. Some of them were left there for winters before they killed them. They lived on the tussock grass.

There was a Norwegian there called Muller who was trying to tie the hind feet of one and she kicked him in the guts and landed him in the harbour, clean off the barge. They had to fish him out in the middle of tying the kye's feet. Then they had sheep that they kept on Mutton Island. They fattened up like anything, you would not have believed it. There was just a layer of fat under their skin. When they butchered them they just felled them with the back of an axe. They did not blood them, they just felled them and let them lie there. They swelled up and it was poor mutton that. When they got that mutton in the galley, they took a big cleaver and chopped it in pieces. As Geordie Cheyne said there was bits of it sticking in the deckhead and it was just full of peerie splinters of bones, you had to watch for it sticking in the roof of your mouth. Then they filled it with that peerie black things like rats' pirls - that peerie peppers. They did the same in Norway because they had tinned Norwegian mutton at the whaling and it was the same, been chopped up with peerie peppers among it.

There was a great big pig at Leith Harbour. I never saw a pig like that before in my life, he was as high at the fore shoulders as a big horse. He was a boar and the hair on him was like floss. He disappeared and we likely ate him I suppose. Nobody knew what became of him. There was another boar they were going to kill one day and he got off from them and they were so mad that they caught him in a drain full of crude oil which was leaking from a tank and they shot him in among it and we ate him too. I wish I had had a photo of that. The ordinary pigs could not put their heads out over the door but it only came up to the big boar's breast and what size of tusks were on him! I have never seen anything like it. He was a massive animal. I was always vexed that I did not take some hairs out of him for sewing with. When you were making thread for sewing your boots, you used to buy the pig bristle but that might have been too big. We all likely had a bit of him or had him in sausages or something. That was the only right bit of meat you got there.

The year the war finished the grub was something serious. You lived on bread and jam for most part but there was an old steward on the *Saluta* who had flogged most of the stores in Norway. He was in the *Saluta* all of the war, him and Andy Smith from Scalloway, known as "Bim". The *Saluta* ran back and fore between Freetown and the West Indies during the war and never saw a thing. There was a Norwegian factory ship lying condensing water in Freetown. She was called the *Vestfold*. They took her out to put in the dry dock somewhere and she got torpedoed and was lost.

I was not back at the whaling again until 1949 and then I was on the *Southern Venturer* for four seasons, one after the other. Then I went back again for one final year in 59/60. The whaling was coming to an end then. The grub was an awful lot better by that time. You had powered milk in a jug on the table and a bit of difference from a spoonful of Nestles or something like that. I did half a season flensing because the flenser got his ribs broken and so he could not work. The first day I was flensing, we did 48 hump back and one blue whale in 12 hours. You could have taken my outside jacket off and wrung the sweat out of it for you were just flat out as hard as you could go. What oil came out of them. They were as fat as could be. We got 4,000 barrels per day. That was the biggest production we ever made. I think we had 28,000 barrels in one week. They always thought that the British could not flense whales. That was Charlie Duncan and me and a Norwegian flensing together who did that. So we managed to do as well as what the Norwegians were doing.

One night we came on shift and there were 16 sperm whales to work up and they wanted them done quickly because we were going to steam somewhere. Old Myhre, the skipper of the *Southern Venturer*, said they were to give him a shout when they had finished the sperm. We did the 16 of them in 4 hours. They gave Myhre a shout and said they would be ready to steam and he said, "They can't be, they can't have done 16 sperm in 4 hours." But we had done. So we could hold up our end with the Norwegians anyway at that rate. It would not have done to have failed. We could not let the side down.

One year as we were coming home on the *Svend Foyn* the Norwegians challenged the Britishers to a tug of war. On a Saturday afternoon they got this lot lined up. The Britishers went with them just no bother at all so the Norwegians started grumbling. They thought the Britishers must have had a bit of an advantage. So Johnnie Harrison said, "Right oh. We'll change ends." But they went with them again and somebody heard a Norwegian say, "Oh, faan. Far too many stoer Shetland man there." We paid off in Liverpool.

During one season I mind them coming alongside with a catcher. She had got a foregoer in her propeller. Myself and a Norwegian, who worked as a lemmer, went on board the catcher. They had rigged up a stage on the after end of the catcher and the blacksmith had made big chisels and long poles. We had to sit over the side and feel down through the water until we felt this rope. It was an awful job with her surging. There were men up above us on the rail with sledge hammers, hammering like the devil, until we got it cut off.

We sat there the whole night until between four and five o'clock in the morning. That was after working all day and every now and then there was this surge of sea which came up to soak us. Very cold. I never knew there was so much marine life down there. It came to the light, there was all kinds of things there. There was things like jointed jelly fish all around our feet, not that we were worrying about that.

When we could find no more rope they said, "Right oh." So we came on board and we had just got back aboard the *Southern Venturer* when it came a full going blizzard. We were very tired after doing a whole day flensing and then doing that job all night. It was tiresome on the arms trying to force the big pole down through the water and when the poles splintered they would come with another one. There was splinters lying all over the place.

I mind the year they found something in a sperm's stomach. Jimmy Robertson, that was his first year there, said, "Whit is yon?" And the boy said it was a sheep's head. "Sheep's head?" he said. The boy said, "Yes, it was an almark from around the dyke ends of the Falklands and the sperm has eaten him."

I did the winter of 51/52. Among the men that winter were Jimmy Nicolson from Quarff, (we called him 'Faeder'), Jerry Dalziel from Sand, Tammy Nicolson from Aith, Geordie Cheyne from Sandness and Andrew Peter Johnson from Nesting. The Norwegian 2nd mate who was there could speak no English at all. His name was Olstrom and Tammy Inkster called him "Gulfstream". There was a Norwegian there and for some reason we called him the Bressay man. He fell off the big winch one day doose down upon the deck. He got up and just shook himself.

Jimmy Sinclair from Snarraness said to him one day, "Boy, what part of Bressay does du come fae?" This fellow just looked at him. Jimmy married in South Africa. He went up with the catchers that time and just stayed. Jimmy was in charge of the gang who scrubbed the bottoms of ships. They used great wooden backed brushes with steel bristles. Massive things. They pulled them back and fore around the bottoms of ships and scrubbed them clean. Then they moved them the width of themselves and started again. This saved dry docking ships and also saved time. They did a splendid job.

There was an old catcher called *Gun 6* up on the slip at South Georgia. We launched her before we left there and she was so old that the spokes on the steering wheel were worn away just to points with handling. She was a coal burner. We took her over to the old coal hulk called the *James Turpie* which lay under Coronda Peak. We put bunkers in her before we left. She went somewhere during the war, I think Newfoundland or Labrador. The bunkers we put in out of the old *Turpie* were just devilry. They had one run around to Grytviken with her but they had a terrible job getting back because with the poor coal they could not get steam up on her and a gale of wind came up on them.

We had some fun at the launching with old Olaf, the slip foreman. He stood on one leg and waved the other one and his two hands for us to heave with three winches at one time. He lived at the top of the slip. There was a winch shed there. He had rigged himself a peerie shack in there and that was where he slept. He always wore leather leggings. He did his boots with tallow and fir tar so if there was any water on them, it just ran off again. He was very worried just after the war finished that he had lost all his money in Norway. When he found out his money was safe, he was just a different man. He was as hard as nails. He wanted to work bell to bell all the time. I said to him one day, "Olaf, this is just a lot of hellery we are working. Times have changed, nobody works bell to bell now." "So I see," he said.

Leith Harbour, South Georgia. Catchers in foreground are at the place known as Jericho.
Photo: T Robertson.

Funeral of Sverre Akseth, Station Manager, Leith Harbour. He slipped between two catchers and was crushed to death. Building in the background is the picture house or 'kino'.
Photo: I Sales.

Inside picture house or 'kino' at Leith Harbour.
Photo: A Williamson.

Well-timed photo of harpoon about to strike a fin whale.
Photo: T Robertson.

The whale has been inflated and flagged. Gunner returns to the bridge as mate prepares to reload the gun and deck boy stows long wooden pole with a blade for cutting the foregoer. *Photo: T Robertson.*

L to R Back row Karl Brown, Yell; a Norwegian; Bobby Coutts, Fetlar; Jim Craigie, Lerwick. Front row: Freddie Peterson, Tingwall; Willie Wiseman, Lerwick; Jimmy Hay, Dalkeith; Peter Copland, Northmavine; Bunty Leask, Aith. Photo: Karl Brown.

The ***Southern Venturer*** *59/60 season. L to R Back row - Norwegian flenser; Henry More, North Roe; Norwegian flenser; a Norwegian; Sonny Williamson, Ollaberry; Bobby Nicolson, Mossbank; Donnie Cluness, Lerwick; 2 Norwegians; Alex J Henry, Yell. Front - Kenny Ross, Embo; Andy Rojano, Mossbank; Alex MacLeod, Stornoway; Davie Inkster, Whiteness; Kenny Mckenzie, Stornoway. Photo: T Thomson.*

L to R Andy Cumming, Walls; Bunty Leask, Aith; Rab Skene, Edinburgh; Tom Robertson, Yell.
Photo: T Robertson.

Christmas Day 1955. L to R Sandy Irvine, Lerwick; Isaac Morrison, Weisdale. Photo taken by Tammie on the ridge of Coronda Peak, South Georgia. The three had been at a large penguin rookery. This was on the return crossing.
Photo: T Thomson.

HENRY MORE

My first trip to the whaling was on the old *Salvestria* and we left Jarrow with her somewhere about 20th September 1939. The skipper was a man called Capt Jamieson from Sandness and on that trip going out we had Norwegians who had come over to Britain to join her. We sailed right away and headed for Aruba. On that trip we had 96 Shetlanders aboard, all taking passage out on that one ship. When we arrived in South Georgia, some men went to the *New Sevilla*, some to the *Sourabaya*, others to the land station and the remainder went to tankers and that kind of thing. In that day and age we had a 90 day season. We would set off from South Georgia down to the South Sandwich Islands and we would spend maybe a week or so on sperm whales, mainly to knock the deck crews and machinery and everything else into shape.

The baleen whale season started on the 8th December and we fished until the 8th March, a 90 day season. We were in two shifts. On that trip I was just what was termed a deck mess boy and you had a mess room with maybe 20 to 24 men you looked after. You had to scrub decks and scrub tables and just look after the men and carry the grub down from the galley and so on.

That trip went past very quickly and I think we had, that year, if I mind right, somewhere about 112,000 barrels of whale oil in the old *Salvestria*. She had been a big passenger liner in her day. Anyway, we got that season over and we came back in convoy. We came up to Freetown in West Africa and we lay there for a bit getting bunkers aboard. We then set off in convoy back for Weymouth. When we got to Weymouth, the Navy men came aboard and fitted the degaussing gear before we could go up the channel. We went to the Thames to discharge in London that time. The *Salvestria* and the *New Sevilla* were lying in at the same time. The *Sourabaya* went to the west coast to discharge her oil.

To me, it was a great experience, that first trip. In those days there were not many by-products or anything like that. All of the whale was used except for its guts and that was dumped over the side. The rest went through some kind of process to get the oil out of it. That year too, we did not do much steaming. We never went further west than the Bransfield Straits I think and lay in the ice. That year we just had eight fishing boats and one buoy boat.

The following year I joined the *New Sevilla* in Bromburgh Docks in Liverpool and we did not get very far with her that trip because she got torpedoed. We were about 20 miles west of Barra Head when she got it and there was one man lost and one man seriously injured. There were some who did not do very much after that but we got off light. We were picked up maybe four to five hours later by a corvette and they took us right across the Atlantic with that convoy and met the home-coming convoy and came back into Liverpool. By the time I got back the *Svend Foyn* was crewed up and I could not get away on her. So that finished me with the whaling for that period of time.

I was home for a bit and as there were no jobs in Salvesens, I joined the Navy and was no more back at the whaling until 1947. From then on I was year about until the end of it. We saw lots of changes in that time with the whaling. As the price of the oil fell, we even had helicopters spotting for us. We had them maybe two seasons and then we lost two helicopters and that was the end of that. Salvesen did not really own the helicopters, they probably had some stake in it to try them out. They had to alter the ship to carry the helicopters which meant they built a hangar between the funnels. We also had to carry engineers to service them.

I did 15 seasons in total. There were some gruelling days among it all. Conditions got better as time went on. It was very crowded accommodation and the conditions on deck were pretty horrible when you were steaming and the spray was flying over the decks which was covered in blood and guts. But there was not much else which could take its place at that time, unless going to sea. When you signed on a ship you had no idea just how long you would be away. You could be away ten and a half months, a year or up to fifteen months in some cases. It had its ups and downs. The passage home on the ships was the best part of it. Getting back and paying off in Liverpool or wherever you paid off. That was the highlight.

Most of the years going out I was on watch and in that position you were in a way segregated away from the rest, you did not come into contact much unless when you were off watch when you could go and have a yarn with them on deck or whatever they were doing. But it was fine when you were on day work all the time. That was better. As the time went on, the seasons lengthened and you were doing away about four months at the ice. One year we went away to hell and gone east and we ended up at the Ross Sea, away east of the Balaena Islands. That was a tremendously long season and a long steam back. I think we were six weeks on sperm fishing alone that trip. The weather was not all that great either, especially off Enderby Land, that is south of South Africa, a very forbidding looking coastline that.

I had a variety of jobs in the time I was on the factory. I would be maybe driving a winch one year or be cutting up for the rosedown - that is for the meat meal plant. Another year I would maybe be on the ribs cutting and the last year I was down I was flensing, second flenser on the after deck. I was with some men who had come from the *Balaena* factory. That company had ceased fishing the previous year. They had different ideas how to work up whales from what we had been used to but by and large they were a good enough crowd to get along with. There were lots of funs back and fore when we were on passage out and home again, that was the time for that. The rest of the time it was a deadly serious business. Six in the morning till six at night, non stop. Six at night until six in the morning if you were on night shift, non stop. Anyone who was on night shift for two months, by the time that two months were up and they came out to go on day shift again, they looked a bunch of ghost-like figures, they were just bleached white being under the electric light and no daylight for so long.

As I told you before there were 96 Shetlanders on board the *Salvestria* and I think I can mind damned near every one of them. Now I think there is probably five of us left, five out of that 96. So the passage of time takes them away and brings everybody down to size. That is 61 years ago now. No wonder we are kinda ancient looking by this time. I think when the whaling packed up a lot of folk missed it but Salvesen, by and large, was a good employer.

After the whaling came to an end I cannot mind how many thousands it was that came to Shetland from Salvesens through a loan scheme. It benefited a lot of folk. It was James M S Tait, the lawyer, who was the Secretary for it. He told me many, many years later that he had never come across a more honest bunch of men in all his days for they all paid up every halfpenny they had borrowed. And that said a lot. Some got fishing boats, some got tractors, etc and they were given a specified time to pay it back. That money is still in circulation yet in Shetland but nowadays anyone can get out of it for that money was all paid back with interest. Originally the interest charged was something like three per cent, a very low rate.

To get back to some of the highlights of the whaling, I did several jobs – cutting, flensing, hooking and driving winches and so on. I was two seasons in the tank gang where you had eight men and a bosun. The layout in a factory ship is different from any other tanker in as much as she had 36 tanks as against 27 on a tanker of that time. In the latter years when we were working with so much meat meal and by-products we used to floor out the centre tanks when they were cleaned and properly floored out with a canvas covering over the bottom leaving a gap of about one foot below the dunnage on the bottom in case you had seepage of water getting in. That tanks would have carried thousands of bags in each one.

The last year I was in the tank gang we had filled the centre tanks from 1's to 8's just leaving the 9's clear for the oil from any sperm whales we took on the way coming home that trip. All that by-products were worth more than the oil she produced that year. That is why they went in so much for by-products. We were also turning out bovril in 5 gallon drums, thousands of them. So it had to be a profitable trip for Salvesen even though the oil had come down in price.

The tank cleaning was a gruelling job. One day you could be working in a centre tank, red hot, with a cloth wrapped round your forehead to stop the sweat blinding you and the next day you could be in a wing tank with ice forming on the side of the ship and you would have to scale the ice off the side before you could get to the oily bits.

Sometimes after being in bad weather the rivets in the side of the ship would start leaking into the tank. Then the head of that rivet had to be burned off on the inside of the tank and the rivet would be punched out. A stage would be rigged over the side above where this leaking rivet had been and the man inside the tank had a piece of bamboo with a line on it and he would push it out through the hole to where the man on the stage could hook it up. This man would tie on what was called a 'fish bolt' with washers and white lead grommets on it. The man inside hauled on the line and the bolt would come in with the pressure of the water from outside. It came in with a click and he could put on all the necessary washers and a big nut on it and tighten it up with a big long spanner. We renewed close on 1600 rivets one season.

The bridge of the factory ship would have been a good 75 feet above the water line and one time as she was being driven hard through bad weather she took a huge sea on board. It cleaned everything off the top of the monkey island, sand buckets and everything and the weather boards off the wings of the bridge and when she came down it was just like the sound of a bomb hitting her. All the bulkheads between the messrooms were made out of tenply marineply and that was squashed as if you had crushed a matchbox. It was shattered and all the stanchions were visibly bent. The bridge itself was set back over by some inches and was bent down at the after end and lifted up at the fore end. Some of the portholes were smashed on the front of the bridge. We were up putting extra lashings on the boats aft when we saw the old blacksmith standing with his hammer in his hand. We shouted to him that a big sea was coming and he was looking around at us when the lump of sea took him. The blacksmith's shop was on the starboard side amidships, what they called Hell's gates. We saw him go down the chute still holding the hammer. The stern went in heavy and the sea came green up the chute and he ended up over at the carpenter's shop on the port side of the ship in the mouth of a kettle, still holding the hammer. That was in the Roarin Forties.

This happened on a Sunday. The night before Fraser Scott and myself were for'ard putting on a hatch at the back of the bridge and the sea swept the two of us along the deck. We had stacks of timber on the deck with the ropes just all hanging loose. We thought that Fraser had gone when the sea subsided and then we saw his arm sticking out through this pile of timber. The sea had lifted the ropes and had pushed him in and when the sea subsided all the wood came down on top of him. But he was all right. I don't know what happened to me but the boys said that I went out at the far side of the carpenter's shop and came in over at the after side with one sea. But I did not know that, I just thought that I had been washed aft along the deck.

I think it was the 1958/59 season and we had two helicopters aboard. We had six pilots and a chief engineer and some engineers under him and they did all the maintenance work. This day it came down thick fog. They had taken out the passenger seats from the helicopter and put in extra tanks which gave them a bigger radius.

The helicopter had been away for a while and by one o'clock when we were turning to on the deck again, they decided that the helicopter was overdue. The Chief Officer came along, John Holtan, and said to me "More, get an accident boat's crew at the ready. The helicopter is overdue. We must stop all the winches so that we can hear."

This was duly done. We went up to the port side. The top boat on the port side was in double davits, and the motor boat was in the top davit. Fryzndorf, a Polish Officer, was the 4th or 5th mate. He was running around there giving out all kinds of orders. We lowered the lifeboat down to the embarkation deck. The two whaling inspectors were there shouting the odds, "Come on, away you go. Get this boat away. The helicopter has ditched." I said, "We can't go until we get orders from the bridge."

Back came Fryzndorf and said, "As soon as the doctor comes aboard, push off." The doctor came aboard with his bag and a bottle of brandy and the two whaling inspectors were shouting, "Come on, get your boat lowered away." "No," I said, "We can't go until we get the order." Back came Fryzndorf and said, "Come on. Push off. Get going." So down we went.

Johnnie Tait from Lerwick, originally from Brae, was on the brake and lowered the boat away and just when we ready to unhook the lifeboat then I could see the propellers of the factory ship thrashing ahead. I thought, "Oh hell, it's down thick fog and we're in the shit here now. We'll keep close into the ship's side." The next thing I saw was the bow of the *Sistra* coming zooming damned near on us. The Captain on the bridge did not know that the lifeboat had been launched. This was Fryzndorf's orders we were working on and he ran up to the bridge and said, "We'll have to watch, the boat is away."

The Captain gripped Fryzndorf and pushed his face in the wheelhouse window and said,"See that? That is the bloody boat there. Who gave the orders for that boat to go away?" Fryzndorf started shouting the odds, "Get this boat back alongside."

It would have been about a 15-18 foot swell running up the side of the ship and it was some job to get both hooks in place at the same time. So I said I would not come alongside until I got a lee side and with the factory moving ahead we could run in and keep her there with her running to get her hooked on again. I never said a word until the boat was back and secured again and then I went for Fryzndorf. I called him for everything I could lay my tongue to and he was backing up the deck and everybody was standing watching. He backed right up the deck in front of me until he came to Holton, the Chief Officer. "Now that's enough," he said, "We don't want any more of this carry on."

I said, "Well, I'm prepared to go up to the old man and see him, just to clear me." So me and Fryzndorf were never friends any more after that. What happened was that the helicopter had ditched in the sea and the crew had got into their liferaft. The *Sistra* had picked them up and they had been lifted on board in the basket. We weren't needed and the lifeboat would never have been launched if Fryzndorf had kept his cool. Apart from the men getting soaking wet, they were both ok. That was the nearest shave we had with that.

One night I was in at the Fiddle & Accordion Club in the Clickimin Centre in Lerwick and I met Capt Davie Polson (who used to be the Harbourmaster in Lerwick). He came over and shook hands and spoke and I knew by the smirk on his face what was going on. He said, "Oh, I have just been having a chat with an old friend of yours while I was away." I said, "Who was that?" and he said "Capt Fryzndorf." I said, "I would have another name for him."

CHRISTIE JOHNSON

I fell in with John Duncan from Aith and Geordie Eunson from Orkney and they said they were going to see about a job at the whaling cause Salvesen was going to take on Britishers again. The reason for that was to destroy the Norwegian Union because the Union was too strong and they were demanding too much in wages and bonus. So in a way we helped to destroy the Norwegian Union. Salvesen had also employed some blacklegs from Bergen and so there came to be three different groups aboard the ship, the Britishers, the Norwegian Union men and the blacklegs. But it seemed to work out all right. I don't remember any trouble on board.

We went down to South Georgia on the *New Sevilla*. We had all signed a contract saying that we would work when and where required and I was put on a whale boat for the season. She was the *Sukha*, an old catcher. A new catcher came down that year after we had been fishing for maybe a fortnight. I think she was called the *Sara* and she beat us. If she had not come down we would have been top boat. When the gunner fired at a whale and missed the Norwegians called that a 'boom' and they used to be ill pleased at the Skipper if he fired a 'boom'.

At that time there was no nylon so the foregoers were made of the very best manila. It was spliced into a heavy whale line and after every time the gun was fired the foregoer had to be coiled down again in front of the gun. It was a job that had to be done properly as it had to go out clear with the harpoon. On there we were on watches, 4 hours on and 4 hours off and you might have got anything from 7 to a dozen whales a day. They had to have air pumped in them and a flag put in them. After getting these whales during the day, sometimes you might spend all night picking them up and delivering them to the factory so in the middle of the summer you had very little chance of ever getting to bed. It was a fine clean job but I thought I could have done with a bit more sleep.

Sometimes we would steam in through the pack ice and come into a huge expanse of clear water and there would always be whales there. If we got four whales then that would be enough for us to tow out through the pack ice again and back to the factory. Coming near the end of the season something went wrong with the gun and the Skipper decided we would have to go to South Georgia and get it fixed. It was very bad weather at the time but we set off steaming at full speed. On the way we passed the *Sevilla*, another of Salvesen's factory ships, and she was hove to. We were all a bit scared on that trip. We were going full belt, it was just madness. I can't remember what the Skipper's name was but he did not know anything about being frightened. We had come from a long way south and ran out of fuel about a day out from South Georgia so they had to send a boat out with fuel for us. We had a day in South Georgia while the gun was repaired and then it was right back to the ice again. No time was put off.

The following year I asked for a job on the factory and I got it. I was on the *Sourabaya* every year from then until the war started in 1939.

In September 1940 we left Liverpool to go to South Georgia on the *New Sevilla* and we were torpedoed 30 miles off Malin Head. I was off duty at the time and was just having a walk along the deck with some others when we got hit. It was then that Tammy Smith from Walls lost his life. I think that he went down to get his life jacket for I'm pretty certain Tammy was with us when the alarm went and that was when the first ship in the convoy was torpedoed but we never saw him again.

The mate, MacLauchlan, was in charge of our lifeboat. He decided we would row towards Ireland. We had no room on board to handle the sail as there were two boat's crews on board her. It was going to take a bit of time to row to Ireland. Then an Icelandic trawler bound for home came and picked us up. They gave us what I think was the last grub they had on board. Then we met up with this armed whale boat and were put on board there. Later a destroyer came up to us and said there was a tug coming to take us off and that we were to help the tug to get a tow rope on a tanker which was nearby. She was lightship and her back had been broken. We tried it but she would not tow very well, she just kept going from side to side. The tanker was the *Empire Venture*. Later we transferred to another tug and we got to Gourock some time next day but we had had a lot of changes before we got there.

I was home for a fortnight and then I decided to go away again. I thought if I could get away down to the whaling I would be clear of a lot of the trouble but it did not work out like that. Just after we left Norway was invaded. We wondered how that would affect the Norwegians on board as there were some who were true Norwegians and others who thought the Germans were all right and some who just wanted to get on with their jobs. The 1st Mate, MacLauchlan, spoke to the Norwegians and told them that there was no need for them to fight among themselves on board the ship as their government would not be worrying about them. It was a little while before it became clear which way the Norwegian government would go but they decided to ally themselves with Britain and the King came to London.

So we set off for the ice and did our season there. But coming towards the end of the season we heard that a German raider was in the area, that was the *Pingvin*. We also heard that she had captured two Norwegian factory ships and their whale boats except for one who had escaped and made for South Georgia but she ran out of fuel before she got there and they had to send a boat out from South Georgia to refuel her. I think what saved us was that we had a lot of foggy weather. Then later, on a fine clear day, we saw smoke on the horizon. This caused a bit of excitement as we thought it was the raider but it turned out to be the armed liner, the *Queen of Bermuda*. She had been lying in the Falklands. They had taken an old Norwegian aboard as ice pilot and how he found us I don't know because, with the war on, you were not allowed to use a wireless. The *Queen of Bermuda* came and stayed close to us for the remainder of the season. We heard that the two ships that the *Pingvin* caught managed to get all the way to France but we never heard what happened to the men.

I did a winter in Leith Harbour. I worked on the whale boats painting down below in the cabins. We also had to clean and service the springs in the bottom of the catchers. They were fixed by wires to blocks up the mast and the whale lines ran through these blocks and they took the strain when the whale had been harpooned but they were some lads to clean, I can assure you. It was a very dirty job and you could get in a right mess but then you got time off to clean your clothes. The winter was ok, you were pretty well off. You did your work during the day and then you had your cabin to go to at night and we generally just played cards. There was a lot of snow and sometimes there were avalanches. I only ever saw one during the day as most of them happened at night. It made a tremendous noise but was well worth seeing.

ALEX PATON

I started off as a deck mess boy on the catchers and after two years there was a shortage of firemen so I took up that job. When I was mess boy I used to go at nights down to the stokehold beside Peter Blance from Lerwick who was a fireman. I picked up all the things about the job and then I was transferred to the engine room after that as engine room rating. After a couple of years at that I was assistant engineer for the last three years I was whaling. It was mostly watch keeping except for when you broke down and had to do repair. The watches were four on and four off. As soon as you went on watch, you checked over your main engine first and then all your auxiliaries and made sure that they were all topped up with oil and everything was all right, not running too hot or else it would burn the bearings out.

We had an evaporator on board for taking the salt out of the water to get fresh water for the boilers. And then there were filters to see to, the water filters and oil filters and all that to clean up. Every watch you had to change them and then once per week you would put new covers on them. You would take off the old ones, it was the heavy terry towelling and it made very good hand towels too. When you were chasing whales you had to put the fires out and fires on as after going flat out, when they rang down to stop the engine your steam would build up and blow off at the safety valve and that meant a loss of water. You had to be ready to light the fires up again as soon as they rang down for full speed. So you were kept on your toes.

I was on catchers called the *Stora*, *Southern Joker* and *Southern Soldier*. The last one I was on was the *Southern Angler* with Martin Olsen as gunner, that was with the *Southern Venturer* expedition. It was when I was on the *Southern Joker* that we lost our gunner Harald Olsen. We were chasing whales and they were on the port side a little bit aft of the gun platform. I think it was the starboard side harpoon that was in the gun and when he fired it meant that the foregoer was going over the top of the gun. This spun the gun around and that knocked him over the side. The tide was taking us away from him all the time and there was just no chance of picking him up.

The winters were a different story altogether. I spent one winter in the Larsen block. There were five or six of us in the cabin. I got an empty sugar barrel which held 35 gallon and put it up in the loft and set a home brew in it and fixed up conduit pipes coming down so we had brew on draught. The management knew what was going on. They had inspections maybe on a

Sunday and then they would shine torches up in the loft and they could see this hole but by that time the barrel was out lying in the burn so that it would not dry up and the conduit pipe was taken down and under the mattress in my bed.

It was a wonder that we did not get poisoned with that because we filled it up on Sunday night and then we would try it on Friday or Saturday night so it hardly stood long enough. The ingredients were all stolen. Sugar and yeast came from the steward's store. When you were unloading stores off the transport ships they had men every ten feet watching that there was none of it being stolen but we always managed to get what we needed. Then we made a still and that worked perfectly for a while. The still itself was alright but the brew that I had made one time had raisins in it and as the brew was bubbling away and going into the still one of the raisins choked the pipe coming up from the end of the five gallon drum. We were all sitting around yarnin' and waiting for this drops of spirit to come out of the still and then all of a sudden the five gallon drum jumped off the electric heater it was standing on. Everybody went quiet wondering what happens now? Then the cork blew out of the drum and five gallon of brew just clined the ceiling and brew was dripping everywhere. What a caper!

Well we had to clean the place up and of course the ceiling, that was the worst of it. With the sugar in it the mess just stuck there. It all had to be squeegeed down. There was an old Norwegian down there, he was an expert with still and he took down with him bottles of essence. You could get what you wanted, flavour wise. He would put in a drop of essence into a bottle of still and that was just like rum, a drop in another one was just like whisky or gin. It was just the pure essence that went in. It only took a peerie drop but it fairly flavoured the whole thing. It was better than the plain gear.

During the winter we were just repairing the catchers, stripping down the engines and doing them up. We had to overhaul the auxiliaries and any job that was beyond you would be put up to the workshop to get the valves all skimmed and turned and that kind of thing. It seemed that there was something in the water down there that would pit the valve faces. You could grind them by hand or with a peerie drill if it was not too bad but some of them had great big holes in the valve seats and it would have taken you a month of Sundays so you had to get them machined out.

You had to go through the whole engine room. Every engine had to be taken apart and we usually used the lead on the bearings so that you got the right clearance on them. We would put in bits of lead and clamp them together and then put in shims so that you had the right clearance on them. If you had to do anything with the bearings on your main engines, they were white metal and that was more or less an art of its own. It was so fine that you had to have maybe two or three thou of an inch difference from the centre of your bearing up to the edge so you kept the oil in, and that kept most of the oil around the main bearing instead of it just spewing out into the bilge all the time. The bearing sort of floated in oil.

There were some damned good men who worked in that machine shops. One fellow I watched scraping one of the main bearings. He had it on a surface plane. It was dead level. He scraped it by hand and then he laid on this micrometer and just pushed it along the bearing for it had to be perfect, dead level.

Some of the men used to make model whale guns about six inches high out of brass. They used to flog them for rum. Speaking about drink, I mind Geordie Niven from Scalloway had made a brew in a gun powder tin. I think he was on the *Southern Gambler* at the time. We were in for bunkers and he said, "Come aboard, I have some brew." So we went aboard and we got drunk on this stuff but he had never washed the tins out properly. After that for a few years when I had a drink, my lips and tongue turned black, even when I came home here some time later. You would have thought that it would have worked its way out of my system by that time. But that's what it was like.

ANDREW ANDERSON

My first trip to sea was on the *New Sevilla* and I joined her at Birkenhead on 18 October 1939. I was put straight into the tank gang under Willie Moncrieff from Trondra and we were cleaning the tanks up to whale oil standard prior to loading fuel oil at Aruba. The idea was that they cleaned her up to whale oil standard and then they sprayed the tanks with a solution of waterglass and some other stuff. This was so that the fuel oil did not actually penetrate the steel which made it easier when they came to the ice and had to do the final cleaning.

We left Aruba with a full cargo of fuel oil. After cleaning the tanks we were in an awful mess. I had hair upon my head at the time and even that was clarted in fuel oil. It was under my fingernails and all over. Our showering facilities were a 2 gallon zinc bucket, a gawpen of soft soap and a sweat rag. We went into the wash place and filled the bucket with cold water and then we put a steam jet into the water to take it up to the temperature we required. We would empty so much of the bucket over our heads and we would scrub ourselves down with soap and make sure there was no fuel oil left and what water was left in the bucket went over the top of our heads again and, if need be, we joined the queue for another bucket of warm water.

Now after Aruba we were put into the rosedown to get it ready for the whaling and that took a bit of time because it was in a steer and there was not very many of us on the job. We had to take all the bales of bags out of the tank and stack them in between decks. That job more or less kept us going until we arrived at South Georgia. Some of the other fellows were sprootin' tatties. My contract was for Leith Harbour and six of us came ashore and got into a room in the Brick Building. In the cabin was John Henderson from Westafirth in Yell, Charlie Sandison from somewhere in the north mainland, Arthur Ramsay from North Sandwick in North Yell, Magnie Williamson from Walls, John Anderson from Neshon, Toft and myself.

A major part of our work was digging coal out of the *James Turpie*. She had been taken down to South Georgia at the turn of the century to be used as a coal hulk but they rather doubted that the condition she was in at the time of the first year of the war 1939, all the coal would have to be taken out of her for a hull inspection. We dug the coal out of the *Turpie* and that went on to the *Coronda* and from the *Coronda* to the shore by what was called a married purchase. So we had to turn to and dig the coal out of the *Coronda* to get it ashore.

After that our next job was in the guano shed. Now, if digging coal was bad, the guano shed was worse because we were nearly choked to death with the dust that came off it. It was yellow stuff and it got into our clothes and hair and all and was difficult to wash out. That job was bagging the meat meal which had come through the factory and into the guano shed. On completion of that, our next job was to put the bags of meat meal on bogies and take it down to the pier. It was loaded onto barges, towed to different ships and loaded into their tanks. Coming towards the end of the season a whole gang of us was sent around the station to pick up whatever timber was lying around and we had to transport this to almost alongside No1 Store. The man who was in charge of the whole operation was Scottie Christie from Bridge End in Burra Isle. The timber was to be used to build a shed. They sent two handymen with Scottie to help him. One of them was Harry Smith from Whiteness and the other was a Leith fellow. Scottie sent them to No 1 Store to get what tools they needed and they came back with all the tools of the day. Scottie came toddling back after them and the only tool he had was the fit eetch.

With the war on, a 4.7 gun arrived. It was lying on a barge. It had to be taken ashore and erected above the guano shed and Tammie Laurenson from Bressay was in charge of that job. We were splicing all kinds of wires together to parbuckle this thing up to the site and that was the last job we did at Leith Harbour before going home that year. I was put on board a catcher which was being taken back to the UK for being converted into a minesweeper, escort or whatever the navy needed.

I was along with Andrew John Robertson from West Yell and we were signed on as AB's. We left Leith Harbour on 23rd May 1940. As we came out past the Black Rocks, Andrew and I were both on watch. The weather seemed to be worsening. Andrew said, "Boy, du'll better go down for wir oilskins cause it is not going to be good when we turn to the north at Cape Saunders." And hear about famous last words but down I went for oilskins and there was a wash place just at the back of the fo'c'sle where our sleeping accommodation was but the toilets were right aft.

I thought I would put my oilskins on before I went up and she started heaving and pitching and I got my right arm through one sleeve but I had to drop it off and I reached for my bucket and then I started to spew. And I spewed, spewed and spewed and I thought I'll have to get out of this so I washed out the bucket and then got another bout. But I got over that and I managed to get my oilskins on and took Andrew's oilskins and set off for the bridge. When I got to the bridge there was nobody there. And then I looked and Andrew was spewing over the other side of the bridge and I said, "Andrew is du sick?" and he said, "Yes, I'm sick. It takes an awful lot to make me sick. Take a hold of the wheel." Well about all I could do was take a hold of the wheel because she was pitching me all over the place.

We suffered that weather for about a week but we were calling at Trinidada Island, that is off the Brazil Coast, to bunker off the *Saluta*. I think there were seven catchers altogether. We lay at anchor for two days until the *Saluta* arrived. The sea had smashed the teak wood doors leading into the for'ard accommodation and they had had a very rough passage. We sailed from there to Freetown and when we came there we found the old coal burner *Shuka* who had left South Georgia almost three months before. We called in at Gibraltar and then on to Avonmouth and from there to Glasgow and home.

I was home for a start and then I was outlined for the *New Sevilla* but I never got any word to join her. After a time I decided to go away and see what was happening. When I came to Lerwick on my way south I met Willie Arthur from West Yell and he said, "Andrew where is du goin?" "Well," I said, "I'm just going away on spec. I have an outline for the *New Sevilla* but I've heard no more about it." He said, "I am the same." Anyway we arrived at Leith and we went into the office and George Adamson who looked after the personnel along with Capt Robert Leask, said to us, "You're two very lucky boys. You were outlined for the *New Sevilla* but there has been a mistake having to call you away. The *New Sevilla* was torpedoed two nights ago." We got a job on the factory ship, *Svend Foyn*, and had an uneventful trip to South Georgia and down to the ice.

I was on watch with Jimmy Peterson from Califf, Alan Smith from Whiteness and a Leith chap. There was one morning that the whale boats reported a strange vessel approaching. They knew that it was not a whaling ship of any kind and it was heading more or less straight for the factory ship. When it was sighted by the *Svend Foyn* the crew took the covers off the guns and put in a shell all ready to do battle. But the ship turned out to be the *Queen of Bermuda*, an Armed Merchant Cruiser. We then heard a story that a number of the Norwegian whale catchers in the Weddell Sea had been captured and one of them sunk. The *Queen of Bermuda* sent up her signal so all the signal books were rumbled out to see what they meant. She came alongside for fresh water and stayed near us until the end of the season. In fact, she followed us right up to Freetown and while we were at Leith

Harbour doing the interchange of fuel, she lay at Grytviken ready to sail. When we left she was lying outside Leith Harbour waiting for us. I was not at the whaling for the duration of the war but always had a desire to go back.

It was now November 1949 and I had gained my 1st Mate's ticket. I wrote to the Leith Office and was offered a job as 4th Mate on the *Southern Raven*, the frozen meat ship. We were with the *Southern Venturer* in the Antarctic. She was fishing very well indeed and the meat was taken off the back fillets from the small younger whales and transported from the *Southern Venturer* to the *Southern Raven* on the converted whale boat the *Sabra*. The fillets, some of them weighed about a ton, were lifted on to the foredeck of the *Southern Raven* and the boys cut them into blocks of about maybe 14lbs weight. From there they went into the cooling tanks which were on the starboard side. The tanks were full of cold salt water and there were 6 of them. It was left there in wire net slings until it reached a certain temperature and then it was passed over the top of the boys using the flensing knives to the hand cutters at the side and they cut it into suitable blocks for going into the freezers. It was all highly controlled by a Meat Inspector. The frozen meat did not seem to take on in the UK but I really did enjoy a good feed of whale meat.

I did another voyage on the *Southern Raven* and then I went as 4th Mate on the *Southern Harvester*. I did the season on the *Southern Harvester* which was uneventful and when we came back to Leith Harbour I was fully expecting to go straight home on board her but lo and behold I was on the night shift on the *Southern Harvester* putting stores ashore. One night I was lying asleep on my bed and I heard the room door opening. There stood the Captain of the *Southern Harvester*, and the Secretary was with him. He said, "I'm very, very sorry, Mr Anderson, but you are signing off. You are going 2nd Mate on the *Saluta*. She is at Stromness and she will be coming around to Leith Harbour shortly." And that is the only time I have ever signed off a vessel lying on my bed. Anyway the *Saluta* was an old wreck, I can't say much about her but she did not break down on the way back, we made it and I have a feeling that that was the *Saluta's* last trip to South Georgia. I signed off at Ellesmere Port.

The next season was *Southern Harvester* again as 3rd Mate. On the bridge of the factory ships the procedure was that at the wheelhouse after bulkhead is a metal disc about 8 feet across. This was graduated 360 degrees and the factory was always the centre. From the centre it was graduated in nautical miles, each ring was 5 nautical miles right out to the outer perimeter and the whale boats. Each whale boat had a number. As did the buoy boats.

Now if a catcher called in that it had caught a whale, that catcher's number was the first thing in the log book followed by the whale number and species of whale - B-blue F-fin S-sperm H-humpback O-others, time flagged (that was the time the whale boat had flagged the whale) and everything you wanted to put on it that was a DF beacon, a light, a radar reflector and a red flag with the boat's number in white, the time picked up and the number of the tow boat which picked it up, the time delivered to the factory, the time hauled up (that was the time it was hauled up out of the water) the sex of the whale, the length of the whale, contents of the stomach, the foetus if it was female in young, the length and sex of the foetus. Now if it was a milk whale, that was a very serious offence. That meant that one or two baby whales would be running all around the Antarctic looking for their mother and they would starve to death. That was all strictly controlled from the bridge and the bosun's office at the after end of the ship.

Now apart from all that and the bridge watch, you did twelve hour watches right throughout the ship except for the day workers, that was the engineers, fitters, carpenters and blacksmiths. The mate on watch had to find out where all the whales were, why they had not been delivered and which boat was towing them in and all that had to be ready for his relief coming on at 6 in the morning. The buoy boats would be contacted and they had to radio in which whales they were towing as each catcher's number was carved into the tail in Roman numerals and also whether it was the first, second or third whale of that day for that particular catcher.

One year we were at Enderby Land when the season finished, that was three weeks steaming from South Georgia. It was not an awfully successful season because the ice was a long way south. We sometimes had difficulty in bunkering and servicing the catchers but we did manage. And another thing, the whales were very thin and the harpoons were going straight through them and when the nylon foregoer was cut, the harpoon would be lost. There was an awful shortage of harpoons to the extent that we sent a whale catcher west to the *Southern Venturer* in the Weddell Sea for more harpoons. I forget thc number they brought back but it was enough to do us, we just managed.

Towards the end of the season, the *Southern Collins* was our tanker, and they had been alongside twice and just before finishing up, they were outlined to go from Enderby Land via Cape Town to Liverpool. So the overwinterers aboard us made the request, in order to be home a little bit sooner, to be transferred to the *Southern Collins* for a straight run through the Atlantic calling at Cape Town. That was duly arranged and they left. We bunkered the whale boats and the bigger ones went for South Georgia at full speed. The smaller ones stayed with us because we had to replenish their bunkers twice on the way to the island. We had to stay close by the ice in case we needed shelter for bunkering the boats. We left Leith Harbour after about three days, cleared Cape Saunders and set our course for Liverpool.

As we approached the UK we heard through the BBC News that the Liverpool dockers were on strike and also the tugs so that meant there would be no berthing for us. But they agreed to take the *Southern Harvester* in because it was the only tide that could float her. So they duly took us into Gladstone Dock. As we went in, lo and behold, there was the *Southern Collins* lying at the Barr Light vessel with all our overwinterers on board and we were home before them.

My last trip to the whaling, I joined the *Southern Collins* as 1st mate on 3rd December 1955. We cleaned tanks to a certain extent and called at Caripito for a cargo of fuel oil. We were outlined to call at South Georgia to put ashore some stores but the *Southern Harvester* was fishing very heavily in the Bellingshausen Sea so were diverted to go straight to the *Harvester* because she was running short of clean space for the whale oil she was producing. Some of our tanks were more or less ready to receive whale oil but when we arrived at the *Southern Harvester* we needed much more clean space than we actually had. I had a word with the mate on the *Southern Harvester*, Magnie Scott, and he said that they could not do a blessed thing for they were full up too. The Leith Office were toying with the idea of us having to discharge 1000 tons of fuel oil over the side but before that could happen we got three days of dense fog and that saved the situation.

But in the meantime, on the *Southern Collins*, we filled the fore and aft cofferdams and that emptied another tank so we could accommodate another 3000 tons of whale oil from the factory which eased the pressure. Washing to whale oil standard was quite something because when you got alongside the mothership the chemist came to inspect the tanks that were prepared for the whale oil. He came on board, went down the tank with milk white gloves on like a surgeon and arrived at the bottom and the first thing he did was look at his gloves and if there was any dirt on them he would say, "No good. Do the lot over again." He would run his hand under all the ledges in the tank and under all the angles and if he came out with even a trace of fuel oil, that was it. The tank had failed. Do it over again. But we always managed to arrive alongside with clean tanks. We have the crew to thank for that because they were excellent, knew what was required and did what they were told.

On the *Southern Harvester* they also filled the cofferdams with fuel oil which was highly illegal but it eased the space on board. We berthed alongside about every third day and I think that was the best season the *Southern Harvester* ever had. I'm sure she was working up in the vicinity of 22/23 whales per day. At this time we were about 72degrees South in the Bellingshausen Sea. The sun's rays reflected off the icebergs with beautiful shades of blue and small lumps of ice, maybe the size of your head or your fist, were rocking on the slight wavelets that were there. Each piece seemed to have thousands of prisms and threw up all kinds of different lights in a ray. It was out of this world, beautiful.

2nd mate on the *Southern Collins* was Gordon Walterson. He looked after the tank washing during the night and I looked after it during the day. We changed over at 6 in the morning and 6 at night. Each morning when I came out to relieve him he would ask, "Are we berthing this morning?" and if I answered, "Yes, we are berthing in three hours' time, alongside the *Harvester* at 9 o'clock," he would have a cup of tea and something with it and he would just keep his seaboots and his boilersuit on, get himself down in the sawdust, draw a piece of tarpaulin over him and go straight off to sleep and I would call him at 9 o'clock. I think he had a very poor time but he never ever once complained. Thank you, Gordon.

Coming back to the factory ship and to production control. All the whale oil was monitored through the separators and there were samples taken every now and again as the whale oil was coming off. When it had run for so long, it was number 1 and when it became discoloured it came under number 2 whale oil. The samples were taken probably every three hours and the meat meal plant was exactly the same. Each bag of meat meal had a batch number. It was a consecutive number and was logged by the man in charge of the bagging platform. He would put a handful of meal into small buckets and the lab boy would come and collect them. The samples were then tested in the lab and if there was anything at all wrong with any batch, they could trace it to the bag and when it was convenient that bag or bags were dug out and it was put through again.

Now for a long time they could not find out where the protein was going but it was actually in the refuse from the kverner cookers. It was pumped up to a settling tank and left there so long to let it settle. Then the liquid was taken off and the protein was left in the solids. The liver plant was a different process. The liver was cut into small pieces. I mind I used to feel sorry for Jimmy Manson sitting up there on the weather side of the front half of the carpenter's shop at Hell's Gates with his backside in the wind as we always lay with the wind on the port side and poor Jimmy Manson was cutting up the liver, slicing it up into lumps small enough to go through the worm drive and into the mincers. From there it went through the processor and it was mixed with a solution of caustic and other chemicals to break it up. Liver oil was clear - something like castor oil - and that went into stainless steel drums and I believe went to laboratories at Hull or somewhere for patent medicine. The only parts of the whale that we could not make use of was the intestines and the bones. We did not have a plant to grind the bones down for bone meal. The cookers were emptied by hand and that went through the shell doors and into the water and that was the only wastage. So this brings me to the end of all my whaling experience.

SAMUEL ANDERSON

The first trip that I went to the whaling I went down with the *Polar Chief*. We joined her at Cardiff. She had just come back from South Georgia and discharged a cargo of whale oil and turned around and took the whalers back again. There were a few of the men who came home with her that were just home for about a fortnight and then they came back with her. I was on the 4-8 watch from Cardiff to South Georgia. We had fine weather all the way and it was a very lightsome trip and there were a lot of the men aboard her that, like myself, had never been to South Georgia before.

We had one peerie mess boy, he was brawly young, that nobody could control. He was just a proper peerie hooligan and was always playing tricks on somebody. One day he jumped off the top of the for'ard galley on to the mate's back. The mate was knocked to his knees upon the deck and then he saw this peerie boy and he said, "Boy, do is a bloody monkey." And that was all there was to it. A night or two later we were going to get a tot of rum. The mate stood in the chart room door and we all had to file past him to get our tot of rum. We had to drink it there and then. As he dished out the rum this peerie mess boy came by for his tot. The mate poured him out about half a tumbler and made him stand there until he drank it all. That was his punishment for jumping on his back.

When we came to South Georgia we went into Stromness instead of Leith Harbour and we who had not been to South Georgia before all wanted to get ashore and have a look around. We went over to the beach where the sea lions were and the big bull ones would rear up and roar at you. The skipper and the mate were with us. We started to throw stones in the sea lions' mouths and they would spit them out again. The following day there was a notice on the notice board that we were not to go and torment the sea lions and it was signed by the Skipper despite the fact that he had been there with us. But that was all that we ever heard of it.

I was put on a whale catcher and as I had been at sea before I did not start right at the bottom, I started at the second year group. I was the mess boy for'ard. The first year's mess boy was amidships. But that was a very long season for we were away from South Georgia for five months and three weeks and we fished away out at Enderby Land. It was a very fine crew on that catcher and I enjoyed the season. The second mate was Bang Olsen and he became secretary in the Office of the factory and he was also in the Office in Leith Harbour when I overwintered one year.

I was in what they called the Fishing Leader's Boat, it was the *Southern Gem* and the gunner did not do much shooting himself. The mates were supposed to be training for gunners and one of them was called Sverre Akseth. He was the first half of the season and for the second half of the season it was Anton Neilsen. I was with him two or three years later when he was a full gunner for a season. I think we had 212 whales that year but I cannot mind where we were among the boats. We certainly were not down at the bottom but we were maybe three or four from the bottom. He became a pretty good gunner.

Then the following year I was on a corvette towing whales. That was the *Southern Larkspur* and when she came down from Britain the mate on her was a George Eunson from Orkney. He was supposed to be the mate but he was the only man who had a ticket that could take her because when they came to sign on, the Norwegian Skipper's ticket was not good enough for that size of boat. When they came to South Georgia the Norwegian said that he was not going to go to the ice on another man's ticket and so George Eunson took the boat to the ice as Skipper. I think the Norwegians did not like the thought of anyone but a Norwegian being Skipper of one of the boats and they did not work very well with him.

At Christmas a transport ship came down with fuel and stores for the factory and to take back whale oil. They sent down a man to come aboard as Skipper. He was a very large man, I would think coming up for 30 stones. He came aboard and on his way across the deck of the factory ship he had fallen on his backside among the whale blood. He had on a pair of brown breeks with a kind of herring bone pattern in them and he never changed them when he came aboard. He was aboard for a while and then they put him in one of the buoy boats and we got another Norwegian Skipper.

At the end of the season the *Larkspur* had to go to Cape Town for dry docking so George Eunson and myself were put on board the *Southern Shore* to go back to the Island and this was the boat our Skipper had been put on as gunner. He was still on board there with the same breeks on. You could still see the stained piece on the backside of them.

The gunner set three watches for the trip back to the Island but on our watch it was just George Eunson and myself. The gunner never came up on the bridge, he just sat in the mess room and drank coffee and if the fog came down we were to call the wireless operator to keep a look out. He came up to the bridge to look at some peerie volcanic isle that we passed and he still had on the same breeks. By this time, there was a hole upon the sleeve of his moorit cardigan and there was a hole on his shirt and his jumper where his elbow was sticking out, as black as a piece of coal. When we sighted South Georgia he came up to the bridge for a look and then he thought that he would have a wash and change his clothes before we came to the Island. He wore a pair of ski boots but he never laced them, he just stuck his feet in them. But he was a very fine man as a Skipper. You could not have been with better. He had been in trawlers up around Iceland during the war on escort duty. The men who knew him there said that he was a very tall, smart man at that time.

One year when I was going down with the *Venturer* I was put in the whalers' accommodation instead of the whale boat accommodation. There were some Newfoundland men on board that year. They had taken an old whalecatcher from Labrador to Glasgow and then they were going to do a season at the ice before they went back to Labrador again. They came in the cabin that I was in. One of them came in one day and said to the rest that they all had to go and pass the Doctor before they could sign on and there was a short stout fellow among them and he hauled up the legs of his dungarees and his knees were just like a pair of polished black shoes. He said that he doubted that he would have to go and wash his knees before he went to the Doctor. When he went out I asked one of the others why his knees were so black. "Well," he said, "he has been a trimmer up in Labrador." It was coal burners they had up there and he had been trimming the coal and it was him kneeling among the coal that had made his knees so black. They had been home for three weeks before they came across with the whale catcher and he still had not got his knees cleaned up. But that men, I would have said, were years behind the rest of us.

I did the winter of 1950 and the following season I was put on the *Southern Soldier* to go to the ice. Salvesen's gunners did not come down with Salvesen's transport ship that year. They wanted a while longer at home so they flew to Buenos Aires in Argentina. They joined the Grytviken transport ship there and they were approaching South Georgia at night when it came on a bad snowstorm and the ship went ashore. They did not know what part of South Georgia they were ashore upon. All the whale boats were lying with steam up ready to go, just waiting for the gunners to come, so they were all sent out to look for this ship to try to get the men off her. The Grytviken boats and Salvesen's boats all went and I'm not sure about the boats from Husvik but I think they went too.

Once the whale boats cleared the harbour they got a DF bearing from the ship and then they knew which way to go. The weather was so bad that they could do nothing about getting the men off for the ship was in a great big geo and her bow had hit one side of the geo and her stern had drifted down around and stuck fast on the other side and they were afraid that she would break in two and sink fast.

They put all the men ashore because there was a pond of still water in past her. They put all the whalers ashore by lifeboat but the banks was so high that they just had to stand where they came ashore, there was no way they could get up. The mate on the *Southern Soldier* had fished for the island. He was a Norwegian by the name of Tony Halversen. He reckoned that he would go into the geo and see what it was like.

So he took the boat in right down to the side of the ship as far as he could venture. Capt MacNaughton was on board. He had been the station foreman during the winter and only came with the *Southern Soldier* to try to help with the rescue. He went on the bow and had a conversation with somebody aboard the ship but there was no way that they could get the men off. When he tried to get out of the geo again the ship would not turn around in the space that we had available so he had to come out stern first all the way. We lay out there until it started to turn dark and there was nothing that could be done so some of the boats went back to Grytviken but we, along with some others, went to an old whaling station called Prince Olaf. There was a pier there that we tied up to and lay all night.

We went out again when the daylight came up and by that time the weather had broken enough for the boats to go into the geo and slip their anchor and lie while they pulled a lifeboat between the ship and the whalecatcher and got the men off like that. They had to ferry the men from the shore to the ship and then from the ship to the whalecatchers. We had lost our anchor when we heaved up at Leith Harbour at the end of the winter so we got no survivors but we were not needed anyway for there was plenty of boats available.

After we had fished for about three weeks we got our new anchor on board and we went to lash it up along the bulwarks where it was usually kept. The anchor slid over the deck and my toe went under the fluke. We got the anchor lashed and then I sat down in the fo'c'scle door and took off my boot. I had on a pair of leather sea boots. The mate came and by that time the blood was coming out through my sock. I got the sock off and then the Skipper came by and the mate said that I would have to go up to the Doctor with my toe. The Skipper looked at the toe and said, "And you can take your bed with you." I went up to the hospital and the doctor took a pair of tweezers and lifted the nail back and the toe was burst underneath. He took the nail right off and bandaged it up but I think that was the sorest thing that

I ever had in my life. I could not bear the wind to blow on that even with the bandage on.

I had to stay on board the *Polar Chief*, she had been lying there all winter. I was along with Karl Brown and Ronnie Manson from Yell. We had to go ashore to the mess room and I managed a few times and then my foot was so sore that I was unable to go ashore and Karl Brown carried grub aboard to me for a week. After about three weeks I went back to the Office and told them that I thought I would be able to work as I could get my boot on again. They said to me that I was to go aboard the *Southern Laurel*. The 2nd Mate was aboard there and I was to help him.

She was lying out at a place they called Jericho. I got the motor boat to take me over to her but I could not find the second mate. I went down to his cabin and there he was lying with his head upon his arms on the top of the table. There was a carton of aftershave alongside him with just a bottle or two left in it. I shook him and he just looked at me with very bloodshot eyes and fell asleep again so I did not have a great lot to do that day. He turned out to be a very fine man and could do his job well. One night he was not in the mess room and I could not find him anywhere. It was a fine night so I took a walk aft over the casing and looked down into the stokehold and there he was down beside the fireman who had a still going. He was brawly drunk and the fireman was trying to get him out of the stokehold. All the time the still was going good.

I spoke to the fireman and when I looked at the front of one of the furnaces the oil was running black down over the front of it. The fire had gone out and the oil was running out. I drew his attention to it. He said he would get the torch and sort it out but I would not let him put the torch in. I did not know much about the fires but I knew that it was dangerous to do that. He agreed with me that I was maybe right. So we got the rakes and I helped him to scrape the oil out of the furnace. Of course, it ran into the bilges and down over the front of the hot boiler. We got it scraped out and he thought that he would try the torch on it then and he stuck in the torch and it went off just like thunder. The oil on the front of the boiler took fire and started to run into the bilges. And then the bilges took fire and we had to get sand and try to put it out. And all this time, there was nobody up top. I was the man on duty and I was in the stokehold fighting this fire. The 2nd Mate had fallen asleep by this time. It could have been a bad job. However, we got the fire in the bilges put out.

The Doctor on board the *Southern Venturer* set fire to his bed with a cigarette and burned his stomach very badly. We were sent from the ice to take him to South Georgia on the *Southern Laurel*. The Doctor there, a

German, fixed him up as best he could and then we had to take the Doctor back to the ice. The burned Doctor did survive and managed to travel home to Ireland.

The next season I was in the *Southern Truce*. She was a buoy boat. At one time during the season, we had more whales than the bottom fishing boat. The following season I was back with that same gunner on the *Sondra* and we had a very good season. The year after that I was with him again on the *Southern Soldier* and we did sperm fishing before the baleen whale fishing started and we fished well. We got a good fishing of sperm and then just when the baleen season started, the boilers on the *Soldier* started to give bother and we went alongside the factory. We spent a lot of time alongside with the engineers plugging the tubes and to finish up with they took us out of the *Soldier* and put us on the *Southern Foster*. She had been put for a buoy boat then because the bow of her was slack and it was affecting the gun so we did not have a good season. I then missed 4 seasons but was back fishing for Leith Harbour on the *Southern Foster* with the same gunner, Otto Tavrsen, in 1959/60 and was to go back with him in 1960 but he died during the summer so I was on the *Southern Wheeler* with Stensines 1960/61 and that was the last year Leith Harbour fished.

WILLIE TAIT

I first went to the whaling in August 1946 when I was 17. I had been working at the Bressay gut factory making it ready for the first season after the war. I saw an advertisement in The Shetland Times.

Along with Bertie Gilbertson from Lerwick, I left to go and work by one of Salvesen's factory ships, the *Southern Venturer*, which was lying in the Middle Dock, South Shields. We were basically mess boys looking after the men who were working on the ship making her ready for the coming season. Bertie and I spent six weeks there and then came back up to Leith to join the *s.s. Saluta* for the trip down to South Georgia. It was my first real trip to sea so it was quite an adventure. We picked up a cargo of fuel oil at Tenerife and then headed for the South Atlantic. After we left three young stowaways were discovered hiding in the *Saluta's* lifeboats. They were desperate to get away from the place as there was much poverty after General Franco had taken over. They worked as mess boys on the ship, the same as us.

On arrival at our destination, Leith Harbour in South Georgia, Gordon Gear from Nesting and I spent the next six months looking after 28 Norwegians in a tradesman's messroom. At the end of the season I volunteered to go to Peru with the *Southern Venturer* fishing for sperm whales. We went through the Magellan Straits, calling at Punta Arenas for stores. Then it was up to the Equator where we spent the next few weeks. We came home via the Panama Canal, arriving back in Britain at the end of June 1947.

I missed the next two seasons and my next trip was in January 1949 for the winter and the season. Twelve of us went to Norway where we joined the *ss Orwell*, an old Norwegian tanker. We sailed from Norway to the West Indies to pick up a cargo of oil and then on to South Georgia. The next 18 months were spent working on the floating dock and the station at Stromness Harbour doing all sorts of jobs. Nearly all the maintenance of the 30 whale catchers was carried out at South Georgia. Two large machine shops could cater for any kind of repair work, whether large or small.

I spent another season at Stromness helping to build a new dock. As catchers got bigger they decided to build a modern one. It was constructed at Middlesborough, I believe, then taken to pieces and shipped out to Stromness where it was reassembled. It was a major undertaking so far away from the UK and it was a proud moment for everybody on the day the launch took place.

I did a season as a wire boy working with the Norwegian flensers.

Working on the plan deck was very interesting as everything was always going at full speed, just like a factory. I also spent a season on the bone loft where the whalebones were cut up into pieces by three large saws. They were then put into kettles and boiled. From there it went to the guano shed where it was processed into bone meal. This was shipped back to Britain for use as a fertiliser.

Most of my time at the whaling was spent in the tank gang. In all, I spent five seasons there. Our bosun was Willie Georgeson from Tresta. Most of the gang were Shetlanders and were handpicked by him. We were classed as Group VII so it was a better rate of pay. It was an interesting job because there was such a variety of duties, including a lot of maintenance work around the stations.

After the fuel oil was used we had to clean the tanks for whale oil. We put one ton of caustic soda in and steamed them for 24 hours. After that they were hosed down with boiling water. They had to be spotlessly clean or the whale oil would have been contaminated and that was not acceptable. We also painted out accommodation blocks. There were between four and five hundred men working at Leith Harbour so quite a lot of accommodation was needed.

One unusual job we had was rounding up penguins to take back to Edinburgh Zoo. We went round to the other side of South Georgia to the rookery. We had to put them into sacks and transport them off to the big ship with a small Norwegian boat, a pram. They were very hard to catch as the flippers were strong and could break your arm if you were not careful.

Another very different job we had to do was cleaning out a tank on a tanker named the *Polar Maid*. She had just arrived and it was discovered that a burst pipe had flooded No 1 tank. All the stores for the season, including flour, butter, jam, tinned fruit, etc. plus all the gear for the slop chest or shop were in there and had been destroyed. When we got up in the morning the night shift men were all drunk. When they had opened the tank to start clearing it out the first thing they had found was a barrel of rum so there had been no work done. Our gang was put to clean out the tank. It was a dreadful mess and took several days to complete. We managed to save a few bottles of gin and whisky so after we had finished there was a small celebration. Normally the bond was mainly for the Officers, whereas we got a bottle of rum among four every month.

One of the most memorable incidents was on board the *Southern Opal*, a tanker which had been converted to a transport ship and could carry about 500 whalers. We left Liverpool bound for Caracas in South America to pick up oil. Shortly after leaving there one of the cylinder heads flew off the main engine. It was as if a bomb had been dropped on the ship but thankfully no one was hurt. The repairers welded a tank lid on top of the cylinder and we limped into the Brazilian port of Pernambuco where we lay for 12 days waiting on spares to be flown out from the UK. After the repairs were carried out we proceeded on to South Georgia with no more problems.

The whaling was a hard job with very long hours but it was a blessing for Shetlanders at that particular time. There was very little work at home so you had no option but to go away.

One of the saddest things I remember was burying a young Shetlander at sea. On the way out Ray Cumming from Gruting took ill with measles and died.

I spent 10 seasons and a winter at the whaling so it was quite a chunk out of my life. But I really enjoyed my time there. There was never any ill-feeling, everyone got on with everybody else. I worked with Norwegians for a season and they were excellent as well.

After getting married in 1954 I did two more seasons and then decided it was time for a change. I bought some crofts and started work as an agricultural contractor, working for people in the community.

L to R Eddie Wiseman, Lerwick; Jim Craigie, Lerwick; Alex J Henry, Yell. Photo: K Brown.

*Whalecatcher, **Southern Runner**, built by Smiths Dock, Middlesborough. Photo: T Thomson.*

Left: Whalecatcher in floating dock at Stromness, South Georgia.
Photo: A Ridland.

Below: ***Southern Lotus*** *being towed by* ***Southern Harvester****. They were caught in a severe storm in the Forties and there were great fears for the safety of* ***Lotus*** *and her crew. 3 Shetlanders on* ***Lotus*** *at the time, A Arthur and B Ramsay, Ollaberry and T Johnston, West Burrafirth.*
Photo: T Robertson.

L to R Back row Hamish Jamieson, Yell; Ivor Johnson, Yell; George Nicolson, Aith; Billy Craigie, Lerwick. Front Alex Hughson, Whiteness.
Photo: B Craigie.

SS Saluta *Transport to whale factory ships 1940/44.*
Photo: A Anderson.

L to R Robert Sales, Ellis Sales, Robert Wiseman, all Lerwick; Dougie Connor, Glasgow.
Photo: R Wiseman.

L to R John R Wiseman, R Watt (Red Robbie), Alex Watt, all Lerwick; unknown. Photo taken at the penguin rookery where the men had been sent to capture penguins for Edinburgh Zoo.
Photo: R Wiseman.

L to R Attie Williamson, Lerwick; Andy Cumming, Walls.
Photo: A Williamson.

View from poop of ***Southern Venturer****. Buoy boat* ***Sondra*** *delivering 10 whales. The line from her port bow is a messenger to the* ***Venturer****. A worthwhile tow for the* ***Sondra****.*
Photo: T Thomson.

Left: L to R Standing Benjie Wiseman, Lerwick; Seated Ian Sales, Lerwick, Jimmy Balfour, Sullom; Name unknown, Edinburgh.
Photo: I Sales.

Below: On ***Southern Venturer*** *60/61 season on the way to South Georgia. L to R Standing Unknown; John Gilbert (Romeo), Newcastle; Seated, Unknown; Albert Clark, Yell; Allan Tulloch, Whalsay; Arthur Thomason, Wilson Coutts both Fetlar.*
Photo: T Thomson.

JIMMY LEASK

The first I knew about the whaling was from my brother. I was working to the Council. I had finished with the Merchant Service and I was in a three foot ditch on the top of the Staney Hill for we worked with the road from the Staney Hill right to Weisdale. I was living in Weisdale then. Addie, my brother, came home dressed with a suit on and a lovely collar and tie and I said "Boy, boy, here's me standin' in the three foot ditch." There were drinks passed around and I forgot that I was with the Council for a bit. I said "Whaur's du been?" and he said, "I'm been to the whaling." I said to myself this is going to be the end of the Council work for me. I am going to go to the whaling. That was about May and I waited until September.

We all signed on in Leith with the Office and were sent down to the Tyne to join the *Polar Chief*. The *Southern Harvester* had sailed from Tonsberg with Norwegians. There were no Norwegians aboard our ship at that time but we went down to Tenerife. In Tenerife you could go ashore and have a dram and most of them had been ashore and had drams. They had a local brew that was just poison. Very, very strong stuff and they drank it like water and it was no time at all before they were all palatic.

I was sent on deck to see that everybody was on board and with three hundred men, I did not know whether they were all on board or not. I tripped over something which I thought was a rolled up tarpaulin and it was someone lying in a deep sleep. There was a salt water hydrant open and water was coming down, hitting his head and going down at each side of him just like a burn. I told Anderson who was the mate at that time.

There was a woman on board who was going to Grytviken to see her husband who was an officer down there. She had a cabin to herself. We were coming into the warm weather and one day, as we passed her cabin port hole which opened up towards the deck head, when we looked up it was just like a mirror and she was sitting on the bench underneath the porthole naked so everyone went past for an eyeful of this. One man wanted to see this and instead of him looking up in the mirror he looked right in the porthole and she let out a scream.

She went right to the Skipper and said that this horrible creature had poked his head in the window and she wanted him brought to book. The Skipper was far more diplomatic than that and he said "There is maybe nobody who knows about this and you would be well advised to forget about it. If I go and call up all the men, everybody will get to know." She said,

"Well maybe that will be the best way." So she said no more about it.

We went right down from there to South Georgia and saw the *Southern Harvester*. She was lying there and when I got my first glimpse of her I thought she was a braw big ship, in fact the biggest ship that I was ever on. We were put on the *Harvester* right away. I had to come ashore and at that particular time they were washing fish that someone had been off and caught. The toilet was open to the sea and he was right along there washing fish. The first times I came down there, it was humble surroundings. There was no sanitation at all. It was only as the years went by that it improved. I was surprised that anyone who stayed there could live without getting some disease. The toilet and the fish were what drew my attention first.

We left there and went to Enderby Land and we started to fish sperm whale. When we got the first sperm aboard I was amazed at the size of it. The sperm was not as big as the baleen whales which came later where you got blue whales up to 90 feet. 65 feet was the minimum size for fin whale and for blue whale it was 70 feet. If you took any under 70 feet, you did not get paid for them. There were some of the gunners who were hot at sizing whales. They could judge them while chasing by seeing how long they could go from when they blew until they dipped their back fin in the sea again.

The *Harvester* was 540 feet long and 74 feet wide. I had been a bosun in Merchant ships before the war finished and at the end of hostilities I left the Merchant Service altogether. I was taken on as a hooker at Group 8 on the *Southern Harvester* because there was no AB's jobs left but the next year I came down I got an AB's job, that was group 7. Before the season was over, someone fell sick and I was made up to cutter, group 6. I think the highest you could go was group 2 and that was bosun and I did end up as that the last two years after Addie Manson left.

When we got our first fin whale on board, I had never seen any animal that size before in my life. It was just after the war and there were plenty of them. Then we got blue whales and they were bigger still. A blue whale of about 86 feet long would have been almost 20 feet high. On the after plan they lay between large chocks. This stopped them rolling and sliding to the side of the ship. Their bellies were away out over the chocks. When they started to flense, they started at the mouth and cut along the side and the belly and the back, what the Norwegians called the fling. They took off the belly fling first and then the back fling but to do this you had a flenser on either side and one man who went on the top of the whale. That man had to cut a line right from the top as you would start a banana and only go as deep as the blubber or the spik, not go into the meat. They took off this fling and the man at the other side got his fling taken off and this being split at the top, both flings fell off. The men at the bottom on both sides did the rest.

The whale was then canted over and they put a wire over the top of it and a wire underneath and the two winches took the strain and turned it over. The wire on top was fixed to the flipper and the other wire was taken around and made fast to the flipper on the other side. Before they canted it over, the jaw bone was taken off and put right to the foredeck where they cut up all the bones. Once that was done they turned it over and took off what they called the last fling. As soon as that was off, the lemmers from the fore plan hauled the whale along there and that is where they cut it up into little bits or manageable pieces.

Once the whale was cut up it all went to different places. There were four big steam saws which were supposed to have come from log cutting in a forest. They could just cut the carcase into pieces. Once the meat was off you were left with the skeleton. The backbone was cut in half and you got a half to each side. The bones were cut up in pieces about a foot and a half wide and then dumped into the kettles which were about 12 or 14 feet deep. They just cooked normally. There were other kettles known as kverners. They were named after the man who designed them. They were steam kettles, the inside revolved around and they had double lids. One lid swivelled, that was the locking lid which came up and shut off the steam. There were two lids, one on each end of them. It was like a barrel lying on its side and would have been 20 or 30 feet long. On the inside was a barrel with holes in it and there was a double lid on that and you folded down this double lids first, screwed them down and then the screwer, before he put the steam on, took this lid and swivelled this lid around, put on two locking bars and screwed that up so the lid came up and when the steam came on the pressure kept the lid in place. You could take the locking bar off until the steam went down again. It was all steam cooked. As soon as it had cooked the men down below took the oil off.

To begin with I did not think I would stay with whaling because I did not like the way the whales were killed by the harpoons and maybe dragging the catcher along before they died. I looked at the deck where we were wading through meat and blood all the time and I thought this is my last year at the whaling. At that time I was a hooker and at the bottom of the pile. But September came and the itch started again and everyone was getting letters to go back. Eventually mine came through and you had to go through the medical and be examined properly before being allowed down.

The seasons were very much the same year after year. When Christmas came around you got your bottle of beer and a tot of rum and if someone sitting beside you was teetotal you would chum them up in order to get their tot too. If you had done some favour to anyone, they would come and hand you their tot. Sometimes you saved it up so you might have a bottle. You could never get enough of this rum because it was always very scarce. Some went to the trouble of making alcohol, not so much on board the ship as there was no place secret enough. Ashore it was common practice to make this booze, especially during the winter.

I did two seasons before I did a winter. I remember one fellow who made booze and when it was brewed he would turn it into spirit by running it through this apparatus called a still. One time while he had the still going he was caught and was taken to the Magistrate's Court in Grytviken. He was charged with stealing sugar from the Company. He was also charged with making spirit with an illegal apparatus and when the Magistrate asked if he had anything to say before he sentenced him, the man replied, "There were some parts of that still that were very hard to get and can I remove them off before you destroy it?" He was assured that this could not be allowed. He was fined £80 which was a lot of money at that time. It would have been nearly half of his earnings for the season.

Brew was made regularly but there were not so many stills around. It was very potent stuff that came out of them. One man had 7 jars set up in a row. He lived in the old accommodation where there were nooks and crannies everywhere. In the new buildings it would have been more difficult to hide because it was more open. This man had his 7 jars set up so that when one came ready another was nearly ready. He made good brew as he kept it for the right time. Some began to drink it before the yeast had had time to work.

The *Harvester* came back down in October and we began another season. I was cutter and then I was made a flenser on the aft deck, along with Jerry Dalziel and two Norwegians. A season or so later they wanted a Britisher to go as a lemmer, that was to dissect the whale. Until that time the lemmers had always been Norwegian. I was made up to lemmer and I got on not too bad. It was hard work the first time but it eventually got easier as you learned all the joints and knew what to do. The Norwegians I was along with were very good. Some said they were awkward but I never found them to be that. Back and fore I learned a bit of Norwegian so I was able to converse with them.

One day someone said to me that they had heard that I was going to be promoted to bosun and later Gerald Elliot from the Office on board took me for a walk along the deck. He asked me, in Norwegian, about the saws and what we did with the other things and I replied in my best Norwegian. He said, "I think we will make you up to bosun." That only lasted 2 years as the whales were getting scarcer and scarcer all the time.

The last season that we were down one of the catchers, *Southern Lotus*, broke down and we towed her with the factory ship from Leith Harbour to the English Channel and then another catcher took over the tow and took her to Norway. In the Roaring Forties we were caught in a terrible storm. That was the worst weather that I ever saw at the whaling. We thought for a time that we were going to lose the *Lotus* and if she had gone she would have taken the factory ship too. There were barrels and gas bottles lashed out on the deck and the sea broke the lashings and things were going everywhere. There was no way we could go out and do anything about it because the men could have been injured or even killed. It was a terrible loss of barrels and gas bottles because the sea took them down the chute.

When it was bad weather down at the ice we could go in to the ice pack, that was like lying in a loch but you had to watch that the pack did not close in on you. There was an old Welshman, an AB, on board the *Southern Harvester* who had only one eye. He was on the wheel this night when they were coming up to the Island and he happened to get a glimpse during what they called an 'ice blink' of an iceberg which was ahead of him. It had not been picked up by the radar. He said to the mate, "There is an iceberg right ahead." The mate said, "Do you think so?" And he said, "There certainly is." So they put one engine ahead and the other astern and the rudder hard over and that was how they came around. She listed right over and just cleared it. The stern came right in towards that iceberg. It was said that if it had been an iceberg in the Arctic it would have been shelved under water and we would have hit it but the icebergs in the Antarctic are steep as if you had cut them with a knife. After that the Welshman would always say, "I can see better with one eye that some of them can see with two." He always made a joke of it.

STUART GRAY

I went to the whaling in 1946 and we sailed from Leith that time. There were a lot of Leith boys that year, just shortly after the war. When we left all the boys went up on the poop deck aft and they were singing and playing and all the lasses were down seeing them off. So it was the best send off we ever had.

There was nothing spectacular about the old *Saluta* except that she was just alive with cockroaches. The trip down was uneventful but we had to live aboard her for a while until the factory came down as there was no accommodation in Leith Harbour in South Georgia. The cockroaches were a pest. One day the rest of the boys had gone to work and I was just slightly behind and I had a pump and some insect repellent and I turned up the steam heating in the cabin and went down on the floor and pumped this repellent on the hot radiator and then crawled out and shut the door and went off to my work. In the cabin next door there was a fellow we called Stornoway Mac. The following day he came in and said, "Lord Jesus for the cockroaches beside us. Have you seen any?" "Yes," we said, "there are a few around us too." He said, "Last night when we came in there was nothing but cockroaches everywhere." This was the spray which had driven them out of our cabin.

I was back at the whaling again in 1947. My brother was going away to sail so we went away together, a week early. I went into the office and they said, "Well it's very good that you came, Mr Gray, because you are sailing early." So I went down to Cardiff and it was three weeks before we sailed. There were engine problems. We went to the West Indies for fuel and then down to South Georgia. There were no problems and the season was very good.

The *Southern Harvester* was on the go then. That was her second year. So I thought that I would do the winter. The *Southern Harvester* came up from the ice with all her catchers. She had been fishing east and was right out of stores. There had been a crooked steward on board and he had flogged a lot of stores before they left. So we had to give most of our winter stores to the *Harvester* as there was over 500 men on board her made up of her own crew and catcher crews going home. We were told that the *Southern Garden* would be down within a month with fresh stores on board. She was going to sail from Liverpool but it was the time of that terrible strike and it lasted for six weeks. That would have been 1948. We were down to the hard tack, there was no milk and no sugar.

We were in contact with the Manager of Grytviken who represented the Falklands government in South Georgia and he gave us a permit to shoot 100 deer. We went with a catcher along the coast to where there was a great valley and there was always a lot of tussock grass there. We went ashore and everybody got 10 cartridges. There would have been a couple of hundred deer right up in the head of the valley which was blocked by a glacier and with the mountains all around there was no escape except coming down towards the sea, past us. We killed 117.

It was a fairly hard day getting that back on board the catcher. We tied their feet and slung them on a pole and carried them between two men down to this small boat and then rowed off to the catcher. And then there was a skinning process. Anybody who could kill sheep and work with that sort of thing was a godsend at that time. They were all flayed and hung up and we ate a lot deer. Sometimes we would go and shoot scarfs, hundreds of them. They hung them up and plucked them and made a stew out of them. I was a young guy so I did not worry about that sort of thing. We were down to black coffee and things were getting pretty low before the *Southern Garden* finally arrived.

Anyway the winter passed and it was one of the heaviest snows that had ever been in South Georgia in anybody's memory. It came on a blizzard that winter which continued for about three and a half days before it broke. The snow was a tremendous height, everything was just snowed in. We had to cut our way out of the hut that we were staying in. We called our entrance the thirtynine steps. Anyway the winter passed and the season began and we started working the whales. They always fished whales for the island a good while before the factory ships arrived. That year the *Southern Harvester* went away east south of New Zealand.

One day my name was up on the board that I was to come to the office along with some other men. We were told that we were to join the old *Saluta*, she was lying at Stromness. I was quite happy about this. We joined the *Saluta* and Capt Alex Goodlad from Westsandwick was Master and the 1st Mate was Magnie Scott from Papa Stour, another nice guy. It took us most of three weeks until we came up to the *Harvester*. She had two whales along her port side for fenders.

We went alongside and pumped fuel oil aboard her. We managed to get on board and spoke with some of the boys and had a dram or two. It took a couple of days to pump the oil aboard. Then we hauled off and we lay there for a fortnight and cleaned our tanks up to whale oil standard. Two of our tanks did not pass inspection but we cleaned them again and they were ok.

We took on a full load of whale oil, said cheerio to the boys on the *Southern Harvester* and set away to the westward back to South Georgia.

We had been steaming for a week and the weather was fairly fine and then it started to blow stronger and stronger until it was just a raging gale and a heavy sea. She was getting difficult to handle and we eventually had to turn her around. We did this just after twelve o'clock on the twelve to four watch and she just lay broad side on and we thought she would never come around but she eventually came around with the mercy of God, I think. So we got her head up and gave her about half speed but that was no use so we put her up to three quarters speed and the gale increased until it was a complete hurricane and we had her up at full speed.

The conditions on board were very, very difficult. There was water between decks and in our cabin we had everything on the top bunk and we slept there too and had to tie our rubber boots to the top rail to stop them being washed away. I shared a cabin with a young Welsh fellow who had been in submarines in Shetland during the war. In the middle of all this we were called out to retrieve the insurance wire that we carried. It had come off the after boat deck and fallen on the lower poop. We took our chance when the deck was above the sea and got it hauled for'ard by and lashed down. If it had gone over the side and gone in the propeller, that would have been the end of us. We got that calamity by with and the weather kept increasing until the seas were reckoned to be about 120 feet high. The greaser had gone aft to grease the steering motor and realised that the stop on the quadrant had broken off. He came dashing to the bridge and said they could not give her any more wheel, just a turn and a half of wheel each way, because the stop had gone.

So the weather did not improve at all and situations were getting pretty difficult and she pooped a terrible sea and lifted the whole of the after lifeboat deck right away, both boats and lifeboat deck and the whole lot went over the side. Things were not looking at all good and it was after that that there was nothing left aft, everything was gone, both lifeboats and the boat deck and then she cracked at No 3 amidships down the fish plate, which is the first plate down a ship's side, and we really did think that she was going to go then. There was some terrible grinding of that steel as she rolled and pitched in the sea but just after that happened it started to moderate.

The Skipper was exhausted and we had to take him down and put him in his cabin and Magnie Scott took charge and he was on the bridge for the next 20 hours. We left her hove to that night and next morning it had moderated enough to put her around and head for South Georgia. We had just turned her around when the fireman came dashing up saying that there was a smell come in the stokehold, that is where the boilers are. What had happened was with her rolling and pitching in the sea, some rockets had gone off and we had a fire on our hands. We got it put out and everything was all right after that and we had a peaceful trip right through till we reached South Georgia.

There was one other thing I remember. This chap had been on one of the *Harvester's* whale boats and he had gone for a walk across to the other station at Stromness and he never came back so we went out to look for him. We found him dead under the lea of a rock. The weather was quite cold then at the start of the winter and he had likely maybe had a heart attack. The carpenters made a coffin for him and he was laid out in the old cinema. We laid him to rest in South Georgia.

One fellow I was good friends with had been a prisoner of war in Germany for four years and he could drop off to sleep at any time. We were working in the meat meal plant and one day when he fell asleep some of the boys painted a big moustache on him and heavy eyebrows before we went for our smoko and when he came into the messroom everybody was laughing at him but he did not understand why. It was only when he came to have a wash that he realised what they had done to him.

A sad incident I remember was when the station manager, a very fine Norwegian man, Sverre Akseth, was killed. A whale catcher had come in from Grytviken, an Argentine station about 20 or 30 miles away, with something in her propeller. This catcher was alongside one of our whale boats and the Manager had gone down to watch our diver clearing it. The rail of a whale catcher was very low and he went right down between the boats. There was a bit of motion in the sea and he got crushed between the two catchers. The men hauled him out right away but he was dead. He was also buried in South Georgia.

MAXIE WILLIAMSON

My first season at the whaling was 1947/48 and my last season was '58, the year we got the fishing boat, *Sceptre*. I joined the *Polar Chief* in Cardiff in '47 and we sailed for South Georgia where I joined the *Southern Harvester*. I had different jobs, just a whaler to start with and then I was a boiler screwer for two seasons. Later I was a cutter on the fore plan, cutting up the carcases. It was fairly steady work and we had some good seasons.

The biggest season we had we were fishing at Peter's Isle, away west, about 2000 miles south of Cape Horn. It was all blue whale we got there, the area had been closed for a number of years. The factory was on 'full cook'. They put the catchers on a quota of 'whales per day' and for a time they had caught their whales and had stopped fishing by breakfast time. You could not handle as many blue whales per shift as you could fin. You could get through a lot of fin in 12 hours but the blue whales slowed you up. There were some big whales, we had one over 90 feet long but they were mostly over 80 feet. When you got one of them cut up in bits, it just filled the deck and there was a lot of oil which came out of one of those big whales.

The factory deck was very dangerous at night with the steam coming off the kettles. You could not see very well sometimes and there would be wires going in all directions from the winches and capstans. Surprisingly there was nothing very serious which happened. I think there was once or twice that someone fell down a kettle but they were not hurt.

Everybody got on very well together. After doing your 12 hour shift, you were glad to get something to eat and go to your bed so there was no time to fall out with anyone. It was always best when there was plenty of work to do. If you had a spell of fog then there might be a week where there was not many whales caught and you would be turned to to do a bit of painting, maybe of the deckhead in the factory or some place like that or you might be put down the forehold to tidy up and that could be a pantomime. Sometimes we would be sent aft to wash cabins. You could either wash them or not, it was just done to get you 'out of sight, out of mind' so to speak. We had a peerie Irish man there and he was always up to a lot of devilment. He would always be tormenting somebody, maybe someone twice his size. Then they would maybe take after him with a piece of wood.

One time the catcher, *Southern Foam*, broke down and we towed her back to South Georgia. She had lost her propeller in the ice. It was rough weather, more or less a gale all the way back. I was on watch with Jimmy Leask from

Weisdale keeping an eye on the tow at the stern of the factory ship. Sometimes you did not know whether the catcher was there or not, you just had to try to judge the strain on the wire. We were near Enderby Land at the time, about 3000 miles from South Georgia, and it took us 3 weeks to get back.

The first winter I did, I was in the station gang with Willie Laurenson from Bressay as bosun. We did just anything that cropped up. Salvesen got some big oil tanks from a derelict whaling station, Prince Olaf, further up the coast. They towed them around from there and we had to dig in anchors and we fixed 3 or 4 fold blocks to them to rig a purchase. We would heave away a while and see nothing happening and then all of a sudden this tank would give a jump when we got enough strain on it. They got all the tanks rigged up for the storage of whale oil. They were hauled up just below where the old football pitch was. It was fine weather when we did this job and I remember them towing around one tank with the snow still lying on top of it.

Just before the 1950/51 season started, about October, a ship was coming down to Grytviken, the *Ernesto Tornquist*. She had on board most of the staff coming down to start the season at Husvik and some of Salvesen's gunners and there was also a couple of women. She ran aground in a snow storm just up the coast from Leith Harbour. The alarm was raised and, as some of our catchers were ready for the ice, we were asked to crew them to go and give assistance. We found her lying ashore just out past the light in the bay where it was very sheltered. She had just missed the entrance to Leith Harbour. She was lying up along the beach with a good list on her. They had got the lifeboats off from one side but they could not get them away from the other side as she had listed too much. We took as many off as we could manage and brought them back into Leith Harbour. Then boats came from Husvik and picked up the remainder of them. The ship was a total loss but I think they got a lot of stuff out of her as she was fairly safe where she was lying.

The second winter I did I was at Stromness working on the floating dock. It was a cold job but it was lightsome. You were always getting a different catcher in and painting in the water line and doing their bottoms. There were two coats of paint put on the bottoms and you got a bit extra for spraying. The first coat you put on was an anti-corrosive coat and then an anti-fouling coat. The bottoms were generally very clean, nothing much ever seemed to grow on them. The paint would come off with the ice. The insides of the catchers were painted at Leith Harbour. In the floating dock there was a hole to drop the rudder down into. You had to be careful and not come too close or you would maybe fall in. One fellow came too close one day. He had just come off the motor boat at the end of the dock and he never noticed this hole and went in right up to his neck. There was a few inches of water swilling around on the dock floor so you had to know where the hole was because you could not see it. We used to catch small rock cod off the end of the dock and they were very good to eat.

There was a bit of snow the first winter I did but the second winter was not so bad. There was always a lot of shovelling to do. Sometimes you would have to go off to the catchers and shovel a lot of snow off them and also off any buildings with flat roofs. The bogie lines would all be covered with snow so anything that needed shifting was done with sledges. There would have been about 100 men in Stromness for the winter.

At the beginning of the winter the block we were living in burned down. It was a 3 storey block in which 30 men lived. We had just had our breakfast and had gone off to the catchers to shovel snow when the motor boat came off and asked if there was anyone here from block so-and-so. They had better come ashore because the building was on fire. But by the time we got ashore the whole building was just ablaze. We got nothing out, we just had what we were standing up in. It was surprising how quickly that building went up.

We got the hoses going as there was another block the same size alongside it and you could see the flame gripping the corner of that one. They had to play the hoses on that one and just forget about the one that was on fire. It was a blessing it happened in the morning because if it had happened at night I doubt there would have been a loss of life. I remember us looking around afterwards and we found what we thought had been an electric fire and the remains of a still so we put two and two together and thought it was probably someone using a still who had gone out and left it on. The heating was all done by steam radiators and the only electrics were the lights. We got £100 each out of either the Shipwrecked Mariners or the Union and went to the slop chest in Leith Harbour and replaced our lost gear. There happened to be a spare accommodation block which we moved into so we were ok.

At Stromness there were all kinds of machine shops with some very good equipment, turning lathes, etc. There were rollers for shaping plates and it was no bother to take a plate out of the side of a catcher and put in a new one. The catchers were all riveted. I watched them doing that and it was a skill of its own. They could have built a ship if need be. We worked a lot of overtime in the winter. I think we worked 4 nights per week up to 9 o'clock which helped our pay-off. We got every second Sunday off to do any washing.

During the season it was not very often that you saw any other factory ships. A rare time you might see one in the distance but of course it was a vast ocean. I remember seeing a few Japanese catchers one time. They were big diesel boats and there always seemed to be a lot of men standing on the bridge and at least 3 men in the barrel. They were big, fast boats.

On the way home from South Georgia I was always in the paint locker usually with a fellow from the North of Scotland, Tommy MacKay. It was our job to dish out the paint. There was a lot of paint used on the way home, the whole ship was done. The main colours were white for the superstructure and grey for the hull. We needed some red and blue for the funnels and then we had some red lead as well. In the paint locker you were always last to finish for you had to collect in all the pots and pour over any paint that was left in them. The brushes would be put in water and steeped for the next day so we were always first to start and last to finish. The men came in a bit before knock-off time. When the painting was finished we had all the brushes to clean.

We never seemed to be short of anything. On the trip home with the catcher there would have been about 500 men altogether on the factory ship so that meant that they needed at least 500 eggs per day. We got a good tot of rum every fortnight. We got an extra tot one time when we had produced the most oil in 24 hours of any factory ship. I think that was the same season as I mentioned earlier when we were getting the blue whales. I don't know if the catcher men got the same or not, it was they who were producing the goods.

I think life on the catchers would have been all right. The men there had to get on together as they were confined in a small boat for 4 months. Occasionally there would be a bit of friction between the firemen and the sailors but it was mostly good humoured.

Whaling was a good thing for Shetland. When you came out of the Forces there were no jobs going after the war so the whaling was the answer and you missed the bad weather in the winter. You got the best of both worlds and just being down for a season, it went by very fast. A lot of your time was spent on the journey down and back again. You could save money as there was no way of spending it unless buying a few cigarettes. The slop chest was cheap and they had everything you might need. Salvesen was a splendid Company and you were well looked after. When the whaling finished, they set up the Salvesen Fund in Shetland and a lot of ex-whalers benefited from it.

It was a good enough life, you always looked forward to the time to go back again.

GEORDIE MAINLAND

I was serving on an RFA tanker lying at Rosyth and I decided to go to the whaling. I went to the Office in Leith and saw Jerry Smith and he asked what my job was and I said I was below, I was a donkey man. So he said, "You come from Shetland?" and I said, "Yes." He said, "What are you doing there, being a Shetland man. That's impossible. But I can give you a job." I said, "When can I get the job?" He said, "There is a ship lying just now in Liverpool and she is needing a crew." And that was the *Southern Raven*. I said that that would be all right and he said, "When can you join?" and I said, "I don't know. I will have to tell the Skipper I am with just now when I get back on board." "Well," he said, "we'll sign you on now." I said, "Well, I'm already signed on with them." He said, "Well, you'll be getting two pays then."

So I went back and saw the Skipper and told him and he said, "Oh well, you can go if it is going to improve you any." So I set off and I went down and there was the *Southern Raven*. The guys I was with were a very rough crowd. They were Liverpool and Glasgow men and the first thing that happened aboard was when we were tipping bales of waste aboard then we threw it down from the top of the engineroom to the plates below. The bales weighed about a hundredweight and this guy was just reaching over a bale of waste when the other fellow up above let a bale drop on him. He said, "I've got him now." And just flattened him. So that was the beginning of it. When we came into the accommodation they were fighting but still, we set off and they settled down and things came all right after that.

We left and we had various bother with her, she was an old ship and had come from lying up and she had what they call watertube boilers. I do not know if anyone is sure about them but there is very little water in them and it's in a drum and it goes through the tubes and the steam is super heated. We had to work the boilers by hand which anybody who has had that experience will know is a very difficult thing to do. It is just a few minutes from full boiler to an empty one. If you get an empty one, you get an explosion.

Anyway, we set off and we got nearly to the Canary Islands when all sorts of problems started so we had to go in there. We lay there for three weeks and got it fixed up and we set away for South Georgia but we went straight to the whaling grounds instead. It was four months before we came in to South Georgia. After we left Leith Harbour, we ran out of bunkers coming by South America and we had to lie for a while of a week before we got a ship to come alongside and give us enough bunkers to get us home. So that was the first trip of the *Raven*.

On the second trip they put two more boilers in her and she was even worse because they put two Scotch boilers in her out of a corvette and the one system was not compatible with the other. The water would all go in one end and out of the one lot of boilers at the other end so it was even worse. We went to South Georgia again. There were quite a lot of Shetland men on her, I cannot mind them all. There was a Willie Tait from Aith, Bobby Jamieson from Yell and Geordie Jamieson and Andrew Jamieson and Jackie Henry from Weisdale. When we came back I was working by her in the Holy Loch when the Chief Engineer, McGonagle, left her. He went down to the *Harvester*. It was not long before he asked me if I would join him. So I joined the *Harvester* in Shields.

We first went to Aruba to take in fuel and I mind the first carry on going into Aruba was that they dumped too much ballast out of her when she went in and she fell on her side and it was very alarming to say the least. I was down below at the time along with a Norwegian and another man, and we did not see the Norwegian for nearly a week. I don't know what became of him, he was in the ship somewhere because he turned up again. We got a terrible scare, the whole thing went over and a big fire extinguisher ran to the side of the ship and went off and we were wading through foam.

Anyway they got the ship righted and our fuel on board and as usual there was hardly a sober man aboard by the time she sailed but we seemed to manage and once we got away, we were all right. She was a completely different ship to the *Raven*. She had two big triple expansion engines in her. They had been meant for a battle ship but were not needed so they put them in the *Harvester*. She could do 11 knots but the drawback was that when the factory ship was at 'full cook' she could not steam, it was either the factory or the engine, one or the other.

The Chief Engineer came down and of course she was an oil burner and the oil was pumped in to the furnaces at a certain pressure and this time the gauges were way above what they should have been. There were 24 fires and 8 boilers and you had to keep the water levels in the boilers by hand. This particular instance, they had the 'full cook' on and everything was going flat out when the Chief came down on an unexpected visit and tapped me on the shoulder and looked at the gauge and said, "I don't want to see that. Hang you cap on that when I come down." That was not to say that I was to turn it back it was just that he did not have to see it.

So that was the Health & Safety you had there. You were your own safety men at the whaling. You had to watch out for yourself, there was nobody else to look out for you but if you were accident prone you did not get a chance to go down next time. If you did not turn the thing up you would not get a chance to go down next time either so you were in a 'no win' situation.

I never did a winter but in the early 50's they used to do tanker runs with the factory ships between whaling seasons. I was asked to go on a tanker run but I refused. So they said, "Well, that's the finish of it, there is no way you will get back." I said, "Well, that is just too bad." Then they came back and said, "Well, if you will work by her then you will get your job back next year." So I worked by and that meant that you just stayed there and told the men from ashore who came and worked the ship about the different valves and that. The valves on a factory ship were a very complicated affair because they had tanks for the whale oil and tanks for fuel oil and you had to know which valve was which.

A fun that I had on the *Raven* was when Willie Tait from East Burrafirth and I would speak to each other up the ventilator. This ventilator came out at the back of the bridge and sometimes when we spoke, unknown to me, Willie would go into the bridge and bring out the Norwegian 2nd Mate and say to him, "Do you hear that noise?" The *Raven* had been a coffin ship during the 1st World War taking American dead back to the States and everybody saw ghosts and things on board her. This scared this 2nd mate out of his life, he thought this was a ghost speaking because he could not see anybody.

Another time, we were lying in Queens Dock in Glasgow and McGonagle, who belonged to Dunoon, had gone ashore. Everybody was ashore except me as I was on watch. I went down and found a burst pipe in the engine room and the water was standing from one side of the engine room to the other. I got all the pumps going on it that I could and that kept it under control until McGonagle came aboard and I said to him, "There's a pipe burst in the engine room and it's going from one side to the other." There was a café up the road where all the notorious women used to hang out so he told me to go up the road and get one of them and stick in it until morning. The water ran until morning but I did not get one of them to stick in it, it ran without.

We had a Newfoundlander aboard. When we were lying in Glasgow there was no heating on the ship. There was no such a thing as putting you into hotels like they do now. We just had to stick it out aboard the best way we could. Everybody went up to the second hand shops and bought electric heaters, there was electricity aboard. This Newfoundlander had his room all fixed up with electric heaters and he was entertaining his girlfriend and some of the boys got to know this. Four of us were sitting playing cards next door and, unknown to us, as the boys went ashore they saw this electric heater on the table so they screwed open the ventilator and put pepper down and they tied the door so this pair could not get out. The Newfoundlander had to smash the door down to get out. By this time we were aware of the noise and somebody realised what it was and we were all in bed when this wife came in. She was supposed to be a very nice girl and she said, "You're nothing but a lot of Highland B———s."

We had a 2nd engineer, an Irishman, who would keep walking around in his underpants in the hot weather. We had ice water down below. We had a big brass syringe, a thing like a pump and as he was walking above me on the grating I shot him with this syringe and he thought he was scalded. He thought it was steam but it was the ice water.

The *Raven* was full of huge rats. They looked big because they lived in the trunking where the ventilator from the blast freezers came out. They were nearly the size of cats. The fur on them was huge. I used to prop up a tank lid with a stick with a string attached and put chocolate under it as bait. When a rat came along I would pull the string and catch it.

I was in a cabin with an Irishman who worked with stills and he also did a bit of crawling with the Officers. He washed the Chief and the 2nd Engineers' boilersuits, their white overalls, in a 40 gallon barrel with the top cut out of it. One of the boys overheard the Chief congratulating him on getting them so clean. "Oh", he said, "I just put a wee bit of caustic in. I know how much to put in." The Chief said, "You certainly make a good job of them." The boys made certain that he made a good job of the next ones. They put 5 gallons of caustic in the drum. There was nothing left but the buttons. They heard the Chief saying the next time, giving Paddy a row, "I told you, you bloody fool, you have put in too much caustic." So he did not get the job of doing that any more, that was the finish of it.

One time just as we were coming on for Las Palmas I said I was going to write and Paddy said, "Oh, I cannot write any because I cannot mind the address. We moved into a new house." So I told him that he could send it to his old address and his wife would probably get it but I cannot mind whether or not he did it. There was one time he was in the engine room and he had on one of those black singlets made out of cotton. We had engines half up the side of the engine room that you had to use a ladder to get on to the platform and Paddy was up there cleaning the engines and when he came down he had no singlet on. He said somebody had whipped his singlet off and we had been on to him about the ghosts which were on the ship. I went up and had a look and the jubilee clips on the fuel pump drive had caught his singlet and just whipped it right off his back. He was some guy.

Him and the cook made a still in their cabin. They used to still the stuff with a Primus stove and when I came up off watch one time they were both lying out for the count. The Primus had flared up and all yon black stuff was hanging around the cabin. I hauled them out and I did not know whether they were full of drink or if they had flaked out with the fumes. Thankfully they came around so that was the end of that still. It was said he made a fortune making stills when he overwintered. That was one thing he could do.

One day he was needing to get a piece of half inch copper pipe bent in a coil and he did not seem to know how to do it. Somebody suggested he bent it around a stanchion which was fixed from the floor to the deckhead. So he bent it around this stanchion and then he could not get it off so the boys said that he would have to cut it with the hacksaw. I'm not sure if they did not have to refrain him from that.

On the road home, the two firemen with me were always Norwegians. They had been on the catchers and were doing their training. They would come down to work the engines and to end up with they were the best guys of the lot because I hardly ever needed to go down, I spent most of my time on deck. The engineers used to have a competition as to who had the most revs on the watch. The throttle was set so anyone who had the most revs was steaming higher than the other one without blowing her off. To end up with I trained up this two Norwegians to steam the ship and one of them would watch until he saw the steam coming near to blowing off and then he would tell the other one and they would steam her like that and I would be standing at the stern.

I was on the 3rd Engineer's watch and the 2nd Engineer was the watch after me. The 2nd Engineer on a ship is always supposed to have the best revs, if he does not have it then there is trouble. So the 2nd started giving these guys trouble and to end up with I got caught up in it because he said I spent most of my time on deck. So they got on to the junior Chief about it and he said, "Well, if he is spending most of his time on deck, obviously the ship can steam herself because it was the best revs. Some of you want to try to stand longer on deck, she might get going better." The throttle was set and it could not alter.

They had a novel way of putting rivets in that ships. What they would do, they would get a bit of stick. The rivets would wear out of them sometimes and there would be just a jet of water coming in. They would go down in the tank and they would push a thin piece of wood out with a string on it through the hole and then it floated up and they had a bolt with an eye welded in the end of it and they would pull a stronger piece of string in through the hole and then pull the bolt in and screw a nut on. That is how they replaced the rivets because they used to wear out with running along the ice. It was a funny thing to be down there below the water and hear the ice running along the side of the ship. It's marvellous how that ships could navigate through that ice at night. They would go full speed with that big ships and yet they just had the basic radar then, that was the early 1950's. There was none of the navigators that we have now. They certainly had to know their stuff as far as navigating went.

Very few people seemed to turn ill at the whaling, they seemed to stay very healthy. There were one or two accidents. The chippy we had on the *Raven*, I think he lost nearly every finger, one by one with the circular saw. He was an old fellow and he would say, "That's another one gone." He was a kind of an Officer so he had access to drink when none of the rest of us did. I don't know how many fingers he had left when he came back but he could not have had very many because every now and again he would say, "That was an accident."

JOHN LEASK

I joined the whalecatcher *Simbra* in Smith Docks, Middlesborough in England, the same place as I joined the *Southern Wheeler* for the previous season. Except for a steering problem crossing the Bay of Biscay, the voyage south was uneventful.

After arriving at Leith Harbour, South Georgia, we took on supplies, whale ropes, harpoons, stores, etc and left in company with eleven other catchers and the new factory ship, the *Southern Harvester*. After two or three days we started whaling and worked our way into the Weddell Sea area of the Southern Ocean, this would have been approximately early to mid November.

After about two months fishing, on the evening of the 11th January 1947, the *Simbra* was lost. With a lot of high speed chasing, fuel was usually taken on every four to six days. On the morning of the 11th we delivered whales to the factory ship then went alongside for bunkers and stores but we were refused bunkers as the factory ship had a tanker alongside replenishing her tanks. It is possible that, with normal procedure, the *Simbra* might not have been lost for with full tanks the stability of the ship would have been much better but as it was we carried on fishing with what bunkers we had left.

The crew were all Norwegians except for the deck boy who came from Edinburgh and myself. I was on watch that evening of the 11th from 4pm to 8pm. We had caught and flagged two whales close up to an area of pack ice. It was my hour in the crow's nest from 6pm to 7pm. We were running before the wind chasing the rest of the pod which had taken fright so it looked like a long chase to catch them up. Perhaps that is why, as I was looking around, I saw the Skipper on the bridge talking to my watchmate probably telling him to turn round and go back to pick up the two whales we had caught before dark because at that moment she started coming round to starboard into the wind and, as is normal when turning sharply, she started keeling over to port – but this time she just kept on going over.

As I realised that things were not right I got out of the crow's nest to come down the rigging but she had keeled over so far I had to come down the rigging head first, on my hands and knees. As I looked down the sea was starting to pour down the hatch. I got down to the ship's side and to get aft to the lifeboat I had to shuffle my way along the outside of the ship which I managed by keeping a grip on the bulwark and going crabwise along the ship's side. When I got to the lifeboat the rest of the crew were already there.

They had got the covers off and my watchmate was cutting the boat adrift from the davits as there was no chance of getting it launched. By this time the sea was coming down the engine room skylights so we all got on the side of the ship ready to jump. That was a bad moment because with no distress signal sent and no lifeboat launched, when we all had to jump it was just like jumping to our deaths.

The shock of the cold water was bad but I managed to get a hold of the lifeboat strongback, the wooden spar that the covers are fitted over. The Skipper and my watchmate also got hold of it. The lifeboat luckily had floated free. It was quite close, but upside down. We started paddling towards it but the Skipper soon lost his grip and went under. It was slow going against the wind so my watchmate let go and swam to the boat. I could make no headway myself as I wasn't a swimmer but I struck out and made it. The fact that I was wearing a kapok lined coat gave me the buoyancy to get me there. The wireless operator also made it and between the three of us we managed to heave her over. After getting on board we pulled another four of the crew on. The boat, of course, was full of water. We tried bailing but it was no use – the sea just kept slapping in over the side.

Three of the men died very quickly so we put them back over the side. Nobody else made it to the boat. The deck boy kept shouting my name but he, too, soon went under. We tried bailing again but it was no good. By sitting right up on the stern of the boat I managed to get out of the water, except for my legs below the knees. I had lost the mitten off my left hand but it wasn't long before my hands and legs were numb. I saw the smoke of a catcher as it was getting dark. I set off a flare but it wasn't seen.

The three men left in the boat with me didn't last long. The wireless operator, the fireman and the mate soon died. It was probably no more than an hour, hour and a half. The mate was the last to go. It was a long, cold night just sitting there. Thankfully the wind had dropped. An iceberg floated past close by and a couple of whales went past. I must have been in a semi-conscious state when the sound of a harpoon gun going off brought me to my senses. I looked round and a catcher no distance away had just shot a whale. I managed to get to the middle of the boat and although I had lost all feeling in my hands and legs, I managed to get an oar with a bucket on it and place it where the mast went. They saw me and it wasn't long before they had me on board – that was about 11am. I spent some time in the hospital on the *Southern Harvester*. My knees were badly bruised and I think it was a week before my legs and hands came right although it was a fair while until my left had got back to normal.

JIMMY MANSON

I left Scapa Flow and went to the whaling in '45. We sailed from Leith on the old *Saluta*. She had been at Iceland and came back to Leith via Norway where she picked up the Norwegians. We sailed from Leith and had been out a day when the freezer broke down and we had to go back in again which was a very fine thing because the war with Japan had finished that day and we had a small celebration. We finally got away and went to Tenerife, there were not many tourists there then. The people were all very happy to see us and I remember our Norwegian Skipper saying that he had been in many ports and seen many men but he had never seen so many drunk men in his life. Norway had been occupied during the war and the Norwegian people had had a rough time. Most of them were in old patched dungarees and when the slop chest opened for the first time they went and got new boilersuits and new dungarees and they would walk the decks. It was like a peerie boy when he got his first long breeks. It was just super to see them.

We got down to Leith Harbour and it was a kind of sad place. There was only maybe a dozen men there. There were two brothers, Willie and Tammie Laurenson from Bressay, and the rest were Norwegians. They were very happy to see us, I know that. And then we got stuck in and did a season. The *Venturer* was new that year. I went back the following year, down again with the old *Saluta*. She was coming past it then, a very sad old ship. At the end of the season that year, I came home with the *Venturer*.

The following year the *Harvester* was new and I went down to South Georgia with her and the rest of my time at the whaling was spent on board her, 14 seasons altogether. I did one winter in Stromness where they had two floating docks. My last season at the whaling, I was deck storekeeper. I worked the winter in the machine shop along with a Norwegian plater, a very fine man, I never had a wrong word with him. I had various jobs on the factory ships. I was a screwer which meant I had to close the lids on the kettles when the whale meat was being cooked and when the sperm fishing was on they took on an extra flenser and I was on that job.

Another job I did was taking the teeth out of the sperm whales. I was along with Addie Leask from Weisdale who now stays in Aberdeen. It was very simple to end up with, once you got the hang of it. And when there were no whales, we used to boil the teeth up and separate them and they were all boxed and taken home. I could have had a lot of whale teeth but I only have 3. I gave away a lot. After we came in to Liverpool one time there were a few of us left to square things up and take the *Harvester* around to the Tyne. One thing we had to do was clean out all the cabins. One day there were two teachers who came on board with 20 or so children. They were having a day out and had come aboard to have a look around. I asked one of the teachers if she would be interested in whale teeth and when she shouted to the youngsters they came running. I wonder if they still have them or not. The last year the *Harvester* operated, Jimmy Leask from Lerwick was bosun and I was storekeeper. We took her across to Norway and I never saw her again.

Despite the kind of work, I do not recall many accidents happening. It was very strange because there were wires running in all directions, up and down and across and there were whales being turned over and heaved up and you name it but I never mind very many accidents. One of the scuppers blocked one time and my old man, Addie Manson, was bosun. He had been bosun for many years and he put caustic soda down and once it started to boil, it just gushed up again and went right in his face. There was a Norwegian there, big Jacob, and he took a bucket of water and threw it in the old man's face. He said later, "That was something that I did not like to do." But it certainly did help. The water washed away the caustic. But he was rushed to the hospital. I was on the opposite shift from him and somebody came and told me what had happened. I went up to see him and his head was all wrapped up in bandages. A day or two later the Doctor asked him how he was and he said, "Oh, I can see you." The Doctor said, "You see me?" and he said, "Yes, I saw you last night." The Doctor could not believe it and he shouted for the assistant and said, "Come here. Come here. I have good news for you." He got his sight back and everything was fine, it did not even mark him. All thanks to Jacob with his salt water.

There was a Norwegian bosun I worked with, a very fine old man. I was with him for a lot of years. He was bosun on the after plan year after year. I forget what happened to him but when we were on the way home he took ill and was maybe one or two nights in the hospital and then he passed away and we buried him at sea. It was a peculiar time of day that he was buried, the sun was just going down. We wondered why this time was chosen for the burial. It was timed to the minute and they lowered him down and away he went. That is a thing that I never will forget.

One season on the way home two men passed away, both Shetlanders. They died within a week of one another. Jimmy Leask, Jimmy Nicolson and myself were detailed to sew them up in canvas and get them ready for burial. And then we got word that they had to be taken home. I don't know if it was to have a post mortem or what but they were taken home and buried in

Shetland. It is a thing that I will never have to do again, that's for sure.

I think it was the last year that I was down and we were among the pack ice when we got a big slash on our bow about 20 feet long. The ice just cut through the thick plate as if it was cardboard. We were on our way up to South Georgia after the season so we emptied out the forepeak and the platers at the island welded on a patch. Our Skipper got into a lot of trouble about it because he never told the Company or the Insurance people and when they found out about it, he got the heave. If he had reported it to the Insurance Company, Salvesen could have made a claim and got it done properly but as things were they had to do it at their own expense.

It was a hard life, 6 to 6 day and night, a 7 day week for four months. When there were lots of whales, the more bonus we got and so it was fine. There was once or twice at the end of the season when the fishing finished that we were put on board a whale catcher and sent to Signey Isle where there was a weather station. There were maybe 10 or 12 British men on this island and they had gathered up 100 penguins. We took the penguins on board the whale catcher back to South Georgia where they were put on the factory ship and I looked after them all the way home. That was my job, feeding the penguins with herring or whatever kind of fish we had on board for them. It was a very interesting job because they used to annoy me when I came in sight of the pens. They would make strange noises and come and flap around your legs as if they were glad to see you. Some went to Edinburgh Zoo and maybe some to London Zoo. No doubt some of their offspring is there yet.

When we rejoined the ship at the beginning of a season and we met up with all our Norwegian shipmates again, the first half of the day was spent shaking hands and they always used to say, "Takk for siste." That was, "Thanks for the last time." A very fine crowd of men.

ALLAN TULLOCH

My first season at the whaling was 1953 when I was 18 years old. I joined the *Southern Harvester* in Newcastle and after a few days there we sailed to Tonsberg in Norway to pick up more crew and stores. The next port was Aruba to take on fuel oil and then on to South Georgia where I was transferred to the *Southern Lupin*. Our job was to pick up the whales and tow them to the factory ship. We had not been many days at sea until it was plain to see that the Norwegians did not like young British boys being employed by Salvesen.

Christmas came and one thing I remember was the Captain, our gunner, came around the crew cabins but did not come to our one. My cabin mate belonged to Glasgow. On Boxing Day we had to pass something to another catcher and, in doing so, they collided and our bows were so badly damaged we had to go back to South Georgia and go in the dry dock in Stromness. As it was New Year all the crew went ashore to friends but I did not have any so I only had the sea lions on the beach when I went for a walk to wish me a Happy New Year. It was very lonely. When the season was finished I came back home on a small catcher called the *Sobkra*. The crew there was good and Willie Watt from Lerwick was in the cabin with me. We came to Smith's Dock in Middlesborough.

I was on the *Southern Harvester* for two more seasons and did a season on the *Southern Satellite*, a transport ship. I missed some seasons but was back for two more on the *Southern Venturer*. I would say that it was a good experience and I met a lot of good men. I always had a fiddle with me so, along with other Shetlanders, we had many a good tune. There were sad times as well. One season we lost our helicopter pilot in the Doldrums. They had been out for practice and to drop mail on the *Southern Opal* on her way north. Only one pilot was saved. Also a Norwegian boy on his first trip died of polio. The engineers and other men on board made a make shift iron lung to try to save him. One Shetland man died of pleurisy. They were all buried at sea. I thought it was very sad.

I remember a Norwegian man coming along the factory deck sitting on a moving conveyor belt, his hands were out before him but he was not looking and his hands went down between where one belt ended and another began. But Harry Paton from Whalsay was near to the controls and was able to stop the belt. When we got the belt reversed, everything on the inside of his hands was hanging from under his wrists so we got him to the doctor. He fixed him up so that the man was able to be back the next season.

One thing I always laugh at when it comes back to me is one night on the way home we joined the train in Liverpool but had to change at Wigan. We had some time to wait. Everybody was in good spirits after a few drams. I remember sitting on a kit bag playing the fiddle and Davie Arthur from Stromfirth was playing the guitar while the old Arab and Eddie Smith did the crab dance. I think the other people on the platform thought we were all mad, but not so, we were just happy to be going home after a long season.

LOWRIE LAURENSON

I am one of the old ex-whalers. I'm getting on a bit now, I'm 73 years old so it's a start since I was at the whaling. I'd been four years in the Admiralty before that and when I came home there was not very much work so the only thing was the whaling. That was 1949/50. We set sail from Liverpool on a ship called the *Polar Chief* a brawly old slow packet with tarmacadam decks and with the hot weather the tar would melt so you had to take care going on the top deck with your bare feet. Anyhow, we got to South Georgia after not a bad trip. It was a start before they got us all placed with what we were going to do. We were all just doing anything on the way down. Some peeled tatties, some painted and other odd jobs. I was along with Lollie Tait from Aith, painting.

Our accommodation was in what they called B Block 21, a lot of the boys will remember that famous place. I got a job on what they called the meat laft. There were a few of us there including Willie Tait, the Councillor from Bigton. Our job was, when the whales came on the plan, the cutters and the lemmers cut them up and then the pieces were dragged up the plan to where we were and cut into a size that could go down into what was called the kettles. It went down there and was boiled and then the water was separated off from the oil which was pumped into storage tanks and the water went to what was called the soluble plant.

It was a new plant. Isaac Peterson from Sullom was the head of that plant. I was three months on that and then I was put on a peerie boat that towed the whales from the buoy into the plan. Kaare Iversen was the Skipper of the peerie boat. That was the first year. I came home on the *Saluta* and we were home a start and the same old way, everybody thought the whalers were loaded. You used to buy an old car so that you knew you had the fare away again when you flogged her.

The second year I was down, we had a bit of a jinxed trip. We left on a ship called the *Southern Opal*. When we were about 90 miles off Aruba most of the boys had gone down with German measles. A terrible thing, they had to make a hospital aft on her as it was contagious. You were not allowed to go in and speak to them but you could speak to them through the port hole. There was one fine big fellow there who came from Gruting, he died. He was Ray Cumming. There was a lot more boys who got the measles. The spots would not come out with the hot weather. They went in and that was really what killed them. There was Buchan Henry from Weisdale and Willie Fraser from Walls, they all had a terrible time of it.

We left Aruba and were going down the east coast of South America when one of the pistons blew up and came right out the side of the engine. It was the biggest cylinder, there were three cylinders each one a different size. We drifted along for 3 days. The Chief Engineer and some of the boys did a repair using 2 tank lids and they made a splendid job of it. They bored the tank lids and put one above and one below the cylinder and put a bolt clean through both, tightened it in place, and took her on two pistons into a place called Pernambuco in Brazil. We were in there and I cannot mind the outs and ins of it but somehow or other they got her all fixed up but it was a kinda slow journey to South Georgia. We did eventually get there after about 6 weeks I think. When we finally got there I was wondering what kind of job I would get, the meat laft the year before and probably the same again, when I saw the old Manager coming flapping his wings along, Skarra they called him. He said, "Ah, Laurenson, you go on *Gambler*. I said, "No, no. I'm OK where I am." He said, "No, no. You'll go *Southern Gambler*. Your brothers go catcher, you will go catcher." So I said, "Well, OK."

So I set off and they got things sorted out and I joined the *Gambler*. It was really a fine life. It was rough but it can be rough as it likes when you are a young fellow. There was one Shetland boy with me, he was the mess boy and he stays here in Scalloway yet. He is Geordie Niven. Anyhow, we left and I thought that this was all right. I was watching the Norwegians going up into the barrel and instead of coming down the rigging they were coming down the stays. I was one of the deck hands. There were only two Britishers on the boat. My turn up the barrel, I went up the rat lines, had to hang on when she came over and when she rolled the other way I climbed again and got to the steel ladder and I gripped him to go aboard but with the ice and the heat of my hands, it was just like laying my hands on the stove. I had in my mind I would not do that again without gloves on.

I got in the barrel and oh boy was I sick, it was like scrambled eggs. There were three holes in the bottom of the barrel and I had in my mind that they must be there for letting the spewings out. It really was for the rain water I think. I mind the first day in that barrel I looked for very few whales. There was a bit of a dodger and I peeped over him sometimes and I thought Gosh I'm just above the fore end of the gun with the rake on the mast.

Sugen Olsen was the Skipper and there was a bit of competition to see who was going to get the most whales. They went for anything they heard or saw. They could not speak much English, you had to try to learn a bit of Norwegian. They did not really want to speak too much English, although some of them could. You had to watch for the whale coming up and shout what side he was coming at. Barboard or Larbord and sometimes you got a peerie bit mixed up with it. You told him the wrong side and if he aimed at that then you shouted the other way then he would turn around and shake his fist at you.

You had to do an hour in the barrel, an hour on the wheel, an hour in the barrel and an hour on the wheel and then you were off watch. If it happened that the other watch which had gone on before you got a 'fast fish', that was what they called it when they got a whale, then you had to get out of your bunk and you had to coil the whaleline. You had to go into the rope locker and walk around with this cold wet whaleline, coiling from the centre outward towards the edges.

The Chief Engineer was usually on the brake which nipped the rope if the whale lived up again for ten to one he used to live up and they would give one shout and you got out of there like lightning and when you looked over your shoulder there was nothing left, the rope had all gone. There were two big springs which took the tension off the boat which stopped her being pulled over. You sometimes had to go through the same toil again. They had a pipe with a compressor and they would stick it in the whale and blow him full of air, flag him and plot the course and set off after the school again. That was the procedure the whole time. The foregoer had to be spliced on to another harpoon and usually the mate coiled the foregoer in front of the gun. Sometimes you wished that you would not get another whale. In midsummer, with daylight around the clock, you kept going as long as there were whales around. It was a braw long day. The Norwegians were good hands with the harpoon guns.

We came home with the old *Saluta*. It was the last year of her, she had to come home, she had been an accommodation ship and she was no longer allowed in this country, they were going to break her up when she came back. We were in awfully heavy weather in the Forties and there was a boy from Nesting called Charlie Tait. I saw him lifting a lot of cement aboard her in South Georgia and I wondered what we were going to do with cement on the way home. He made solid cement blocks so that as the rivets went she could be cemented. When she came to Immingham or somewhere they whipped the funnel off her right away and the masts and she was just like a barge and they took her to the breakers yard.

The next season I joined the *Harvester* in Norway. We went to Tonsberg and loaded a terrible lot of hutting and stuff to be taken down to South Georgia for accommodation. On the way back from Tonsberg, I did not feel very well. I got pains and the old doctor we had reckoned that it was appendicitis, or threatening appendicitis. So I was put ashore in Southampton and I was never at the whaling again. That was the end of my whaling experience.

L to R Bobby Garrick, Sandness; John W Abernethy, Walls; Alex J Henry, Yell.
Photo: A J Henry.

L to R Teddy Wiseman, Lerwick; Ronald Manson, Yell; Freddie Johnson, Selivoe; Samuel G Anderson, Whalsay on board ***Polar Chief****.*
Photo: K Brown.

L to R Mitchell Arthur, Ollaberry; Norwegian mess boy; Ellis Sales, Lerwick.
Photo: R Wiseman.

Winter 1960. L to R Bobby Nicolson, Mossbank; John Nicolson, Yell; Tammie Thomson, Yell.
Photo: T Thomson.

Floating factory ***Southern Venturer*** *showing helicopter and hangar between the funnels which are side by side.*
Photo: W Watt.

*Whale catcher **Southern Main**. When **Southern Broom** broke down off Enderby Land in 1960, the **Southern Main** towed her to Middlesborough via Cape Town and Dakar, a total of 11,000 miles. D Clark, Yell on **Southern Main** and G Fraser, West Burrafirth on **Southern Broom**. Photo: A Anderson.*

L to R Andrew Sutherland and Willie Arthur, both Yell. ***Svend Foyn*** *1940.*
Photo: A Anderson.

L to R Alex Hughson, Whiteness; Jimmy Watt, Jimmy Johnson, both Lerwick; Andrew Arthur, Ollaberry.
Horizontal John Gilbert (Romeo), Newcastle.
Photo: R Wiseman.

Left: L to R Back row Alan Watt, Jim Craigie, Eddie Wiseman, all Lerwick; Christie Tait, Aith. Front row Bertie Henderson, Unst; Robbie Watt (Red Robbie), Teddy Wiseman, both Lerwick. Photo: K Brown.

Below: L to R Back row George Cheyne, Sandness; Jimmy Nicolson, Quarff; Jimmy Leask, Weisdale; Tammie Inkster, Ollaberry; Front row Andrew P Johnson, Sefster; Sonny Williamson, Ollaberry; Jerry Dalziel, Sandsound.Photo: J Dalziel.

KAARE IVERSEN

I had to go back to Norway with the boats after the war and I was in Norway for a year before I was demobbed and I took my wife over and she was in Norway for a year. Then I could not get a job, I was engineer but did not have any certificates and did not have a ticket. So I asked to be released from the Navy to emigrate but that was refused. My wife was back in Shetland by this time so I wrote and asked if I could go on holiday to Shetland and that was granted. I packed my kit bag and escaped again and I arrived in Shetland on 12 November 1948. I worked first of all for Capt Hay at Blacksness slipway. Then I worked with Henry Goodlad and Bobby Walterson heightening the bulwarks on the *Hazelbank*. That was in the summer of 1949 and I got a job on her at the herring fishing.

I applied for a job in Salvesens in the whaling industry and left here in early August and went to Glasgow and joined the *Polar Chief*. We lay in Glasgow for a fortnight or so. Then we went to South Georgia by way of Tenerife. When I signed on in Leith I was asked to do the winter. I said, "I will have to see how it is first." But I did the winter on the motor boat. The men who were going home were Jimmy Peterson and Angus Ridland from Lerwick. There was one motor man needed but I refused to take the job at first as it was just to be for the winter. Finally I persuaded them to let me do the job for the season as well.

I came home after that and then went back whaling in 1953. I was again on the motor boats along with Gibbie Clark this time. Some days there was not much to do so we did painting in the barracks. Then we were sent on board the *Polar Maid* to do some clearing up. The skipper was Willie Spence from Yell.

We worked away and then the Skipper came down and saw that everything was cleared up. He said, "It's nearly knocking off time. Would you like to have a dram?" Gibbie said, "After a job like this we are needing a dram." We went to his cabin and he came out with a bottle with very little whisky in it and poured it into half tumblers and Gibbie looked at it and said, "Willie, do you call this a dram?" "Yes," he said. Gibbie said, "If that's all the whisky you have we'll leave it with you." He said, "No, I've got a whole bottle over here but I don't touch it myself. I like a drop of wine".

Gibbie says, "Aye, aye, I always thought you were a bloody plonkey." So before we went ashore, over half the bottle was gone and we were feeling fine. Capt Spence had a lot of respect for Gibbie and he was a first class man.

While I was on the motor boat I had to go one night about 6 o'clock with some people to the Norwegian station at Husvik, a few miles away. I was to come back at 10 o'clock again and pick them up. Josie Manson was with me on the boat at the time and we got there and there was no sign of them so we thought we would wait five minutes and that five minutes lasted until five minutes past five in the morning. We did not have anything on board to eat so we went up to the galley in Husvik and got some sandwiches and a cup of coffee or something. But it was a very long night and then we had to go to work the whole of the next day.

One of the catchers, I think it was the *Southern Lily* who broke her thrust bearing at the ice and she almost sank. The *Southern Main* took her alongside the factory and put a wire underneath her and kept her up until they got the bulkhead stiffened up. All the after cabins were flooded but they got her pumped out and towed her up to Leith Harbour before taking her to Stromness to the floating dock.

Putting a catcher in the floating dock was a job for a motor boat. One day we managed to get her around to Stromness. It was a fine flat calm day in Leith Harbour but a good breeze of wind in Stromness so they could not get her into the dock. They tied her up to one of the buoys there and kept a fireman aboard day and night to keep pumping her out. I was over there at half past five in the morning with the relief fireman and it was flat calm, there was not a breath of wind. When I got back to Leith Harbour I went to the villa where Capt Mhyre lived and I said, "Well, if you're going to dock the *Lily* you had better get ready to go now because it's no wind but before breakfast time at 9 o'clock it will be blowing a gale". "Oh", he said, "it is very fine here".

I said, "You see Coronda Peak?" "Yes, what about it?" "Well, you see the dust flying off Coronda Peak? It is blowing up there and when you see that there it is not long before it is blowing right down here as well." So he got men and the *Bouvet* over and took the *Lily* in towards the dock and by this time the wind was beginning to freshen. We were just approaching the dock when a gust of wind came and she went the wrong way. But we took a complete turn out of her and got her in next time. By this time the spindrift was coming from the graveyard where the old catchers were tied up. After the *Southern Lily* was safe in the dock, Captain Myhre came and thanked me for ordering him as Captain to get the men and dock the *Southern Lily*.

He asked how I knew that it would blow a gale in Stromness Bay. I just answered that when one had been a motor man and worked with whale catchers in the season and the winter, you learned to take notice of cloud and as for Coronda Peak, that was a sure weather forecast all to itself.

In 1963 Salvesen left whaling. I stayed on in Leith Harbour as Salvesen's representative for a time. Then when I finally left I came home via Japan on a refrigerated ship. From there we flew to Anchorage in Alaska. We left there and flew over the north pole and over my home country, Norway, and finally got back here via Hamburg. That was the end of my whaling.

ALEX JOHN HENRY

I got a job as a Group 9 whaler on the factory ship, *Southern Venturer*, in 1948. She was lying in South Shields. My job was working in what was known as the rosedown. That was bagging and stowing bags of meat meal below decks. It was very warm. I wasn't that taken with the heat but it was a job and a start.

The next season I was on deck Group 8 and the job was feeding the rosedown with lumps of whale meat for the meat meal plant. We had a fairly good season. However, when the season ended I had put my name down and went ashore to Leith Harbour for the winter and was in what was known as the station gang. The man in charge was Ertie Ramsay from Ollaberry. The work was looking to all the maintenance needing to be done on the shore station there, and any other jobs such as going to Grytviken when the ship would come from Argentina with stores.

The weather was fairly good, snow but not too bad and we had a good crew of men in the gang and any time off was spent on the skis. I mind one fine night with the moon shining going from Leith Harbour to Stromness on the skis. It was quite a distance across there but was a great experience. That's where the drydock was so there were a number of men stationed there for the winter as well.

However, as time passed the winter came to an end and when the *Southern Venturer* came back down I was back on board her and I had the same job as the year before once we started to fish. The following season I was with two Norwegians, one on the capstan, me the hooker and the head bone sawman. My job was to take the head into position, then steady the saw blade which, if I remember, was about eight feet long. Once the head was all cut up, we put the bones down the kettles for cooking. I got on well with the Norwegians and did a turn on the saw for the sawman when he got hit with a hook and was off work for a time. I was with that sawman for three seasons, then the following season I got a cutter's job which was group 6 and cut the meat up to feed the meat meal plant.

I again, before the end of the season, put down for another winter and was accepted. That winter I got a job doing the maintenance on the whale catchers. The man in charge was Bjarne Olsen, Norwegian mate off a catcher. We again had a good crew and Peter Manson of Urafirth and me worked together. When the winter came to an end, the factory came back down and we were placed for our jobs. I was back on the same as before, cutting the meat for the meat meal plant. The next season I was on the afterdeck cutting up the spik for the kverners – that's the boilers it was cooked in. There were four of us on that job, two cutters, a hooker and a capstan man. The final and last season I was on the same job.

The biggest whale I saw coming on board the factory ship was a 98 foot blue whale. My best week's pay was £45, that was at group 6, overtime, bonus, the lot. It always had its dangerous moments as well on the factory deck. It would have looked worse for anyone seeing it for the first time – wires everywhere. You got to know it all and were always on the alert and would give a shout to anyone if you saw something about to happen. There were many near misses but never more than a broken leg with running spik or someone getting burned with oil.

The trips down to South Georgia were spent getting everything ready, a lot of wire splicing to do, tail strops, etc. I remember us doing the factory's insurance wire. Charlie Duncan and me worked a lot together on that job. We had a rough trip down to South Georgia once. A very bad storm for two or three days, the wind registered 128 miles per hour. The weather boarding was cleaned off the bridge, all the port holes on the front was gone, the forecastle head deck came down, one of the bits on the fore deck was broken in two like a match, the bulk heads between the mess rooms were all burst. It would appear she was being driven too fast at the time when she took a lump of sea.

When we did get to Leith Harbour, one of the repairers, Jocky Manson whom I helped with it, put in 300 rivets in the forefit. Another trip down I was looking after 80 pigs and 30 hens which we took on board at Newcastle. The man the bosun put to work with me was Geordie Robertson from Walls. The pigs were for our own use and the hens were for Leith Harbour. We slaughtered the biggest pigs before Christmas and the rest before the main whaling season started. I mind the big ones all hung up at around 200 pounds, they did very well and we did not lose any.

The bosun I had for most years was Magnie Christie, originally from Cunningsburgh and on the afterdeck when I was cutting up the spik, it was a Norwegian bosun. During the season we were on 12 hour shifts and changed at half season so if you were first on day shift, it was night for the second half. There were usually 4 from our shift that did tank cleaning if and when the tankers came alongside. That was usually another 3 hours on top of the 12 we had already done. Then Magnie, the bosun, would take us to his cabin and give us a good glass of rum after the job was finished. This was a known practice. It was an issue given to him for this purpose. It was all good team work and everyone appeared to get on very well together, especially the Shetlanders and the Norwegians. But I suppose, like everything else, it had to come to an end for during the latter years you seldom ever saw a blue whale at all. Another job I did in the station gang was fishing for rock cod with a chap called Willie Couper. We would get so many then we would go ashore and fillet them so all in all there weren't many bits of whaling work I wasn't involved in.

DAVIE LAURENSON

I had been working here in the building trade with Halls of Aberdeen. Before that I had been with the Zetland County Council. I was called up and did my two years in the Army and when I came back all my brothers were away at the whaling. It would have been about 1950. There was nothing much doing here so I thought I would maybe go to Salvesen too. I went down to Bernard Street in Leith and got a job. I was mess boy, maybe group 10. We went to Glasgow and joined the *Southern Opal*. She was a tanker transport and that was the ship we went to South Georgia on. I was looking after the whale catcher engineers' messroom and some of the mates and skippers - they were all in one messroom. I was 'Peggy' for them as they called it.

When we came to Leith Harbour I got a job on the plan as a winch boy, driving a winch when they were hauling ashore the whales. They had three winches going which pulled the spik off the whales. I was there with Willie Tait from Bigton. I think I was about two months there when the old station foreman came along and said, "Oh, you're a very big strong looking man, they are needing an engine room rating on a whale catcher - there is somebody coming ashore off the *Southern Guider*. Will you go?"

I had heard about the whale catchers and how awkward they were and you would probably be seasick but I decided I would go and that was what started me off in the engine room. She was coming in at midnight and taking bunkers and that is when I joined her. There was a fellow who came and said to me, "So you're the new engine room rating?" And I said, "Yes." He was the man we called the Whiteness Norwegian, Bjarne Karlsen. He said he was married to Lillian Smith and shook hands with me and said, "You will be in the same cabin as us. Get your gear aboard and I'll show you the ropes."

I duly went aboard and we sailed at the back of midnight sometime. For surely the most of three days after that I was seasick and that was my first experience in the engine room. The work we had to do was to keep the plates clean and change the water filters and sometimes assist the fireman. When they chased and harpooned a whale they stopped the engine, then the steam pressure would rise and you would have to cut the fires to stop her blowing off steam. I would generally take one side and the fireman the other. You then started the air pump. The air line went from the engine room to the gun platform so that the men on deck could inflate the whale to stop it sinking. There was one fireman on duty at a time.

The engine room rating was on day work, a 12 hour day with no overtime - 6 in the morning to 6 at night. If they needed help after 6 at night you had to give them a hand but none of the crew got overtime on the catchers. I was on the *Southern Guider* for two seasons. She broke down on us now and then, there was always trouble with the engine so we took over the *Southern Main*. By that time I had been promoted to fireman and was doing 4 hour watches during the day and 6 hour watches at night – from 8 to 2 and 2 to 8. Then I was back on the *Southern Guider* after that as fireman. You could have got promotion to maybe 4th Engineer or something but I did not fancy it.

There was one time that we picked up survivors off a Norwegian sealing ship. It had gone ashore on Willis Island. We picked them up from a lifeboat one night we were coming in. We had got a wireless message from the shore that this had happened. It was in the early hours of the morning. Two of them were making their way for Leith Harbour to try to get help. There were no other Shetlanders aboard with me except Bjarne Karlsen. The old gunner was Knocker Nielsen. Later we got another gunner, Kjelstrom, he was Swedish. I came from Nesting and the mate's name was Axel Nesting. One time he said to me when I was sending home a letter to South Nesting, "That's my name." We did not get any big whales that season, only a couple of blue whales that were any size but they were very scarce. We caught mainly fin on the island catchers and also some sperm and humpback and some peerie sei. It was a difficult job to shoot them, they were zig zagging all over the place.

When I left the whaling I came home on the *Southern Garden*, she was some ship. We were in the engine room of her coming home, what a mess – black reek. My brothers Herbert, Elliot, Lowrie and Charlie were all on catchers. Lowrie was on the *Southern Gambler* and Herbert was on the *Southern Runner*. A serious thing happened there when the gunner was shot with his own harpoon. The gun had been slewed inboard and the rope from the harpoon carried away. It came up and hit the trigger and set the gun off and the gunner was in the way. This gunner's brother was lost in a freak accident off the *Southern Joker* when he was knocked overboard by the harpoon gun or the foregoer.

The *Southern Main* was a fine catcher. I liked her but she had a dangerous stokehold. It was not in the engineroom as on the normal catchers, you had to go through a tunnel into the stokehold as on the corvettes and the boilers were face to face. They were Babcock & Wilcox steam drum boilers. When I joined her the old Norwegian fireman told me to watch when I flashed up the fires. I asked why and he said, "or you will never come out, she fills the stokehold with flame." And that is what happened.

There was something just not right. When the engines were stopped and the fires were cut and they rang for full ahead we had to get the fires on as quick as possible. You started in and you could just reach the levers on each boiler and you could flick on the four fires, the two bottom and the other two and get out of the stokehold and there would be just a sudden 'woof' of flame. If you had stayed in there you would not have had much hair left. Maybe it had something to do with the fan system because you could get a blow back on all boilers if the fan was not opened first. If you turned the oil on first, you had the chance of a blowback. You always had to get air first so that if the fan was screwed in, you had to open her up before you turned the fires on. I think we were on her for the whole season as the *Southern Guider* was waiting for bits coming for the engine. The *Main* was a lovely ship.

When the *Southern Guider* was ready we took her over again but she was still as bad, she never was right. She had a Frederikstad Steam engine, a high speed one. They did 144 revolutions which was fast for a steam engine. They were what was known as 'double complement'. Our sister ship, the *Southern Gambler*, never had any engine problems. They are both still going as fishing boats. The *Southern Guider* has been in Lerwick.

During the season when the gun went off everybody was up there working in all kinds of weather. When I got promoted to fireman, Bjarne Karlsen went as assistant engineer on the *Southern Broom*. He was a good guy.

One story which comes to my mind was when the whole crew got very drunk on champagne and I've never had such a hangover in my life. It was during the making of the film, 'Hell below Zero' starring Alan Ladd, that a ship called the *Kista Dan* came to South Georgia with a film crew, but none of the big stars. She was anchored off in Leith Harbour to prevent the whalers getting booze. Our Skipper, Kjelstrom, however, went alongside her and Bjarne, having collected all the money we had, went on board and bought the champagne.

TAMMIE THOMSON

When I first started at the whaling it was 1953 and, as usual, we went down to Leith and had to wait for a day or two before we were accepted or given a job. I went down on the *Southern Venturer* and went ashore and started working at Leith Harbour. The first week or so we were just doing cleaning duties and then Geordie Sales from Lerwick had had an accident and I was sent in as a replacement for him. The spik plan was the place where the blubber was. It had been taken off on the main plan and sent up there and the cutter would cut it into strips and the hookers, of which I was one, would fork this down through a hogger and it was chewed up and melted down in the cookery. That was my job for that year.

I was actually at the island for three seasons and every one they managed to make the quota, so I certainly picked the right seasons to be there. At the end of the first season I went home on the *Southern Opal* and then came back for the following season. I think the *Southern Opal* left about August or September and the island fishing season started about October. It was a six months season at the island. The second time down I was on the rib plan working along with Bertie Ramsay from North Roe or Lochend I believe he was and a Murdo MacKinnon from Stornoway, both cutters, and there was a Jimmy Mackenzie from Stornoway who was the hooker and I was driving the winches.

We had a derrick winch and the cutter would go out with a winch hook and hook into this sheet of ribs and cut it clear of the side of the whale once the lemmers had split it up and they would heave this up and you would lift it up on the derrick and they would cut the ribs into singles and then they were taken up on the bone loft and sawn up and put into the kettles up there to be boiled for bone meal. That was more or less the carry on for that season.

Then I decided to overwinter and applied for a job and got one. During the winter I worked in the machine shop. When I started there I was just doing bits of small jobs or helping anybody who needed a labourer's assistance. One of the men who was working there was Charlie Nicolson from Aith and he was a repairer/fitter. He was a very handy man to have around for he had a good kit of tools and if you needed a loan of anything he was always very willing to give you it and any information you needed. He was well informed and a very good fitter. At the beginning of the winter the machine shop foreman said, "Anything you want to find out, ask Charlie."

Then, a while into the winter, I was asked to go and work as a labourer with Theo Hunter from Weisdale and the main job we did was repairing whale boat telegraphs. The gunners used to get upset during the season and very often they would use their feet instead of their hands to send information and usually it meant broken glasses and stretched wires and all the rest of it. So our main job was putting in new glasses in the telegraphs and of course they did not have any so improvisation had to be brought in. We took sheets of corrugated plastic used for putting in along with corrugated iron for skylights and if you laid them between two sheets of metal in a tub of hot water and screwed the sheets slowly together as you boiled it up, the plastic would flatten out and then they would cut it on a band saw and make new glasses for the telegraphs. So that had to be done and all the wires adjusted and repaired so that everything was back to good condition by the time the following season started.

The following season I was back on the rib plan again but it was now changed from down on the main plan up to the roof of the bone loft but it was still the same derrick system – to bring the ribs up there you had to hoist them up and cut them but they had put in a hogger which was a tube down which you dropped the ribs end on and a wheel flying around like a chipper that chewed them up and this was fine while it was the ribs that went down but when bits of harpoon went down along with the ribs then the men who had to do the repairs were not very happy. Sometimes you got very rotten whales at the island and when the ribs went down and there was no meat on them, they would bounce around and very often a piece would come flying out again so you sometimes had to stand clear.

At Leith Harbour you worked a normal 12 hour day and when busy often 4 hours in the evening and weekends. Sometimes when there was a lot of rain and wet snow, a 12 hour day in full oilskins was heavy going. Also with rotten whales the rain reduced the rotten meat to the consistency of clay which stuck to your boots and oilskins and made a hard job even harder. The team that time was Bertie Ramsay, cutter and Tommy Edwardson from Lerwick was on the winch and I was hooker. And then at the end of the season, Bertie had done two winters, I think, and he was sent home a bit early for he had had enough of it and Norman Tulloch from Tingwall had come ashore off the factory to do the winter and he came and did a week or so as cutter. He was a very entertaining person and could do the job very well. He was not very happy at some of the knives they had because they were old secondhand flensing knives. One day he decided he would get a better one and he went down to the winch house and came up with a better knife. But it was the end of the season and none of the flensers really worried. Otherwise, I suppose there would have been a complaint about it.

When the season finished and we set off for home on the *Southern Opal* again, I applied for a transfer to the factory ships and so from 1956 and on to 1961 when I finished with the whaling, I was on the *Southern Venturer*. The first year on there I was hooking on the kverners aft which was sort of like a colander steamer inside a metal boiler which worked horizontally. You put the whale blubber, which had been cut in strips, down the kverner and this perforated drum was revolving inside a steam container and it cooked for about 11 hours to bring out the oil. Sometimes when there was not enough spik and there was too much meat on the foreplan they put down the back meat and it was different job to work on.

Another job we had to do sometimes when there was a lot of spik around was put it down the press boilers which were big kettles at the back of the blacksmith's shop and the back of the carpenter's shop. They would pile it in there until there was very little headroom. When you were putting down a big sheet of spik and you got it running down the kettle, once you saw it was going then you pulled the hook out and ran for your life because when the end swung around you were better not to be there. There was one of the Stornoway fellows who got his leg broken with that. The end caught him and broke his leg and it was not very good because bones were very, very slow to mend there. But anyway, that was the three things that you basically did and when there was no whales you had to do bits of painting or chipping if the weather was suitable or maybe serving tail strops or cleaning accommodation. That used to have to be done after you had had a spell with a lot of whales.

After the first season I went on the claw winches with a Kenny Mackenzie from Stornoway. We had to drive the claw winches down on the poop to pull the claw down and drop it on the tail of the whale and then you had to slacken away until it was up on the plan and then you had to go full speed up to the plan and connect on the canting winches for turning the whale once the top two pieces of blubber were off. Next you had to go and drive the winches to turn it over and then on to the derrick winches and take the claw off and take it down on to the plan and land it at the top of the chute. Then it was full speed down aft and pull it down with the claw winches all ready for another whale.

I worked on the three winches and if it was smallish whales then you were certainly going fast. We did that job for three seasons and then I did the 1960 winter working in the catcher engine rooms along with a Peter Porter, an engineer from Edinburgh. The work varied. You had to start off by cleaning the engine as it had all been covered with oil to keep it. You had to wash this off and take off guards and so on and work on the engine and then put all the guards and that back when you finished. It was a fairly cold job down there. You had a bogie right enough run on diesel oil and it was very warm when you were sitting alongside the bogie but once you got about six feet away you were back to Arctic conditions. But anyway it kept you under cover for the winter.

Then it was back to the factory ship for the 60/61 season. This time I was boiler screwer on the after plan so I had to open and close the kverners and keep the doors and all the lids in good order so that you did not loose steam when everything was going flat out. Although you were classed as a boiler/screwer, you also gave a hand with driving a capstan or doing the hooking or whatever was needed. At the end of 1961, the whaling was getting pretty well through so I transferred to the Merchant Navy and that was basically my finish with Salvesen's whaling but I worked on the coasters after that for a good few years.

HARRY PATON

My first season at the whaling was 49/50. I worked with Angus Ridland on the motor boat. We towed whales in from the buoys in the harbour and put them ashore at the plan. The following season I was on the motor boat to start with and then I left to join Jimmy Johnson in the soluble plant and was there for the rest of the season. I then overwintered in Leith Harbour. I was back in the soluble plant for part of the season and then I was put in the station gang discharging and loading ships.

When the whale meat was cooked, the water and oil which came off it went into a settling tank outside and sulphuric acid was mixed in with the oily water to separate the water and oil and meaty residue. It then went into another settling tank and from there into the soluble plant where all the solids were removed using a machine called a de-sludger. The oil and water were pumped to another tank and the solids were put onto a conveyor belt to the dryers to become meat meal. The water and oil mixture was heated up and it went through oil separators which removed the oil from the water. It was then pumped into separate tanks. The remaining water was pumped into evaporators and it boiled away until it was brown just like treacle and once it came to a certain gravity, it was pumped to a holding tank outside. It was a concentrated protein and eventually used for animal feeding.

In the 1950/51 season we left Glasgow on the *Southern Opal*. We broke down at the tail of the bank before we got clear of the Clyde. I forget how many times we broke down before we got to Aruba. 13 of us got the measles. Edgar Gray from Yell got it first and he was put ashore in Glasgow and then Willie Fraser from Walls, who now lives in Orkney, and Magnie Hughson from Yell and I got it. We were all in the room together. Sadly Ray Cumming from Gruting died with the effects of the measles and he was buried at sea. It was said that the spots went in on him instead of coming out. . Our cabin was right aft above the engine. You got the heat from the engine room and being in the tropics made it worse.

Magnie and I were the only two who were fit to have a run ashore in Aruba when we got there. We left Aruba and then we broke down off Pernambuco. That time they reckoned that it was a nut that had come loose somewhere in the valve chest of the engine and come on top of the piston and burst the cylinder head out. They drew the piston and then they took a tank lid and bolted it on to the cylinder head and put strengthening bars across it and we made it in to Pernambuco under our own steam. We were only 60 miles off when it happened, and by that time, Willie Fraser was not well at all. He had got a relapse and was put ashore there. I believe we lay there 10 days before they got a new piston and bits and pieces flown out and got her all repaired and working. I do not remember if there were any more breakdowns between there and South Georgia.

My last season on the island was in 1952. I came home on the old *Polar Chief* and on the way home the engine broke down several times. While the ship was drifting we could see whale oil leaking from loose rivets but I knew about that as I had helped to clean the tanks at Leith Harbour. I was told that approximately 60 tons of whale oil was lost. We arrived in the Mersey, Liverpool and went up the Manchester Shipping Canal, all the way to the discharging berth. After discharging the oil we took the *Polar Chief* to Glasgow to be broken up.

I worked on salvage boats from then until 1954 when I was back on board the *Southern Harvester*. My job that year was stowing the bags of meat meal down in the tanks. It was not a very healthy job but it was warm. I worked along with Alan Tulloch, John Thomson and Bob Davidson and a man from the Western Isles, I cannot remember his name now. When the season finished that year we were away east of Enderby Land and you could see the shore. It took us a fortnight to get back to South Georgia and then we came back to Liverpool on the *Southern Harvester*. I worked by a while at Liverpool and then I came home and that was the end of my time at the whaling.

TOM ROBERTSON

I first went to the whaling in 1959 at the age of 22. I had done my apprenticeship as a joiner and had spent that summer on the *Explorer*, the Fishery Research ship. The Army was chasing me for National Service and I had to get further than the *Explorer* to dodge them. So whaling was the idea and I was lucky to get a job. I went down to South Georgia on the *Southern Opal*. I put in for a winter as carpenter more or less as soon as I got there. During the season I was Group 9 hooker on the rosedown. The rosedown was the section which cut up the whale meat and fed it into a conveyor and it was eventually made into meat meal. I was lucky to get the carpenter's job for the winter and it put me up to Group 5 which was a better rate of pay.

When the winter started, I was given a helper. The first job I got to do was to put a new gun platform on the *Southern Guider*. I had just taken off the old platform and everything was in an upheaval when the helper arrived and said, "Boy, does du know what du is doin'? Every gunner is a different height and that platform has to be right for them." I said, "Yea, they have told me about that." I had already got it all sussed out.

Our work was mostly to do with the catchers but we did some work in the piggery. That was a fine job. It was maybe a bit smelly but it was warm and all right in there. Another kind of an unusual job we got to do was to make a cru. They had sheep down from the Falklands and the day they went to caa the sheep, they asked us to make the cru so we did not have much time. The caaing of the sheep was a bit of a carry on too because there was as many men as sheep, all this men and only one dog. Everybody on the station was caaing the sheep while the carpenters were making the cru. We had got this pen just about finished when they were approaching with the sheep. I mind the foreman carpenter saying, "Come on, let's get to hell out of here." We bailed out while they penned up the sheep. They took them all in and they slaughtered them all in one go.

During the winter we used to do a bit of brewing and stilling. It gave us many a spree. One day some of the mess boys came along with the bottom springs of a bed and mattress and two big jumping skis. As I was the carpenter they came to me to see if I could put the skis on the bed for runners. So we got it rigged. It could go like the devil. They used it for a while and I think that some Norwegians borrowed it one Sunday and went rather high up the hill with it and came down and laid it in pieces. So that was the end of the sledge.

On one occasion the carpenter's helper got a little too much to drink. To save him from being spotted, we laid him under the bench and covered him with wood shavings. The only danger was if he snored and you could see the shavings move as he breathed but he was never spotted. Another incident that winter was when two boys noticed that the chief steward had set out an empty rum barrel. They thought there was maybe a drop left in it for the boys so they arrived at my cabin with it. We tipped the barrel up but got no rum, just a drop of water so they had to roll the barrel all the way back.

At the end of the winter just before the factories arrived, there was always a rush on with little odd jobs that had been missed out during the winter. When the factory or the transport ships came to the island, the men would come for the catchers, get the steam up and go off for trials with them. That was a bit special for me because I had never been on a catcher. Some days we would be working on board when they went out and that was always quite a good day. We got the job done and the rest of the day was a bit of a holiday. When the boys came down again they had a bit of a dram and a good bit of a spree that night. We met our old friends and heard all the home news. When the expedition left for the ice I was back to the rosedown again for my second season.

There was a sad incident at the island that year. The Station Manager, Sverre Akseth, fell between two catchers and was crushed to death. It was a sad time because he was a gentleman and nobody had a wrong word to say about him. It just happened that it was Christmas Eve.

And then the time came to go home again and that was when I met my wife. That would have been in 1961. I spent the summer at home casting peats and whatever I could get to do. And then it was back again to the *Southern Venturer* and that was a new experience. The job I got that time going down was splicing and making ready all the flag poles for the whale catchers. There was a gang of us on it and it was a fine job. During the season I was driving the lemmer winches which was a fine job but a cold job on a bad night.

Once the whale had been flensed on the after plan, the boys took the wire down and fastened it on to the whale's tail and I pulled the flensed whale up on to the fore plan. I then went to one of the side winches depending which way the whale was lying and pulled the meat off it. We completely dismembered it. So that was my job that season other than a spell when the fellow who pulled the wire out, the main wire boy, hurt his hand and I relieved him and he took the winch and I did his job.

On one occasion I was standing at the winch and they had opened up a big kettle to put the meat and bones in. The steam came out and a young Norwegian boy went across the plan and he just walked into the kettle. Being up at the winch, I was the only one who saw him going. We had a bit of a panic fishing him out and wondered about him because the water was usually hot. It was hot right enough but not enough to burn him. We got a big ladder and one of the boys went down and helped him up and he was back again on the plan a few days later. But it could have been a nasty accident. We nearly had a cooked wire boy that night.

There was a funeral I was at during the winter. That was a young Highland man who I knew extremely well. In fact he was the fellow who taught me the names of all the Norwegian grub, the baccalao and all the different stuff. He had been at the whaling since he left the school and would have been a man about my own age. He just slipped and fell down some steps and died the following day from head injuries. So that was a sad occasion.

That was my last season on the *Venturer*. We all thought that the whaling was going to end so I was surprised when I got a letter to go back on the *Southern Harvester*. That time, on the way down, I worked laying the plan deck with the carpenters. I did not like that job so well because we were handling jagged wood in the tropics and I did not enjoy it. We also tried to fish sperm whales in the tropics on the way down which was a bit of a disaster because they were all undersized. I think I was called out two nights and it was a good job that it was during the night because the oil was running out of them before you got them opened up. But it was an entertainment seeing someone with shorts on working on the plan deck.

The job I got was hooker on the head saw that year. And that was a fine job, we had a good gang that year. We could lash a head through and have a smoke before the next one came, no problem. That year at the end of the season we had to make a tow rope to take home the catcher, the *Southern Lotus*. I was not involved in making up the tow rope but Rab Skene, who worked the saw, had to go for several nights and make ready the rope and I was put on his job. I enjoyed that, it was something new.

When we left Leith Harbour we took the catcher on tow and set off for home. We had a really bad storm in the Forties which was a bit of a nasty experience. I was not too sure whether it was a common occurrence to get weather like that but it seemed extremely bad to me. I woke up one morning with the bangs of something on the deck. It was the gas and oxy-acetylene bottles going down the chute. There must have been hundreds of them. With this kind of weather, it was impossible to go across the deck, you had to go through the factory.

Everybody was extremely quiet and very concerned about the catcher which we lost sight of for long periods of time and every time you wondered whether she was going to appear again or not. But she always appeared, thankfully. It was later on that day that the bosun, Jimmy Leask, called some of us out to help Bobby Odie and John Georgeson to catch some of the penguins which we were taking home to the zoo because they had escaped from their run. But the weather got better and the catcher was all right. We towed her up to Lands End where another catcher took over the tow and went to Norway with her. And that was the end of the whaling for me – and for Salvesen.

JOHNNIE POLSON

These are a few memories or anecdotes from the 1954/55 season at the whaling with Salvesen's *Southern Harvester* and on the whale catcher *Southern Actor*.

Even the trip to Aberdeen was an experience for a young man like me. Luckily I was in the company of other older men who had made this same journey many times and who could tell me what to do and where I needed to go.

From Aberdeen we travelled on to Leith where we went through the usual medical and were signed on, in my case as a mess boy. From Leith we went on to Newcastle and joined ship. All these towns were places I'd heard of but never been to before. These things seemed to happen so quickly and really very little of this part seems to stay in my mind but the trip to South Georgia on the *Southern Harvester* was very enjoyable, especially the warm weather in the tropics and the company of other young Shetlanders of which some were my own age like Alan Tulloch, Peter Irvine, Willie Johnson, John Thomason and Gordon Smith.

There was always plenty to do clear of your work on the trip down and with many other men from Shetland, several from Whalsay, you seemed among friends all the time. We had the use of a swimming pool for a while until some engineers made a blunder and pumped the bilges into it. It was just a heavy canvas affair but could to the job ok. Our accommodation or cabin was on the aft part of the factory ship and looked out on the tunnel where the whales were hauled up. We had a stop at Aruba mostly for bunkers I think but that was an experience again and well worth seeing. I expect some of the men saw too much and suffered for a period afterwards.

South Georgia itself was something else – mountainous, barren and cold – and Leith Harbour left a bit to be desired – all clutter and mess I felt – but you were young and didn't dwell too much on that. While at Leith Harbour I managed to get a trip to Stromness and, along with several others, we visited Shackleton's grave, a lonely place thinking back on it but when you read of men like him and their endurance and experiences you realise just what driving spirit they must have had.

I joined the *Actor* as mess boy. There was one other Shetlander, Tammy Nicolson from Aith, he was an AB. Other Britishers were the Asdic man, a Robert Fairgreaves from Edinburgh, the 'Sparky' came from Berwick and the 2nd and 3rd Engineers were English. I'm afraid their names escape my memory now. I can remember the 3rd Engineer telling me that he was going to buy a new car when he got home and he sent me a photo of himself standing by it while he was on holiday some place or other, I think it was at Lake Windermere.

For a good job I had been on fishing boats before this so I wasn't bothered by seasickness. Several other crewmembers were and it was no wonder for the catchers took some getting used to especially with rough weather and when they were really pushed during a chase after whales. I can't say I really enjoyed the catcher part of the season but it was a real eye-opener to me, the chasing and harpooning the whales, killing them outright before getting them alongside to mark and buoy them. This work needed experienced men and you felt while this was going on that nothing else was considered. The gunner Ole Christensen was a decent enough man and rarely ever got out of sorts but when the pressure was on or something not right according to his liking, everyone got a piece of his mind mostly in Norwegian so for my part I didn't understand most of what was said (probably a good job). As mess boy I wasn't involved too much in the deck work but helped here and there when needed and truly I felt it a cruel and brutal job.

One thing I particularly remember about was once while bunkering alongside the factory ship, the fuel hose burst (it was pretty rough that night and I remember they had whales for fenders and needed them) everything was covered in stinking black oil and it took days or rather weeks before the smell wore off and it caused a lot of extra work on the crew getting rid of it.

Another thing I can remember was later on in the season when there was less daylight we sighted a whale fairly late on in the day. The gunner decided against trying a shot at it so we followed that whale all night on the asdic and when daylight came up he got it. According to what I remember about this, the whale hardly ever altered course and speed during the time we followed it; it travelled at a good few knots but I can't be sure to put a number to it.

After this when the season ended we had some rough weather on our return to South Georgia and had to hove to and clean down ice, sometimes in the shelter of icebergs or just in the open sea. It was more or less every watch for a spell. It was unbelievable how fast the ice formed, it seemed to get thicker every time you looked at it and was a very real danger but with the steam hoses the worst could be cleared away fairly quickly, you had to watch out though for sea, falling ice and scalding steam. We were glad when we got back to Leith Harbour.

After leaving the *Actor*, I joined the old tanker *Southern Garden*, she was a down-at-heel vessel and the cabins were filthy. We gradually got the worst cleaned during the return and part of the time was spent chipping and painting the bulwarks. Some places they were so thin that holes appeared when you got right down through the rust. We called along the Cape Verde Isles on the return and saw the 'bum boats' come alongside with goods to sell, everything you could mention plus booze and monkeys. Fruit was very cheap and there was a much better variety, better than what you usually got on the catchers and factory ship.

I felt very homesick on the return and I think some others felt likewise. Some called it the 'Channels'. Some men were hardly every sober after leaving the Cape Verdes until we got to Tilbury Docks in London. I was not greatly impressed with that part either and was very relieved to get clear and on the train for Aberdeen and then home. It took a while to get back to your old self and feel comfortable at last.

Another thing worth mentioning was years later while on holiday in Norway along with other whalers we went to Sandefjord and saw the *Actor*. She had been sold to a company in South America and had ended up in Spain. A Norwegian Merchant Officer had seen her lying a derelict but had recognised her as a catcher and he contacted some people in Norway who were interested in getting hold of a craft like this to restore as a museum piece as part of Norway's Marine history.

They eventually purchased her and she was brought home to Norway and they completely restored her to the original setup more or less and last year she made a crossing to Lerwick. While in Norway I spoke to the gunner, Ole Christensen, then a man in his late 80's. It felt a bit emotional meeting up after thirty odd years. He said he hoped to come across for the trip on the *Actor* but sadly he died before that took place. A pity because he seemed so interested in the restoration work going on while we were there. Most of it was done by ex-whalers with them giving their time free.

HENRY ROBERTSON

I went to the whaling in 1960. We went down on the *Southern Opal* and I was mess boy. Stuart Gray, down the road here, was the mess man but I did not have a table. My job was in the sink washing up the dishes for two sittings in the big mess room of the Opal. When we got to South Georgia I was put on the *Southern Guider* as galley boy and we were buoy boat for the season. It was a bit scary to begin with when you were in bad weather, you did not know what had hit you sometimes.

There was one day, I came up in the afternoon to the bridge and Billy Ramsay and the 2nd mate said as it was a lovely day I was to go up to the barrel. The 2nd mate said, "Now do not look down." I got on OK until I got to the peerie ladder at the top of the rigging and then I got stuck. This ladder was very narrow to get into and I looked down and that was me finished, I had to come down. They started ragging me about it. I got a cob on and I said, "Right, you so and so's, I'll do it this time." So up I went up without stopping and from then on it was no problem, the worst was over.

Seeing the first whales was something else. It was very exciting. Being a buoy boat, sometimes when there were no whales to pick up, if we came on whales we could chase and shoot them. On one occasion we were chasing when a whale was reported. We had to stop chasing and go to pick it up. It was very disappointing. The next day we were in Leith Harbour delivering the whales. We were alongside taking bunkers and stores. The mate went up to clean the gun. It had been cocked the day before when we were chasing but he forgot and pulled the trigger. The gun went off, the harpoon went up the beach and the grenade went off. It was a mercy nobody was around or they could have been killed. We had to start up the winch and heave the harpoon back again.

We came home again on the *Opal* and docked at Tilbury. It was on a Sunday night at tea time and as we were mess boys, we had to wait and serve up the tea and wash up the tea dishes. We had just finished doing that when they took her off into the middle of the harbour to turn her around and put her with her opposite side to the quay so it was between 9 and 10 o'clock at night before we got ashore. We got a taxi to the station and a sleeper on the train for Leith. We had to pay over and above the amount on our railway warrants for the sleeper but it was better than sitting around there all night and it was the last train that we could get before 3 o'clock in the morning. When we arrived in Leith, my brother Tommy and Billy Morrison both bought motor cycles and then we made our way to Aberdeen. The bikes were shipped on from Leith. Billy Morrison's bike is still on the go. She is in the museum for the whaling exhibition, an Ariel VB. So that was that season.

Anyway, we were home and likely had a wild summer. We set off again in 1961 and went to Shields and joined the *Southern Harvester*. I was signed on again for the catchers as galley boy. When we were just a day or two out they called for me to come up to the mate's office as they were an AB short for the catchers so I got that job and was delighted with that. The catcher I was to go on was the *Southern Angler*. My job as AB was coiling the foregoer and splicing in the new harpoon. Coiling down the foregoer could be a tricky job because they paid no attention to you. You were right up in the bows of the boat, on your knees in front of the gun. You would be chasing at full speed and there were lumps of water hitting you. You would be coiling the foregoer down and she would just bury her head into the sea and the next you would know you were up along the handrail at the back of the gun platform, swearing.

I remember one time the gunner shot a sea elephant or whatever it was lying up on a lump of ice and they decided to have the liver out of him for tea. The 2nd Mate went down on the ice and got a rope around the sea elephant's tail and we heaved him aboard. The gunner came down and cut the liver out of him and the cook took it to the galley. I did not fancy the idea of it and when the tea was ready I did not eat the liver, I just ate gravy and tatties but I don't think it was half an hour until the whole ship's crew broke up with the diarrhoea, including me. Danny Morrison from Leith was mate and he took a piece of the skin off the sea elephant and cured it and it came very bonnie.

One day we were going to pick up whales to deliver to the factory as there were too many for the buoy boats to handle. The gunner said he would take the wheel and I was to go down and give the men a hand on deck. Danny Morrison told me to go aft and slip the end of the wire which was lying along the casing. I had got to the step of the galley door when the gunner came hard over with her and she dipped her side in and I jumped up on the step of the door. The cook was in the door and he laughed and said, "He nearly got you that time." She straightened herself up and I had taken three strides along the deck when in she went again and I grabbed the handrail and the cook said afterwards that all he could see was my knuckles and I was streaming straight out. We were doing about fourteen and a half knots through the water and when she dried herself that time, I got down on the deck and I had a severe cob on, oilskins torn open and I was soaking to the living hide and frozen.

I called them all the shower of so and so's that I could lay my tongue to and said that I would not be back on deck any more that night and I did not go. Thankfully I had on that rubber mittens and they helped me to grip the metal rail. If I had just had on the woollen gloves which I wore under the mittens, they would have slipped. It was so cold in the water there that you would not have lasted long. We did not have a great season at all. The gunner thought that the gun was not right and we steamed all the way from the ice back to the island and got a new gun. This took an awful lot of time off us and when we got back to the ice things were no better. We thought it was him, not the gun at all. We were a full catcher that year.

Normally we got a tot of rum every fortnight but this season we had not taken it and settled for a bottle each when the season finished. When we came in to Leith Harbour, the *Venturer* was just about to sail for home and Tommy, my brother, was on board her. I grabbed my bottle and, along with Andrew Arthur, we set off going to give Tommy a dram before he left. But we were too late, the gangway was up and they were just slipping the moorings when we got there. But we got rid of the rum, that was no bother. We were in there for about a week and then we left for home. Some of the catchers came home that year. We had to stay handy with the factory ship and we bunkered twice from her on the way home. We did not get the second bunker until we were just in the mouth of the English Channel and then it was full speed for Norway. We went to Tonsberg and they kept us in a hotel for three days before a charter plane flew us all back to Edinburgh. There was about 80 of us on the plane. The stewardesses came around with baskets of duty free fags and scent and all that hellery but nobody wanted any of that. We had plenty of fags. But when they came around with the same basket full of half bottles, duty free, that was much better.

We were met at the airport by a fleet of buses and although it was after office hours when we arrived, 8 o'clock at night or so, we were taken down to the office at Bernard Street and given subs. We set off to the pubs and then caught the train to Aberdeen in the early hours of the morning so we had a whole day there. That was the last year I was down. By the next season only one factory ship was operating and I was asked to come away on spec, which I did. I did not get a job and I went back to Aberdeen and joined the pool and went to sea after that.

The whaling was a good life, very exciting on the catchers when you were among the whales. I would not have liked to have missed it.

IAN SALES

I went to the whaling in '54. We left Glasgow on the *Southern Opal* and went to Tonsberg and picked up the Norwegians there. We went on to Antwerp and then straight down to South Georgia from there. I was a mess boy on the whale catcher *Southern Gambler* and then I overwintered. The following season I was on the whale catcher *Sondra* fishing for the island until the factory ships arrived and then I was on the Gambler again.

When I went back to the whaling in '56 we sailed from South Shields. We thought we would go and see Jim Craigie from Lerwick who lived in Shields. He took us to the pub for a dram while his wife made dinner for us. We had to be back at the ship by 2 o'clock. At about 1 o'clock we started to phone around for a taxi but it was a Saturday afternoon and we could not get one anywhere.

Tammie Tulloch was with us and he decided that he was not wanting to go anyway, he might as well just go home. But eventually we found a place that would send a car if we were ready to go right away and when it arrived it was a wedding car. So we went down to the ship with ribbons and balloons and the whole lot flying and there were big cheers. Just behind us came Geordie Gray and I think Attie Williamson was with him. They were standing in the back of a truck, rigged in oilskins. The man had given them oilskins because it was a day of rain. And that was how we arrived at the ship.

I was on the *Gambler* again that season and I overwintered and then I did another season on the *Gambler*. In '58 I was on both the *Southern Rover* and the *Southern Foster* and for the last year I was on the *Southern Wheeler* fishing for the island. I was mess boy when I went first and worked my way up to AB on the catchers. Tammie Nicolson, Jimmy Balfour, Geordie and Ellis Sales and Peter Goodlad were all AB's on the catchers at the island about that time. I was at the whaling right up to '61. The first winter I was mess boy in the hospital and the second winter I was working on the catchers and painting them. It was a good life and you worked along with a lot of fine men.

NICOL THOMSON

I went to the whaling when I was 15 and a half. I went down on the *Southern Garden* with a lot of boys from Shetland. We arrived in South Georgia in early December. The whalecatcher I was on was the *Southern Rover*. The gunner was a very religious man but good to sail with and I got on with him very well. By the end of the season we were top boat. The weather made life on a catcher very hard sometimes. I came home on the *Southern Venturer*.

I went down with the *Southern Venturer* again the following year and did a season as mess boy on her. In 1958 I went down on the *Southern Garden* again and did the season and went ashore and did the winter along with my father and quite a few boys from Yell. The winter weather was very bad, snow storms and what have you. I was in one of the mess rooms there so I did not have to go outside too much. Sometimes at night I would go and visit some of the boys in the various cabins and we would have a fry-up about the night, sometimes bacon and eggs that someone had been able to pinch from the galley. You were not supposed to cook anything in the cabins but it went on. Once or twice during the winter a boat would come from the Falklands with mail on board. The winter passed by likely not too bad and at the end of the time I did the season again and then we came home. I was away about eighteen and a half months altogether.

On the factory, I did a season in the liver plant and when we came home I had somewhere in the region of £800 pay off. It was a lot of money then but it is not a lot of money to what you get nowadays. The next season I was back on the factory working in the tank deck. I worked along with Jimmy Henry from Sellafirth and it was a hard job humping bags of meat meal but I got the season put in. We played a lot of cards at nights. Sometimes we gambled for cigarettes and of course we made home brew.

The foreman on the liver plant was John Clark from Mid Yell and there was a fellow there whose name was Jimmy White. He had special days that he would celebrate, St Patricks Day and so on when he used to throw a great big booze up for himself. He used to come staggering down the ladder many a time and sometimes I would say to him, "Jimmy, I think you had better go back to bed." And he would say, "No, no. I'll be all right." He would sit down in a corner and fall asleep. It made things a bit harder but we managed without him. We kept going until the next shift came on. The liver plant was a kinda dirty job. Sometimes the liver would choke up the mincer and then you would have to take it all adrift and roll up your sleeves and clear it all out. That was the worst side of it.

We used to swipe yeast from the baker to make home brew and we used to put in apples and oranges and God knows what all into a five gallon drum out in the locker and leave it for a while to ferment. But it tasted all right. During the winter we would make a brew and then put it through a still to get pure alchohol. There was a hatch in the toilet that you opened and went down a short ladder to where the still was kept. Only the few who used it knew it was there. Willie Spence who was a Skipper with Salvesen came in every Saturday and he always tried to find the still. He stood many a time on top of the hatch and he would say, "Boys, I know there is something going on and if I can just find out." But he never did. It worked out that you got a bottle of still from a gallon of home brew. Every now and again during the process, we had to take a little drop in a saucer and set a match to it and if it lit up it would be all right but if it did not then it was poisonous. But it was very strong stuff, there was no doubt about that.

One of the other times that I went down to South Georgia, I went down on a whalecatcher, the *Southern Rover*. Wilbert Hoseason from Yell was on the *Southern Broom*. We called into Dakar and took bunkers. When we came into the Roaring Forties we got a really bad trip through and it took 9 days instead of the 5 we were expecting. There were seas running like mountains, sometimes I was wondering if we were going to get there but eventually we sighted South Georgia and we got in but we had a really bad trip that time.

One year on the way home, we were just about a week out from Britain. We were sitting watching a film on deck and this man came tearing up the stair calling for the bosun. They went down below again and then the bosun came up asking for men to come and help him. What had happened was these four men had thousands of cigarettes packed in a tank on top of the meat meal and with the film showing on deck they thought it would be a fine quiet time to retrieve their cigarettes. They opened the lid and the first man went in and collapsed. There was no air in the tank, just the gas off the meat meal. The second man went down to help the first and the third one went down too. It was a good job the fourth man ran for help but it was too late. It was a sad episode and put a damper on us coming home.

On the *Southern Garden* every Saturday was inspection day when the Skipper, Chief Engineer and Chief Steward would come around and check that we were keeping things clean. With serving up breakfast and getting the mess room cleaned we were likely running a little bit late. By the time we got the mess room floor swept we did not have time to take the rubbish away so I just swept it under the mat. Then in came the Skipper, the Chief and all the rest. They had a look around and thought that everything was all right. The Skipper was standing right on top of the sweepings. He lifted up the mat and saw all the rubbish and said, "What's this, Thomson?" So I got a bit of a talking to that morning but it passed by eventually.

L to R Gordon Smith, Effirth; Robert Wiseman, Lerwick.
Photo: R Wiseman

Southern Venturer *Foreplan bone saw 1960. L to R Harry Johnson, Bixter using knife. Centre Ian Strachan, Yell driving capstan. R Willie Johnson, Eshaness, bone saw man.*
Photo: T Thomson.

L to R Willie Watt, Lerwick; Jake Nisbet, Jnr. St Abbs.
Photo: W Watt.

***Southern Venturer** 60/61 season. Ship's cat inside a baleen whale's mouth. The Captain of **Southern Venturer** was Per Virik. He had come to Salvesens from the factory ship **Baleana**. He wanted a cat on board before the ship sailed.*
Photo: T Thomson.

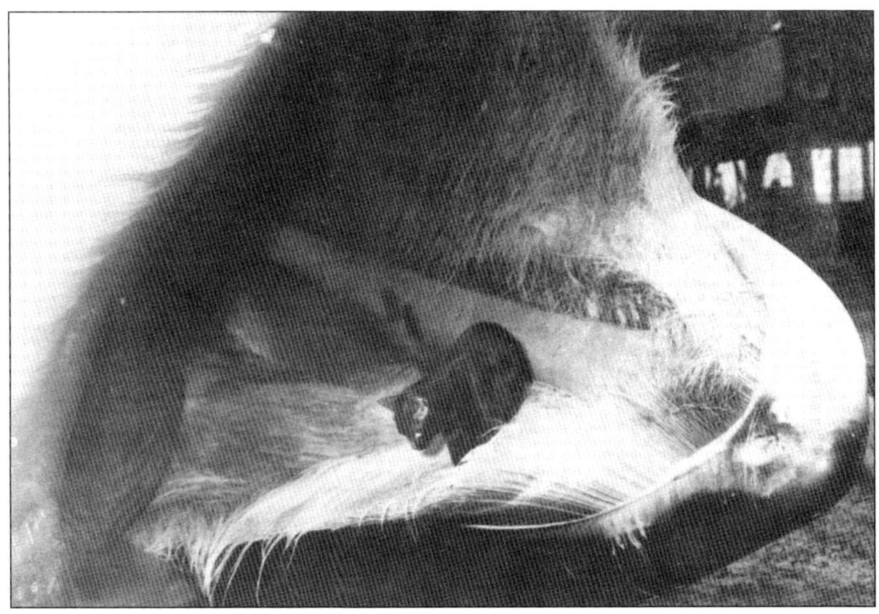

Left: L to R Lowrie Laurenson, Nesting; John Henry, Foula. Photo: L Laurenson.

Below: L to R Back row John R Goodlad, South Shields; Bertie Henderson, Unst; George Leask (Cleek), Lerwick. Front row, Jim Craigie, Lerwick; George Cheyne, Sandness. John R Goodlad survived the sinking of the ***Royal Oak*** *in Scapa Flow. He swam ashore. Photo K Brown.*

L to R Back row Unknown; Andrew Cheyne, Westerskeld; Andrew Nicolson, Eshaness; ? Abernethy, Kincardine O'Neil; unknown. Front: John Hay, Aith; Sonny Williamson, Ollaberry.
Photo: A Ridland.

Whale catcher ***Southern Truce****. Photo probably taken towards the end of season. Ice beginning to form on lower rigging.*
Photo: W Watt.

*Foredeck of whalemeat freezer ship **Southern Raven**.*
Photo: A Anderson.

*The only means of access between catcher and factory. The catcher is modified to transport whalemeat from **Southern Venturer** to **Southern Raven** for freezing, hence the bins.*
Photo: A Anderson

Barges being loaded with meat meal before being towed alongside a transport ship by the motorboat. Photo: A Ridland.

*Stromness, South Georgia. Salvesen's repair base with two floating docks, platers and engineering shops and accommodation.
Photo: N Thomson.*

WILLIE WATT

The first year I went to the whaling was 1951 and I was a mess boy on the factory ship. The following year I was on the whale catchers and I was on them, more or less, right up until it finished. I was with different gunners. As I said I started as a mess boy or galley boy but I ended up AB. It was a tough life but you got used to it after a bit. If you were chasing whales and you were on watch your job as AB was to be an hour on the wheel and an hour up in the barrel, an hour on the wheel and an hour up in the barrel. When you were supposed to be off watch, you were still working because if you got fast to a whale you were up working with it so you did not get a lot of sleep during the season when it was light around the clock. But it was just the way of life. My father was at the whaling and he had been at the whaling for four years before the war started. I was there one year with him and then he finished.

I did the 1957/58 winter, that was just before I married. It seemed a long time, especially the last season but I did it. The job I was on in the winter time was on the catcher gang and you did a bit of everything. You did painting, I was on the spring gang for nine weeks when you renewed all the springs, the wires that needed to be done and you finished at 5 o'clock but you booked in till 9 or 10. You got paid to that. This was because you were on the spring gang and it was supposed to be a dirty job and you got £2 extra per week on that so that was on the nine catchers, £18. The worst time was when you saw the factory ship and all the ships leaving and you were there, there was no way home then, you just had to stick it out.

Then after I had finished the winter, I had two months' fishing on the island catchers and that was something else. Two months for 13 whales. You saw them but you could not chase them for the weather and I was glad when the factories came and we could go to the ice. There were a lot of Shetland men there and a lot of Highland men and ones from all over the place. Some of them were very fine people. We used to have sprees and bits of laughs. There was this old fellow, Attie Williamson. We had just come back from the ice and he was second man on the motor boat in South Georgia and he saw me so he came and spoke. I had not seen him for a few months and, all of a sudden, he just turned round and said, "It would be fine to have a bit of saucermeat." I thought it was very humorous because you never saw saucermeat there.

I mind another time on the *Southern Garden* when we were on the way down and we were painting around the bridge and you could see into the pantry and the steward was working with three cooked chickens. This was for the Officer's sandwiches and their tea and coffee in the afternoon but there was nothing for the boys so we thought, well. So Norman Jamieson from Yell nipped in and whipped one and I can't remember the name of the other guy who was with us but he nipped in and whipped one too. The steward came back and saw that the two chickens had gone and he was not very well pleased. From where I was I could see where he hid the last chicken so when he went out again I nipped in and took it and hid it in the cabin. We had a chicken each for tea that night and the bones went out the porthole and they never knew what happened to the chickens.

Sometimes accidents happened. There was a fellow I was very acquaint with, Peter Gillies from Mallaig. He was AB on the whale catcher, *Southern Archer*. One morning he was climbing the rigging to go to the barrel. He had reached the top of the rigging to where a steel ladder went up the last 15 feet or so when he lost his grip and fell on to the deck. He was very lucky because when he fell he hit the catwalk and it, in a way, broke his fall. I think the catcher was going down into the trough of the sea at the time so that benefited him. Among other injuries he burst his spleen. He was in hospital on the factory for a while and when we were in for bunkers I used to go and see him. When he got more able he used to come and give me cheek from the stern of the factory when we were delivering whales. He was a very fine fellow, very humorous.

One time when they had the pool rigged up for the Father Neptune ceremony I grabbed hold on him and dumped him in the pool and he was fairly mad about this. Sometimes on night on board the *Southern Garden* we used to sit on a big anchor and have a cup of tea. This night there was a few of us there and Peter knew I was among them. So he nipped into the big fridge that was aft and got a jug of cold water and came over the poop, it was in the dark, and the next thing I knew was this water was about me and I can tell you my heart stopped completely. But this was the kind of tricks we played on each other to amuse ourselves. I have never seen him since the whaling finished but I believe he is still on the go.

There were a lot of fellows from Shetland who went to the whaling and there were some happy times and some sad times. One year there must have been about seven or eight deaths. A young mess boy on the factory died of polio not long before the end of the season and there was one or two who jumped over the side. There was also one who went over with the wire with the whale. I think that was the same year that Alex Bruce from Lerwick died.

For a burial at sea they stopped work for an hour's time. They put two harpoons, one on each side, and over you went and that was it. I suppose in the back of your mind you were hoping that you would be all right.

When we were working on the catchers during the winter of 1957 there were three Norwegians, a Highland man and myself on a painting job. One of the boys lit up a cigarette and it ignited the paint remover. Two of the Norwegians got badly burned, it burned the skin on their hands and faces. From where my accommodation was I could look down into the hospital. They used to take them in every day and take dead skin off them and it was not very nice. They were sent home by the first available transport.

I remember a fellow called Jack Sheridan. He was an Irish man married to a Shetland girl and he just termed himself a Shetlander. They later emigrated to Australia and he died out there. He was a number of years at the whaling on the motor boats in Leith Harbour. Others that come to mind are Tammy and Geordie Nicolson from Aith and Norman Jamieson, Peter Irvine and Bertie Tulloch from Yell. First when I was there, there were not many Shetland fellows on the catchers but it got more as time went on. You had laughs but it was a tough life on the catchers. On the factory it was not too bad, they had their 12 hours on and 12 hours off. On the catchers if you were off watch and you caught a whale, 'fast fish' as they called it, you were up there working whether it was your watch or not. So it was hard life and a lot of bad weather. I don't think there was any other small ships of that size that went through the as bad weather as the whale catchers. Some of the days you could feel the hair on the back of your neck rising up. They were fine sea boats but the only time I did not care much for them was when they were a bit light with bunkers. When they had plenty of fuel on board they went through a lot of weather. You got icebergs and you could take shelter in the lee of them but if there were no icebergs around it was just a case of head up to wind and dead slow ahead until the weather eased.

There was no bother among the crews although they came from different backgrounds, they just all got on with the job. And there were very few accidents really with the quantity of things that were being used on the factory. Sometimes when you shot a whale and did not kill it, they would have to put in a killer harpoon, sometimes two or three before it died. Occasionally they were lucky and hit it in a vital spot.

The first year I had on the catchers I thought to myself, what is this I've let myself in for here. When I went aboard it was bad weather and as a young fellow, I was very sick. I did not know what I wanted to do and I thought about packing it in and going back in the factory and then I thought if I do that I will be called a chicken so I stuck it out. Once I got over the sickness, it was ok and after that if it was an exceptionally bad day and she was jumping all over the place I would get a bit of a sore head. Other than that I do not think that I will ever be seasick again.

JIMMY JOHNSON

I started going to the whaling when I was about 22. I was working at the docks in Lerwick and Jimmy Watt, a friend of mine, said why did I not go to the whaling because there was no future in me lying around the docks. He thought I would do all right at the whaling. So we went up and phoned Salvesen. I got a job and had to go away that night so I never got back to the steamers' store that day. We went away that night and got down to Leith and they gave me a job as machine boy on the *Sigfra*, that was the same as being a greaser. Then everybody kidded me on about the *Sigfra* and I thought, boy this must be some boat. We got the *Southern Garden* going down and my first recollection of the *Garden* was me standing in this maze of passage ways and I did not have a clue where I was, just completely lost. I had never been aboard a boat this size in my life before. Then I heard a voice at my back, "Boy, is du lost?" and this was Scottie Christie and Victor Inkster. They took and showed me to their cabin and got me something to eat. I'm still good friends with Scottie yet. Sadly Victor died some years ago. That was the start on the *Garden*.

When we got down to South Georgia somebody shouted, "Jimmy, come and have a look at dy boat." And I looked over the side and here was the *Sigfra* and I said, "Yon canna be my boat, yon bloody thing is sinking." But she turned out to be a lovely sea boat. My first day at sea on her, I was running aft going on watch and I missed the foot of the ladder and before I could get turned back, a lump of water hit me and took me right aft so I had to climb back right up over the steering engine because no way was I going back the way I had come. I was standing up there and I was shivering and it was not just with cold. And that was my first day on a whale catcher.

The first night they started up the capstan I shot out of bed because I thought that someone had dropped a bomb on the deck. In that cabin there was just one peerie light. You could not leave your shoes on the floor of the cabin because every time the water came in over her, it hit the capstan and came down the shaft right into the cabin and it did not run out the bottom or anything, it just shloosh, shloosh, shlooshed the whole time. The steward aboard there was called Scabby Head, I never knew his right name but he was Norwegian and he was brilliant. The grub that man dished up was really good. But I liked the *Sigfra* so I spent three seasons on her. I worked myself into a really nice job on her and then I missed a year and went to the salvage and when I phoned up again I got a job on the *Southern Terrier* and the boys who were down with me at that time, Mitchell and Andrew Arthur and Billy Ramsay, they called me for all the jammy buggers under the sun. I had never heard of the *Terrier* so I thought to myself, with their reaction, was this another bloody *Sigfra*.

When I saw her she was so different from the *Sigfra*, much bigger, and she had been a corvette in the wartime. When I went on board her and went down to the cabin which I shared with the Fireman, with a wash hand basin, man I thought I was in the Ritz. I went down below to the engineroom and after the *Sigfra* it was so big and spacious with the same type of engine as the *Sigfra*, it was just really, really good. I was put on day work on her instead of being four on and four off. I was on the whole day and the 4th engineer came on all night. This was because the 2nd engineer, he was an old guy, would not stop the engine from turning as soon as the gun went off so we got a rope in our prop twice in one day and the gunner came down to see what was wrong. I told him what was wrong. It did not matter what steam you had in the engine, as soon as the gun went off you had to jump up and grab this lever and haul it down and that stopped your engine dead. The first couple of times you did this you thought the cylinder head was going to lift right out the skylights. Everything creaked and groaned and then you had to get the steam off it and then rock it back and fore so the prop did not move.

I was on day work the two seasons I was on board her and it was a brilliant job. We had one of the best gunners I ever knew, Arne Mikalsen, but he came to a poor end. When we were coming back to the island after the season had finished he was on the gun platform shooting shag with a 303 and stepped back and fell and hurt his back and I am led to believe that he never worked again. He was a gentleman to sail with. We went in to some island where there was a hot water spring and a weather station and they had a doctor who had a look at him. We took him back to Leith Harbour and he was carried aboard the *Southern Harvester*. But I heard through the grapevine that he lost the use of his legs, whether that was right or not I do not know. He was in a very poor state when we took him to his cabin.

My job was to look after the engine and make sure it ran, oil everything, grease everything and when we got bunkers I was responsible for taking the machine oil and diesel and things like that aboard, I had nothing to do with the fuel oil, that was the Chief Engineer's department. In fact I just had a splendid peerie job on that thing. That was really good.

The firemen on that boats were really good guys, they knew how to handle steam. Everybody was really good and we had two top-notch AB's on deck, Jake Nisbet and Danny Morrison because they were on the top catcher. I twice had the offer of getting a job on the *Southern Harvester* as fireman but I would not take it and I would not do that job on the catchers either because there was not enough to do. I always liked to be pottering about painting this and cleaning that and when you were fireman all you did was sit there and look at bloody gauges and then when the gun went off you had to take off like a bat out of hell. I remember that from my *Sigfra* days.

The *Sigfra* was a buoy boat and we did not get many whales, 19 the first season and 27 the second season. We just picked up the whales after the big boats had shot them. The fireman, he was very much at leisure and I thought it was an awfully easy life and I could not be bothered with it so to keep myself interested I got this greaser's job and it suited me fine. I got on great with the Norwegian engineers and the firemen as well. The first year I was on the *Terrier* the gunner went out and shot three albatross. We turned around and picked them up and he hung them up to dry. I had never seen an albatross that close in my life before and when the maggots started coming out of it I was thinking to myself I'm putting that over the side but I never got around to it. One day I noticed they had gone and I thought to myself, they have dumped them over the side. The following night we came in and had lovely strips of meat I thought was venison or something and I made such a pig of myself I could hardly rise from the table. The rest of the crew were all sitting there having a good laugh at me because I had been on about putting this albatross over the side and then they told me what I had just eaten. This was the albatross that the maggots had been crawling out of and it was delicious. It is surely the same as grouse, you have to hang it up until they are bloody rotten and then you cook them. But that was really good grub. The stewards aboard that boat, they were out of this world, they could make some marvellous grub.

A thing that never bothered me then was seasickness, I never knew what it was. I used to go by the messroom and take two slices of loaf and put half a tin of corned beef in between them or a kipper or whatever was there and throw it on top of the fire and turn it over two or three times to make a sandwich and away to my work with a cup of coffee in my hand. Now I can't even go out in my peerie boat without spewing.

All that years I was at the whaling, I had seen Norwegians who had been there longer than me spewing in the bilges and I was thinking what's wrong with these guys. I mind the first time I was seasick I was going to Aberdeen on the *St Clair* and it did not sail at five o'clock on Saturday night it only sailed on Sunday at dinner time because it had been bad weather. I was never so ill in my bloody life. I thought I was going to die.

MITCHELL ARTHUR

I was 17 the first year I went to the whaling. I had been weaving at Ollaberry and the arse had gone out of the market and there was no sign of any much work so I asked Sonny Williamson at the Lubba if there was any chance of getting to the whaling. He wrote to Salvesen and I got a job but Sonny was not going away that year so Charlie Duncan took me with him when he went. I was mess boy that first year, washing dishes and keeping the mess rooms clean. I worked for a while in the big mess and then in the Petty Officers' mess. We came home to Liverpool and I had to stand by the ship and that's where I ran into Davie Clark for the first time. We were three weeks in Liverpool, an exciting time I can assure you.

The following year, when we went back I thought that I would like a change so I asked Salvesens if there was any chance of getting on the catchers. They put me down as deck mess boy and I joined the *Southern Sailor* washing dishes again and peeling tatties and you helped at night when you finished your stint to wash the cartridges and reload the shells for the gun. You started at 6 in the morning and finished at 9 at night, with a couple of hours off in the afternoon if there was no whales. You heaved the capstan for putting on the tail rope on the whale and so on and you gave the mate a hand to load the gun.

I went ashore for the winter that year. I started off in the big mess room there and then they needed somebody in the engineers' mess so I wintered in the engineers' mess, two Norwegians and myself. Jimmy Mieklejohn was in the engineers' mess, he was an engineer for the winter and he had a class that a lot of us went to to learn Norwegian. The boys in the messroom of course helped me. There was a fellow there called Tyjire Gundersen who came from a place called Fliza away up close to the Swedish border and he spoke slightly different from the Tonsberg men.

During the winter Tyjire taught me to ski. It was some laugh that. We went up the side of the hill and he would show me how to turn by laying the skis over on their sides and you were kinda tippin on one ski with the other, like lying over on a motor bike. Of course the first time I tried it one ski went under the other one and I did two peerie whirls around and fell upon my arse and my hand struck a rock, you can see the mark on it yet. "That is not the way to do it, " he said. I went to the doctor and I said, "I would like you to examine my hand." "How did you do that?" he said. I said, "Oh, learning to ski." "It's not your hand I should examine," he said, "it's your bloody head."

That was all the sympathy I got.

At the end of that winter the *Polar Maid* came down with all the stores for Leith Harbour. I do not know what they did but they turned a wrong valve or something and flooded the hold with all the stores and destroyed the whole lot. They had put the pigs' meal on the very top and it got through everything. They had to discharge it all and dumped it on barges which they hauled away outside of Leith Harbour and dumped it over the side. We got furry boots and leather jackets and dungarees and I don't know what else out of it. When they got to the bottom of the hold, they came upon the rum. At Leith Harbour they had their breakfast at half past eight in the morning and everybody knocked off at twenty past eight to get ready for their breakfast.

Old Willem Johansen was the foreman and he went for his breakfast at twenty-five past eight and came back at a quarter to nine. Then he found the barrel that they had set upon the barge before he went for his breakfast was empty. I always mind it because I was working in the engineers' mess and there were forty men in the mess and we had a big aluminium bucket that we fetched the porridge and the soup from the galley to the messroom in and this man came in the door and said, "Have you got that white bucket, Mitchell?" I said, "Yes." He said, "Give it to me." I said, "I can't. It's covered with porridge, man." "Just give it to me," he said. And he came running back with it full of rum.

We got it bottled and hidden away. It was brawly cloudy, I can tell you with the porridge in it but it was drinkable. And then they came upon the beer and it was something which we had never seen, tins of beer, it was something new. And with the heat of the pigs' meal and all fermenting among the stuff, the paint had come off the cans; they were fairly bright shining with the ends of them blown out. So we did not know what kind of beer it was or how to open them but we got screwdrivers and there was foam everywhere.

After a while there was a big search on. They found that one boy had four hundred cans on top of the lockers in his room and he got the sack on the spot. It really was funny because they shovelled the cans over the side of this barge and then the boys went to the radar fixers and they got magnets with long pieces of string and they fished for the beer cans. Somebody wondered if the rum would be all right. So they took a bottle and went up to old Dr Mac and poured him out a glass. He sampled it and drank it all down and said, "Is there any more of it?" He did not analyse it, he just drank it.

The following season I was on the *Southern Runner* with Egil Abrahamsen, gunner. I came home a rich man and bought a peerie car, that was in 1957, the year I married. I went back galley boy on the *Southern Soldier* the following season, with the *Southern Harvester*. The season after that I was whaler upon the *Southern Soldier* again. I wintered out in '59 working on the whale catchers. The number of whale catchers was cut down for the following season and I was put back upon the *Harvester* hooking meat on the rosedown. They speak about hard work, by God that was hard work. Great lumps of meat, they cut them up and you hooked them and put them down this kverner, a big mincer that minced it all up.

At the end of the first two days my shoulders were so sore that I did not know if I would manage to lift a hook again, I was just aching. That same season I was also doing relief work upon several catchers, the *Southern Runner*, the *Southern Briar*, and I ended up on the *Southern Wilcox*. I came back up to Leith Harbour on her at the end of the season and came home on the *Southern Garden* in charge of the mess boys, the same job I always did going down and coming up. She was another experience. Boy it was some heat in that mess room. No air, no ports, no ventilation of any kind. The cabins were built on the tank deck, you could hardly bear to set your bare feet on deck and you could not open the portholes because they were so close to the sea.

The season of '61 when I came aboard the *Southern Harvester* Addie Manson said, "What's du doin this year, Mitchell?" and I said, "Well, I'm just whaler again." "Naa, naa," he said, "I'm needin' a boiler screwer, I'll go and see them in the office." So I was boiler screwer on the after plan with a Norwegian. You had to open and close the kettles and go down and see the guy who was in the factory and tell him how much was in them. By that time they had found out that I spoke Norwegian so whenever we were doing anything, tying up or letting go, I got a fine job. I sat aft with the phone so it did not matter whether it was a British Officer or a Norwegian Officer that spoke, I could tell the bosun, Ole Mhyre, what was going on.

When I went back in 1962 Ole Myhre asked what I was doing this year and I said I was back boiler screwer again. "Oh no, you're not," he said, "I'm needing a cutter." So that was me up a group again to Group 6. I had to learn how to sharpen a flensing knife and how to cut up the spik. Going down you spliced wire tail strops for the whales. First eight strand wire and then six strand wire and all different types to make all kinds of peerie strops for various jobs - Jerry Dalziel, John Georgeson, Bobby Odie and myself.

I learned a lot of seamanship from them. We had to go over the side in Leith Harbour to paint so you learned how to rig stages and bosun's chairs and all different things. The following year we spliced wire going down again. Close to the back end of the season Ole Myhre came to me and said, "There's not much doing this dinner hour and there is a whale on the plan. Get the winchman with us and we'll teach you how to flense." So I flensed that whale and then every time there was a chance after that he would put me through my paces and say, "Next year you will come back flenser." But there never was a next year because that was the end of it.

That year coming home, I was in charge of a squad to do all the after end of the ship, painting the lifeboats and the funnels and the helicopter deck and all around that areas, the two after samsons and all the way down the chute. There were 12 Norwegian and 12 British men and some Highland men. So there was the three languages going on around you all the time. I could make nothing of the Gaelic at all. That was the year we towed home the *Southern Lotus*. We spent the time in Leith Harbour making everything ready, getting the towing gear put together and making the 'tigers', that was the folded rope with the toggles on each end with the knot, dog's heads, on them. It was a very interesting job that, getting all that made ready, especially splicing the eyes of that nine inch insurance wires, they were only six strand. That was a heavy job, that one.

We left Leith Harbour and picked up the *Southern Lotus* just before we came to Mutton Island and got everything ready for towing. There was the two anchor chains from the boat and then the 'tiger', and then there was 120 fathom of double six inch rope and then two of the bridles and then 120 fathom of nine inch insurance wire out from each quarter of the *Southern Harvester*. She was a long way behind us. We set away and we were likely doing ten knots so we thought that it was not going to be so bad and then we hit the Forties and I think that of all the weather I ever saw, that was the worst. We had loaded a lot of empty gas bottles and stuff on the deck of the *Southern Harvester* and the whole lot took off and knocked down one of the rails of the penguins' enclosure and about forty of them got loose and they just vanished down the chute. Boy, they were delighted to get away.

The weather got steadily worse. You could see nothing but the white spume and spindrift everywhere. One minute you would see the *Southern Lotus* away out to port, we were supposed to be towing her astern of us and she was nearly ahead of us going up first one side and then she would swing around and go up the other side. We saw the lifeboat nearly going off her. My brother was one of the ABs on her and the mate came aft and said, "If she goes you will have to find some way of letting this go." The bosun said, "You cannot very well ask Mitchell to cut them clear because his brother is one of the ABs on there." Anyway, we got through it, how I do not know. It was not just a night and a day, it was two or three days. It was hurricane force winds, the worst weather I have ever seen.

On the factory, they made bovril, that meat extract and put it in barrels. All the meat extract off the *Southern Harvester* had to go aboard the *Southern Venturer*. We were in Leith Harbour first so we had to put ashore all the barrels of bovril and we built it up outside the big mess room. When the barrels came ashore Jerry Dalziel and I stacked them up and then we got a plank and rolled them up and stacked them on top of each other. They weighed about four hundredweight each. Boy, that was heavy work, twelve hour shifts. Jerry sang the whole time. I did a lot of work along with Jerry, a good shipmate and a good seaman. Of course we had fun in the messrooms playing cards with John Thomson, known to all as the Arab. We gambled for fags. That was an education, there was a lot of one-liners that came off John when he was playing cards. For three seasons running I had to sew the turnups on his breeks. "Will du sew the turnups on my strides," he would ask. He was always first in the queue to get ashore. "I'll see you in the 'Legs of Man'," he would say. That was always where he went and when I came in, there he was with the paddy hat on the back of the head and six inches of the leg of the breeks out underneath the shoes again. A waste of time, I might as well never have bothered.

The first year I was on the *Southern Venturer* she hit one of that awful lumps of water in the Forties and laid in the portholes at the firemen's mess and set the bridge back about an inch. There were rough times on the whale catchers lying hove to, climbing first one mountain of sea and then down the other side, the big grey fellows rolling at you that had never seen land since they started at one side of the world till they came around by you and went on their way. When you think of that peerie boats, the ordinary whalecatcher was maybe about one hundred and forty feet long, by God it learned you how to steer. We used to look forward to it because if you had had a busy few days and had had a lot of whales, if you got a storm then you got a chance to sleep. You jammed yourself in your bunk with your knees up along one side and maybe your pillow or something between you and the other side and slept through it.

It was hard going in the middle of the season when it was daylight all round the clock. I mind going up in the barrel at two o'clock in the morning and not a hundred feet from us there was a whale that blew; I could not believe it. I shouted and they had to get the gunner out of his bed. When it was dark you could hear the blows of them as they went by.

And there was four days in the season when we fished humpback whales.

When you think of that now it just was a crying shame. One day they shot one and did not kill her outright and the rest of them turned back to see what had happened to her and he just shot them off one after the other. I don't remember how many we got, somewhere in the teens. They all came back to see what had happened to the one who was still blowing on the end of the starboard foregoer. Just sheer slaughter. But then it was all money; the more tails the more dollars.

The first year I was down I did not think a lot of the Norwegian food but when you had been on watch on the whale catcher you could have eaten anything. When you came down from the barrel after being an hour on the wheel and an hour in the barrel from two o'clock in the morning until eight, you could eat fish balls all right. I enjoyed the grub on the whale catcher, it really was good. The last years on the factory, the grub was not nearly so bad as it was the first year I was down. It seemed to improve. Whale meat was good and I enjoyed it but some would not eat it, they would rather have corned beef. And there was many a time that whatever we were having in the British mess, I would have sent the mess boy with a plate to get a plateful of whatever the Norskies were having instead. I liked that smoked sausages and in the British mess all you got was the tinned three cornered ones. I did not care for them.

You got meat cakes or fish cakes or whatever and onions done in brown thin gravy. And when the weather was too bad to make a proper meal, we had storm soup – a big pan with a vegetable soup. I always mind the first time I was mess boy on the catchers, in at the back of the stair in the store room down aft by the steering, there was always a box of raisins and I always had a handful of them as I came up by every time.

One day I said to the steward that my birthday was on the 2nd February. "Oh," he said, "we'll make cakes then for your birthday." I was vexed I ever mentioned the damned thing. After clearing up after breakfast time he came with a three gallon enamel bucket and he cracked in 19 eggs, one for everybody who was aboard and a lot of sugar and he gave me a whisk and told me to whisk until the bucket was full so you got the eggs and sugar all mixed together. Then he put in flour and he made sponges and he split them and made them 3 layers and put cream and fruit in each layer and it was just beautiful. But it was the beating; I beat for about an hour in this bucket of eggs to get the eggs right before he put the flour in. My arm was just aching.

They always made cream from the evaporated milk. Some had an electric drill for a whisk but we were never that far advanced, it was just the hand whisk. When the AB was down for his cup of coffee he used to get a spell at it too. Some of the waffles were good, with heavy syrup and pancakes. I still make them yet. I mind Attie Mouat and me getting the steward to keep a bit of salt ling before they steeped it for making what they called 'lutafisk' and we just boiled it the way we do at home. We used to catch what I suppose would be blue whiting and with that livers we made crappin. They were very soft that fish, you had to be careful with them. We used to draw bucketfuls of them. That was good fun.

When you look back on it, the deck of a whale boat was not really a very safe place to be at times. The lumps of sea that used to come in over - alongside the factory delivering the whales - was the worst place.

The bosun on the aft end of the factory ship would be directing the claw to fall on the tail of the whale and drag it up the chute on to the aft plan deck. He would be directing three winches, the winch that was holding the whale which was known as the fishing winch, and the two capstans which were holding the claw in mid air and when the whale was in the right position, he let the claw fall onto the tail of the whale. The two big winches heaved him up the chute. It took 20 minutes to take the blubber off. The barder out of his mouth went over the side but occasionally some was kept.

As he came up the chute the flensers began their work. One walked up the back and made a long cut near the back bone, another just about knee level along the back and the other about knee level up the belly. Then the cutters would do the middle of the belly and they hooked in the winch and hauled the spik off and then the flensers flensed off the two upper sides. Then they used the two canting winches as they were called, one on to the top flipper and one on to the bottom one and turned the whale upside down and right over and that pulled off the layer of spik which was on the other side so it came off in three strips. They then came with the winch wire from for'ard and put on the tail and hauled the carcase up the foreplan and took the meat off the bones up there, lemming they called that. It was taken off in great big chunks and then they stuck in a hook at the bottom of the hindmost rib, a great bugger of a hook with a kind of a sharp edge on the inside of him and put the winch on for'ard on that and heaved him along the rig bone and cut the ribs clear of the backbone, turned him over and did the same on the other side. That came aft to the starboard side and they cut the head off and that went off to the port side.

Then the steam saws cut up the jaw bone and the head and the back bone was split in two and put to each side. The guts were dumped over the side but that was the only thing not made use of. And when you looked at the whale, he was just exactly the same as any other animal; the heart and the liver and the kidneys were there just in the same position as it is in either a sheep or a cow. The kidneys were just like a cow's kidney but they were absolutely massive, the liver was huge and the heart was about the size of a Volkswagen beetle. Then all the lumps of meat were taken for'ard and cut into squares and ground up and made into meat extract and bone meal and meat meal and put in bags and stowed in the empty tanks. There was a gang washing tanks the whole time, they did nothing else.

The Scott boys from Papa Stour, Alex, Fraser and Bruce, who stays in Lerwick, did that job along with Jimmy and Ernest Tait from East Burrafirth. It was nearly all Shetland men in that tank gang. They cleaned the fuel oil out of the tanks after they were empty and then had to line them with dunnage before the bags of meat meal went in. There were other tanks that they stored whale oil in. It was pumped over to the transport ship when she came alongside in mid season and then the tanks had to be cleaned out again and fuel oil put in them. It had to be absolutely spotless because the whale oil was going for human consumption; it was used for making margarine.

The bags of meat meal weighed 140lb and they all had to be stowed and that was heavy work. The boys in that gang worked half an hour on and half an hour off. It was long enough as the heat was something unbelievable. The boys who drove the bone saws were expert at their job, especially cutting up the head. If it was not cut exactly right then it would not go down the kettle. Hughie Murray was a lot of years on that job and when he left to become bosun on one of the transport ships, Rab Skene took over from him. Some one of the boys said to Hughie one night, "Du's cut this bone ower big."

"Look round you, son," he said, "there's no bones lying here from last year." There was a knack to putting the bones down the kettle. Joe Gray from Lerwick was with him and said to Hughie this day, "Which end of this bone do I put down, Hughie?" "Any bloody end," he replied. So Joe lifted the bone and tipped it into the kettle and it got stuck. Hughie looked at him for a moment and said, "Not that bloody end." There was one day Joe Gray fell right down into a kettle which had not been long opened. Hughie took the capstan wire and said to the winch boy, "Full speed" and he lowered the capstan hook down to Joe and said, "Pit dy fit in the hook and grip da wire," and up he came. He came to where Hughie could get hold of him and he heaved him right out.

The second mate was Fryzndorf, he was Polish. He would not put spikes in the heels of his rubber boots. He would come now and then if there was not an awful lot doing and speak to us boys up at the rosedown where we were cutting up the meat. Then he would walk aft the deck usually looking for Addie Manson because he just liked to upset Addie. Either Rab Skene or myself would speak to him and always somebody had a length of thin nylon twine and we would tie it on to the back of his boilersuit and on to a stanchion and he would get maybe 40 fathoms down the deck when this would come tight and down upon his arse he would go. He would feel behind him to see if this string was there. We got him I do not know how often. It was just a delight. Bertie Sutherland from Yell said, "He'll be sacking you yet."

Working on the rosedown really was a good place for you were right up in the fore end of the plan outside the galley so you were sheltered all the time. The boys who sat at the capstans all the time and the bone saws had a cold miserable job. The blood going out the scuppers blew all over them. An awful mess that boys got in. You were far better off down on the deck doing something. The strips of blubber, sometimes about sixty feet long, were heaved by the capstan up to the mouths of the kettles. When its own weight began to take it down, then it would zig zag and swirl around and you had to stand well back.

The belly blubber on the big fin whales was maybe 18 inches to 2 feet thick and on the bigger blue whales an awful lot thicker than that. We did not see very many blue whales to end up with. The last years it was nearly all sei and the blubber on them was just like pasteboard. The big whales were gone. But it really was magic to watch, there was so many peerie gangs working, everyone had his own job it worked like clockwork, putting 36 whales through in 24 hours in two shifts, when she was on 'full cook'. It was heavy work when you were really going but you got used to it.

The whole secret of cutting blubber was to be able to sharpen your knife. It is something that has stood me in good stead all my life for filleting fish and gutting fish, being able to sharpen a knife makes life a lot easier. There were two men who did nothing but grind the knives, one on each shift. Everybody had six knives so you tried to use three on your shift and put them to the grinder and you used the other three the next shift so you always had three sharp knives. When you were working with sperm whales you needed a well worn knife because the blubber was very hard, especially on the head. It was cut up into squares of about a foot square and it was an awful job to cut it. There was a layer of easy stuff about four inches deep and then a two inch layer of really hard stuff which went right back from the nose through the head until you met up with the blubber in the body.

The head was solid oil. It was made like that to take the shock of pounding the squid on the bottom. And right in the centre of all that blubber there was likely about a big bowl full of just pure oil right in the centre of the head. It was a hard job to cut that head. I never liked to see too many sperm coming for that really was hard on you and the knives. Occasionally through the season you would get them. If there had been no big whales for a time then they would give permission for the whale boats to shoot sperm if there was any about. So you occasionally got them in the middle of the season. And if you did they would keep one for a fender until he was just absolutely muck rotten and then when they cut into it, the blubber was alright but the flesh just went over the deck like custard and you had to sweep it down the holes with squeegees. That was some smell.

And when the season finished you had to wash the whole ship from top to bottom with caustic soda. That was a dangerous job. Bobby Odie got burned one season brawly badly with it. It left a mark on his arm for the rest of his life. Sometimes you were swinging from bosun's chairs away up the masts and the samson posts and down the derricks and everything. We had a peerie pump on a barrel and a great long hose with a spray nozzle on the end of it for the job. From the time you left the ice until you came to South Georgia, that is what you did. You also lifted all the old plan and dumped it overboard. That was the wood they put out over the main deck of the ship to protect it.

That was another job I marvelled at, watching the Norwegian carpenters laying that plan deck on the way south. They never used a hammer; it was always an axe. All that fitting around the mouths of the kettles. It was all done with the axe and they hammered the nails in with the back of the axe. I never saw one of them with a hammer. They covered the whole of the deck with soft wood so the spikes on the heels of your boots could get a grip and that saved the main deck. The deck was washed with caustic every now and again from the time we left the ice until we came to South Georgia and then every Saturday morning on the way going home and then we had lifeboat muster or fire station drill on Saturday afternoons.

The bosun on the *Southern Venturer* was known as Caustic. He came originally from Cunningsburgh but stayed in Leith. He was Magnie Christie and he was some character. We left South Shields and there was this young fellow who was just straight out of the army. He went and asked Caustic what he was to do and he said, "Take a brush and start at the galley door and sweep right aft until you come to the chute." So the boy swept manfully on and got to the chute and then came back and said he had finished. "No you have not, sonny," he said, "you just go back to the galley door and start again." The boy said, "How long will it take?" and Caustic replied, "When you come to the metal, come and see me." That was the boy's job all the way down to the ice, to keep the decks clean. There was some who did nothing else. They swept up where the carpenters had been working, all the sawdust and bits of wood. It all had to be done.

On the *Southern Harvester* Gilbert Sharp was the carpenter, now that was a character. He was very, very precise with his measurements. I went up one day and asked him for a bit of wood as I was going to cover the grill above the door of the cabin to stop the light from shining in when we were on night shift. He said, "What size of a piece of wood do you want?" I said, "I'm wanting a bit about this long." "About", he said, "there's no such measurement on my rule as about." So he measured between my fingers and cut my piece of wood. He had good hands on him and he had a beauty of a peerie panel saw and one day we were fitting dunnage in a tank. He took the saw down into the tank and big Jacob, one of the cutters on the for'ard plan, a Norwegian, picked up Gilbert's saw and he made a couple of cuts through a piece of green wood and broke it. This great man who should not have been afraid of anything laid Gilbert's saw down very carefully, went up the ladder and vanished.

Gilbert was not pleased about his saw. He made a beautiful front door for old Myhre's house, a work of art and then he made a peerie tool chest like one of those things you would have seen on an old sailing ship, all brass bound and with locks and all on it. We came into Liverpool and the Customs men asked him, "What's in the box?" He said, "Oh, odds and ends." "And what does odds and ends consist of?" they asked. He replied, "Bits and pieces." The Customs man looked at him and said, "What's bits and pieces?" He said, "Oh, just this and that." "Oh, for Christ sake go ashore with the box," he said. Gilbert was a very fine man and a good carpenter.

There were a lot of interesting times through it all. I mind the first time they put me up in a bosun's chair, I had no idea what to do. We were painting the funnel so you sat in the bosun's chair and three or four men heaved you up and you came up to this hanging block which had hung there since the ship was built. The block was open ended at the bottom. You would sit up there and hold on to the two ropes and put a hitch on to keep yourself in place. I thought it would be the end of me but you got used to it.

That was what killed Alex Bruce. He came down off the funnel and sat down and died, heat exhaustion killed him. You were coming into the tropics before you got around to painting and the funnel was very hot. It was certainly a shock to the system from down in the ice a fortnight before and then into the sweltering heat. Then with my colour of skin I could not stand the sun. I had to have something cotton to wear all the time, a cotton shirt with long sleeves otherwise I would have been roasted.

Old Mac, the doctor, was another character. This boy came up to him and said he was suffering with Asian flu. Old Mac gave him four tablets. "Take these two when you go to bed tonight," he said, "and if you wake up tomorrow morning, take the other two." I did a trip down as his assistant. It was a bobby dazzler of a number that.

I did the first trip with the *Southern Garden* as galley boy, that was the year they lost all the drums of petrol. They had tied all the drums on the deck and we hit a godless sea in the Forties and it just cleaned the lot. We could hear the rinkle, rinkle, rinkle, ding and away they went. There was a big Norwegian cook on board and she shipped a lump just aft by the centre castle and it swept aft along the deck. The cook was just coming out the galley door and the sea came in and picked him up and put him right past the stove and straight out the other door. I can see him going yet, two great number eleven shoes. Peter Gillies from Mallaig was the other galley boy and I could hear him laughing, he was just in stitches. We were in by the stove, up on the raised bit. It put out the galley stove and I thought there would be an explosion before we got it all switched off.

ATTIE WILLIAMSON

I had been on the Ben boats and came home for Christmas. I was supposed to go on another Ben boat and then I heard that there was a boat going down to the whaling. That was in 1956. So Ellis Sales and I wrote to Salvesens and we got a job with them. We joined the *Teie* in Rotterdam, she was a Norwegian tanker with accommodation built above deck, and we worked our way down to South Georgia. When we got there it was the start of the winter and I got a job as mess boy in the big messroom. We had 20 men to look after for the six months, 10 British and 10 Norwegians.

That winter my brother-in-law, Alex Paton, was doing the winter along with Jimmy Balfour from Brae and Geordie Nicolson from Aith. They were always on at us to bring them as much sugar and fruit as we could get our hands on and we could not understand why. We thought there is something going on here and unknown to us this was for making home brew. Then we were invited to sample the stuff. It was kept very quiet, everything was very discreet. We had to take up cups with us because there were no glasses. We would start drinking this home brew and it was not very quiet maybe two hours after, the roars of Balfour and the grunts of Paton.

We got the winter over and then we all went on different catchers. I was on the *Foster* fishing for the island and I was coming ashore with the laundry when Tommy Moore called me into the office and asked me what sort of a cook I was. He said the *Southern Satellite* was needing a second cook and baker and if I took the job it would get me home a bit earlier. So that was what I did. We went direct from Leith Harbour to Liverpool in 21 days. It was a good job with plenty of overtime. Alan Tulloch from Whalsay was a fireman on board, and Jimmy Jamieson from Lerwick was there too. We took home 3 sea lions. There was one for London Zoo and two for Edinburgh Zoo and it was Jimmy's job to feed them and keep the salt water hoses going to cool them.

I spent the summer at home and then I got a job on the factory ship, *Southern Venturer* and was there for the following 5 seasons. One season I was on what they called the expellers. Another season I was stowing meal along with Nicol Thomson from Yell and then the last year I was on the pumps, so I just did a few different jobs.

I think it was in 1958 when we were at the fishing grounds that it came a storm which lasted for 2 or 3 days, it was just a hurricane. The sea was as calm as a loch, and then the wind fell away and then all hell broke loose, it was just mountains of sea that came up. They thought that there was some volcanic activity in the area. As one old Shetland man who came from the sailing said when they asked him what he thought of it he said that the seas were like the hills of Weisdale. That was really bad and the mess room and galley were washed out, the steering gear was all buckled and the rails aft on the poop deck were damaged. The water came right up the chute and flooded the decks and a Russian catcher sheltered in our lee for 2 or 3 days until the weather eased down. The *Venturer* catchers were sheltering behind some huge iceberg so they were safe enough. The 3rd mate on the *Venturer* was a Pole by the name of Fryzndorf. Captain Myhre from Norway was on the bridge and one of the AB's was at the wheel when Fryzndorf came up laughing and Myhre asked what he was he laughing at. He said, "Oh, the slop chest man is very, very frightened. He is crying, he is so frightened." Myhre said, "Are you frightened?" "Me? No", he says, "it don't worry me." "Well, you're a bigger bloody fool than I thought you were. Get out of my sight. Get off this bridge. Get out. Get out. I don't want to see you. Away you go." And he chased him off the bridge. That was Fryzndorf for you.

Holtan was the Chief Mate. He took all the cats and kittens and banged their heads along something and then threw them over the side. When the boys were aft chipping the bollards they would red lead them and then paint them with white paint. Holtan would come along and ask if the bollards had been red leaded before painting. He did not believe the boys when they told him that they had and made them chip it off again. That was the kind of a bugger he was. After that he went as Skipper on the *Southern Harvester* and then he was starting to see icebergs in the tropics and that was the end of him I think.

In 1960 we had two burials at sea, Eddie Hutcheson from Lerwick and a Norwegian mess boy. He was in the fireman's mess, a great big fine like chap, 16 years old and he actually had his birthday in the hospital aboard the *Venturer*. We used to go up and see him. He had paralysis and it just crept all through his body. When his arm fell down we had to lift it up for him and he could not hold up his head. Some suggested getting one of the buoy boats or even the helicopter and putting him to Cape Town or some place to try to get him home but Myhre reckoned that it would interfere with the season and he would not wear it and we buried him at sea.

I thought the whaling was all right. Of course, thenadays we were all young guys and there was not much work here. It was, for a lot of us, whaling or Merchant Navy. In the summer time we would go to the seine net. We used to go with Ellis' uncle, John, on the *Reward* or whatever boat we could get and then away back down to the whaling.

MICHAEL JAMIESON

I went to the whaling on 8 August 1948. I went down on a ship called the *Polar Chief*. I got to South Georgia in one piece and from there I went on the plan as a winch boy. I was there for a few months and then they put me on a ship called the *Saluta* going to the ice, as a mess boy. It took about four weeks to get there and then I transferred from her to the factory ship. The *Saluta* was a kind of an old rotten tub and when it came bad weather the fuel oil would shoot up through the deck in the mess room when she started to roll. She was so rotten that on her next trip home to Britain she cracked across the front of the bridge. I was not on her at that time. They went into South Georgia with her and eventually got her home but that was the end of her I think. I was now on the *Southern Harvester* until the end of the season. I was working down on the factory deck, it was fine and warm down there.

When I came home, I found the army was after me for National Service so I phoned up Salvesen to see if I could get down a bit earlier because they were going to take me to the army. I went down to the island again and decided to do a winter this time. Before the winter started everybody usually put their names in for a job and stated what job they would like to do in the winter time. I never put my name in for any particular job and the others were always saying to me, "Have you never got a job yet? They are maybe not going to keep you for the winter."

The last day before the factory closed my name went up on the notice board that I was to go to the Office. I went into the Office and they said, "You have never put in for a job?" and I said, "No." They said, "Well, we have a job for you if you want it." And this was laundry man, the finest job on the island. Wasn't some of them mad. Anyway I did that winter and got on fine and then they kept me in the laundry all season. I did 5 seasons and a winter. Then I got married and we had a family and then I did three seasons after that.

After the three seasons when I did not go whaling, I went back and got the same job as a boiler-screwer, that was screwing the lids onto the kettles. I was pig man going down that time. Then we thought we would do winters, Andy Smith and me, and there was a quite a few of us. We ended up in the dry dock doing the bottoms of the catchers.

About half way through that winter the *Southern Garden* came down with a load of oil and they came to Stromness to pump it out. They got all ready and got it all started up and pumped away and they were going to pump all night. There was an old Norwegian who was supposed to watch this oil line. Anyway, he surely fell asleep and the line burst and she pumped for about six hours into the air so you can imagine what the pier was like and all the surrounding catchers and dry dock and the whole voe, it was all covered with oil. Then there was a fun next morning because we were supposed to clean it up.

We had got all rigged out with hoses and everything and gloves and we had just made a start when the motor boat came back from Leith Harbour and Kaare Iversen came along and said, "Is Michael Jamieson there?" and I said, "Yes, I'm here." "You're wanted in Leith Harbour right away to go into the laundry," he said. The boys did not think much of it. There was them with fuel oil to clean up and I was going to wash clothes. I was in the laundry for three weeks that time and when I came back to Stromness, the oil was all cleaned up. We had a good time that winter. It was fine over there and there was not many folk. Then I went back on the factory ship for the season. I think that was the time she hit an iceberg. I mind a hole in the bows of her that you could have crawled out through. It was fog and she was steaming brawly fast. It was a lump of ice called a growler.

I think it was the last season I was down that we had crib tournaments, one on the way down and one on the way home and I won them both. I don't mind how many folk I played but in the final game I played against a helicopter man and beat him. Didn't we have some night that night among the helicopter men. They were crawling out the porthole and onto the deck.

It was a good life, a very good life and it never will be again.

KARL BROWN

When whalers arrived at Leith they had to pass a medical examination and sign a contract agreeing to work when and where required. I spent seven seasons on the factory ship *Southern Venturer* from 1948 to 1955. She was built in Britain, 540 ft long, and she operated first in the 1945/46 season. She was broken up in Japan in 1964. There is a good painting of her in the Lerwick Museum.

It was not easy to find work in Yell in the 1940's and 50's and at that time over 80 Yell men were going to the Antarctic to earn a living. Some went for only one season and others did possibly 20 seasons and a few winters from the 1930's to the end of the 1962/63 season.

The first two seasons I worked in the meat meal department where the whale meat was minced up, dried and ground into meal and then bagged and stored in tanks. From 300 to 600 bags weighing 120 to 150lbs each were usually done each shift. During my third season I operated hydraulic machinery that removed all the liquid out of the meat before it was dried. I worked on deck during my 4th season feeding the raw meat which had been cut into blocks into the machinery below. During my last 3 seasons I worked at a job known as boiler-emptier, we worked in pairs emptying large boilers when all the oil had been removed and only bone was left. We emptied that on to a conveyer belt to go over the side.

During the season two shifts were operated – night shift was from 6pm to 6am and day shift was 6am to 6pm. Work went on Sundays, Christmas Day and New Year. The ship and work did stop for possibly half an hour if there was a burial at sea taking place. The body was sewn into canvas with two harpoon points at the bottom and then placed at the ship's side on a wooden board and covered with either the British or Norwegian flag. The Captain, in uniform, would read the burial service. The board would then be tilted up and the body dropped from under the flag into the sea. I think we had one burial each season during my time. One year there was two, one was our Captain, a Norwegian.

In bad weather if we had to take shelter there were plenty of icebergs nearby. In the Guinness Book of Records the biggest one is said to have been 208 miles long by 60 miles wide. I made two trips on the *Southern Raven* – a four hold refrigeration ship carrying mixed cargo. Our first mate was Willie Spence from Yell. On one trip south I looked after 60 pigs. The pigs and pens were hosed down with salt water each day in the tropics, something they really enjoyed. At feeding time I carried a broom handle in my rubber boot to keep order.

I stayed for two winters in Leith Harbour in 1950 and 1952. I worked at different jobs, cleaning and painting the accommodations. I was also on No 3 motor boat with Gibbie Clark from Yell doing a variety of jobs around the harbour. In 1952 I spent most of the winter in the power station along with a fitter overhauling diesel engines. I also spent some time as a blacksmith's striker and found that a very interesting job.

One winter I thought I might try skiing but when I saw a notice in the office window saying that no more skiing was allowed until beds became available in the hospital I gave up the idea. A lot of craft work was done at nights in winter, carving whale teeth, painting ear drums, making cribbage boards, weaving mats from nylon string, canvas caps and bags and even some trout nets were made. I took material from home and made a halibut line. There was a picture house which was well used. Food was plentiful but you had to take what was going or do without.

Looking back on the whaling years, I'm inclined to think that the winters spent in the Antarctic were a waste of time. You were leaving home in September and were away all the following year and only getting home about May the next year. So much had happened during that time, people dead, bairns born, some married, others moved away and as you only got some of your mail after you got home you only heard of these things long after they had happened.

Leaving home for more than half a year at the whaling could be a traumatic experience, especially for a married man with a family. Once when we were on board the steamer at Lerwick, ready to cast off, one man took his kit bag on his shoulder and marched down the gangway to rejoin his wife and family who were there to see him off.

A whaler's pay in the late 1940's for group 8 was approx £250 for a season, seven months, which seemed a lot then but I wonder what today's generation would think of either the pay or the work.

There are some interesting books about whaling in the library in Lerwick. I have read the following ones – Antarctic Isle, Of Whales and Men, The Call to the South, Salvesen of Leith and From 70 North to 70 South.

RONNIE NICHOLSON

I was demobbed out of the Army on 8th January 1955 and returned home to Yell without any prospect of getting full time employment so when some of my neighbours prepared to go to South Georgia to the whaling I thought I would try that too. Without making further enquiries, I packed a few bits and pieces and joined the boys who had got word to join the *Southern Harvester*.

The morning we left home, there were fourteen of us heading for Leith and a few like myself were just going on spec. When we arrived at Bernard Street, Leith, all the regular whalers were ushered into the Office and signed on, but us chancers had to hang around for some time. One thing us Yell boys had to our advantage was the well known character, John Thomson, (better known as the Arab). Instead of him going down to Shields to join the *Harvester*, he stayed around Leith (had a little dram) and tormented Salvesen's office staff on behalf of Douglas Brown and myself until they signed us on to join the *Harvester* too. After signing on, there were about a dozen of us who caught the train for South Shields.

On arriving on board, I was amazed to see how many Shetlanders were there already, and almost all of them were strangers to me. First we had our details taken and were allocated a cabin. I shared a cabin with Douglas Brown, Kenneth Cheyne and Andrew Johnson. Andrew really belonged to Sullom but he had lived and worked in the Newcastle area for most of his life. The job allocated to me was working in the factory on the liver plant.

There's an old saying that first impressions last and I can still imagine the horrible smell and strange sounds that met me on my first visit into the factory. The whole place seemed to be packed full of tanks, pipes, electric motors and all sorts of unfamiliar equipment, but we will return to the factory later.

About a week after arriving at Shields we set sail for Tonsberg in Southern Norway and anchored or rather tied up in a small bight like the head of Dale's Voe. There was no jetty and the mooring ropes were made fast on shore, both bow and stern, and everything had to be taken out to us by barge or freighter.

Let us look at the deck structure of the factory ship. There were access lids to the factory kettles (for cooking the whale meat and bones) down both sides of the deck. Quite a lot of those lids were opened and the kettles were filled with all sorts of tinned food stuff, cleaning materials, etc. I was surprised how often one or two crates of tinned fruit or a crate of soap would mysteriously appear down in someone's cabin! I remember on my last season at South Georgia, we were coming up the Mersey heading for Liverpool when I visited a cabin and I enjoyed a few pieces of pineapple rings, but the occupants of the cabin must remain anonymous – there's no way that I'm going to tell that it was occupied by Bobby Bruce and Willie Johnson! After the kettle lids were screwed down, both fore and aft plan decks were built high with timber.

Once our cargo was properly lashed down, we set sail again for Aruba in the Dutch West Indies to take on fuel. Now that we were on our way, we settled down to do some preparation work. I was assigned to act as assistant to the plumber, Jock Mcafferty, who was a rather odd looking individual. He stood no more than four and a half feet high with a little fat body and very short legs (very well suited to working underneath pipes in the tank deck) and he always wore a stupid little hat and a very tight little boilersuit. We must have looked an odd pair. I remember Bertie Sutherland drawing a very good recognisable cartoon of us. Well, little Jock and I spent weeks crawling through the main tanks doing what was termed 'changing the bends'. This was blocking certain pipes so that when the season began in earnest the oil could flow through the correct pipes. Not a nice job going through the tropics.

I wondered what all the timber we had loaded in Norway would be used for but when we got further south and came into better weather, parts of the deck were cleared, three big power saws were set up and scores of men turned to and the whole deck was covered with planking to protect the original deck. This also protected the cutting edge of flensing knives and gave the deck workers a better grip with their spiked boots.

At this time the factory ships were supplied with a small helicopter to be used for spotting schools of whales. Late one afternoon the pilot and navigator took to the air and entertained us to a few landings on the small helicopter deck, then headed off to port and soon disappeared in light cloud. As time west past all radio contact was lost. Further time went by and it got dark and by this time the entire ship's crew were on deck scanning the darkness when all at once we saw a red flare climb into the sky and hang for a few seconds. When this was reported to the remaining helicopter personnel, they said that it could not be our helicopter because they were not supplied with flares.

About an hour later the *Harvester* got a radio message from the Norwegian factory ship *Kosmos III* saying that they had been in the vicinity of the flare and had picked up the navigator who was floating in a little rubber dinghy. After some difficulty, a lifeboat was lowered and then it was discovered that the helm couldn't fit the rudder so that had to be taken to the machine shop and made up to fit. Next the engine wouldn't start so an engineer had to do some work on it before it could be coaxed into life. On returning with the navigator, it was discovered that the lifeboat couldn't be hoisted back to the davits as the blocks on the falls were seized up with rust and paint.

It did cross my mind that if this had happened in the Army, someone would have been Court Martialled. Apparently the engine had stopped and the helicopter had begun to sink as soon as she hit the water. The last the navigator saw of the pilot was when he passed him out the small inflatable liferaft.

The weather got gradually worse as we got further south and the day we were due to arrive in South Georgia dawned with low cloud and rain. The first glimpse I had of South Georgia was the point of Coronda Peak which lies at the back of Leith Harbour.

When the whaling season began, my job was working on the liver plant boiler where the liver oil and liver meatmeal were separated. I do think it is worth recording here that for almost seven months at sea I paid off with £426.00 when my slop chest bill for £22.10/- had been paid.

For the whaling season of 1956/57 I joined the *Southern Venturer* and two amusing incidents come to mind. One day, after leaving Norway, a few of us Shetland boys were standing on deck when the 3rd mate, a Pole by the name of Fryzndorf, came along and asked us to move a few steel plates for him. When we had finished he said, "Thank you veerie muuch, I would have liked to give you a leetle drink, but I get so veerie little and I like it so veerie muuch."

After leaving Shields for Norway, Wilbert Henderson from Gloup became unwell and had to be put into the ship's hospital so we took turns to visit him. After a few days, he came out in a rash and was diagnosed as having measles. By the time we had reached Aruba there were five of us in the ship's hospital namely Davie Clark, John Clark, George Hunter, Jackie Hendry and myself. Now having a disease like measles with such a high temperature, in tropical conditions it was difficult to control.

One night about 10 o'clock the hospital door burst open and Campbell Gray and Ronnie Aitken came in. They had been ashore for a peerie dram and Davie Clark and I must have had a peerie dram with them for the next day both our temperatures had shot up to 104 degrees. Dr Richardson was going around not sure what to do. I really didn't remember much for a day or two but I think Dr Richardson did tumble to what had happened.

I must admit I enjoyed my two seasons at the whaling and still enjoy meeting and having a yarn with my old shipmates.

L to R Alastair Thomason, Yell; Cecil Craigie, Lerwick; Bertie Ramsay, Collafirth, Northmavine; Bill Mouatt, Scalloway.
Photo: L Laurenson.

L to R Teddy Sandison, Nesting; Christie Thompson, Weisdale; Robert Thomson, Scalloway; Jimmy Stove, Edinburgh, formerly Sandwick.
Photo: L Cassidy.

Leith Harbour under snow in winter.
Photo: A Williamson.

Accommodation blocks in Leith Harbour in winter. The buildings are two storeys high.
Photo: A Williamson.

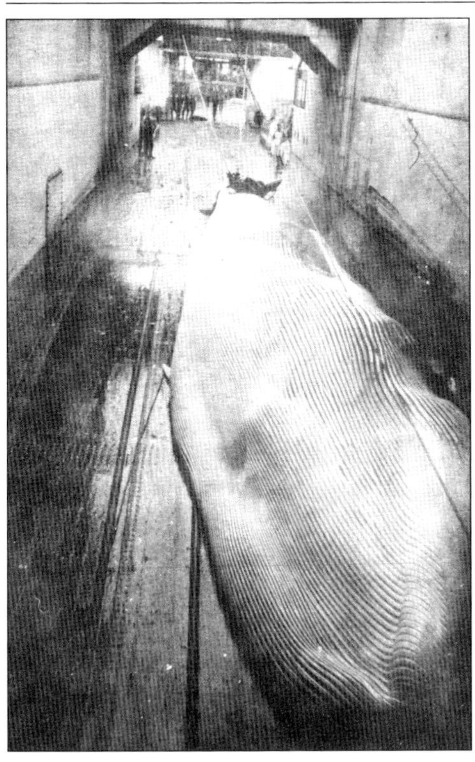

*A 90ft blue whale being hauled up the chute on **Southern Venturer** in 1949.*
Photo: K. Brown.

A catcher AB goes up to do his hour watch in the barrel.
Photo: A Anderson.

*Transport ship, **Ernesto Tornquist** arriving in Leith Harbour on 1st October 1941. She later ran ashore in a snow storm just outside the harbour and was wrecked. All on board were saved. Photo: S Williamson*

***Southern Garden** refuelling **Southern Raven** in mid Atlantic. Photo: A Anderson.*

Left:
L to R Harry Johnson, Semblester; John Johnson, Tresta.
Photo: J Johnson.

Below:
L to R At the gun in Leith Harbour. Lollie Johnson, Eshaness; Peter Pole, Sandness.
Photo: P Pole.

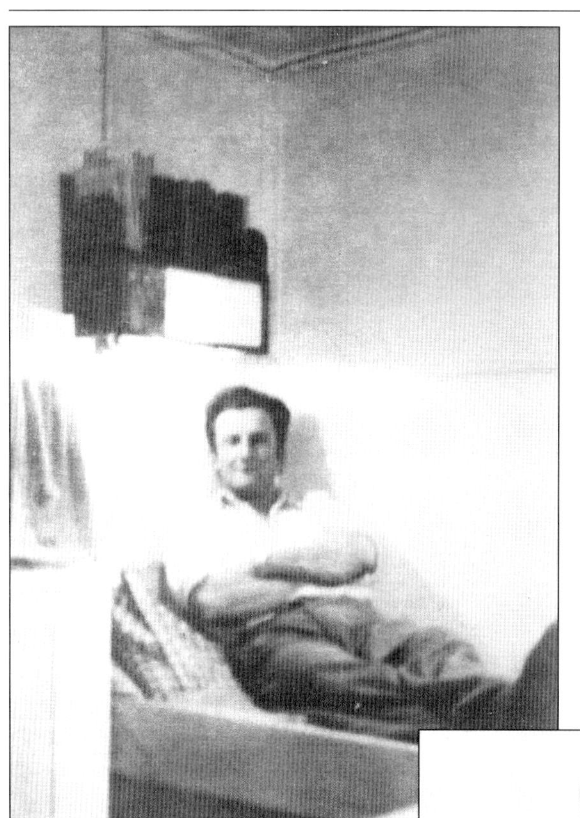

Above:
Willie Mail, Walls.
Photo: R Wiseman.

Right:
Alex Peterson, Voe.
Photo: A Peterson.

WILLIE MAIL

I went down to the whaling in 1949. We went down on the *Southern Harvester* from South Shields to Tenerife. When we got to Tenerife, myself, Peter Walker from Yell, Andrew Hawick from Lerwick, Bill Crooks from Orkney, Alex Walker from Barra and another fellow from the Western Isles joined a tanker called the *Southern Collins* and we went to a place called Mersematrew in the Persian Gulf to load fuel oil for the *Southern Harvester* down at the ice. We discharged the fuel oil aboard the *Southern Harvester* and then steamed back to Leith Harbour in South Georgia.

When we got to Leith Harbour the six of us that joined the *Southern Collins* in Tenerife went ashore for the winter and they loaded whale oil and went back to the UK. We were in the station gang for the winter and most of the time we were clearing snow off the tops of the oil tanks and the roofs of all the sheds that was shut down for the winter with no heating on. We had an awful lot of snow that winter.

When the season started we all went to different jobs. I went to the tank gang. There were six of us in the gang and our job was to clean out the tanks after fuel oil and make them ready to load whale oil. I was in the tank gang all the time I was down there except for the last two years when I was driving a motor boat towing whales or towing barges.

The first winter I did there was very little mail but you could send a telegram home and get a reply back for about £2 so we used to do that regularly to hear how everybody was at home. The food was mostly Norwegian and some didn't like it but I thought the food was ok. There was a crowd of men on the Island all the time but they all seemed to work well together and there was very little trouble. There was a picture house in Leith Harbour so we had pictures about three times a week during the winter and nearly everyone was making something - penguins out of whale teeth, trout nets out of old nylon rope and lots of other things so it helped to pass the time away during the long winter nights.

The weather in the winter could be very bad at times with snow and blizzards but the work went on just the same. The weather during the season was not much different from Shetland. I came home a month early from the 1959 season as my father was very ill and I didn't go back to the whaling any more.

DAVIE CLARK

My first season at the whaling was1952/53. I was on the whale boats all the time I was down and did 9 seasons in total. The first catcher I was on was the *Southern Hunter*. I had been used to boats all my earlier time but yon things, the accommodation was for'ard and obviously the speed it went you certainly got rattled about a bit.

When the season started at Leith Harbour we had not got out past the Black Rocks and with her heaving about I felt sick right away. I was mess boy and the fellow who was in the room with me was Alex Paton, he was the engine room rating. I went up the ladder to the companionway and of course, no breeks on just the bare hams, and came out and the first that got me was the cold. I spewed on the deck and came back down the ladder. I was in the upper bunk in the two berth cabin and Alex was in the bottom one. A peerie while after I was sick again and went up the ladder and spewed again. When I came back down Alex was reeslin with this galvanised bucket and getting it stuck between my pillow and the bulkhead and he said, "Now spew in dat and let's get some bloody sleep." I thought to myself, "My God, du's a right coarse so and so."

He'd been a season before me and done the winter so he was used to it. However, I struggled on with it and, thinking back, one thing that I hated was the smell as they roasted the dry coffee beans. The smell still turns me up. It took me a while to get over the seasickness. It was a lot of motion the day we got the first whale for the season and I mind me struggling up to the bridge with a cup of coffee to the gunner and the mate and hanging on like grim death. We came back into Leith Harbour and came to the buoy. My old man was in the motor boat so he came to pick the whale up and I stuck my head around the corner of the housing and with my pale complexion he said, "Davie, du can pack yon in and come ashore." But I said, "No, I'll stick it out."

Later the *Southern Hunter* went to the ice with the *Southern Harvester* expedition. The catcher I was to go on was the *Southern Joker* and she was on her way down to South Georgia. She had been a Kosmos boat until Salvesen bought her. When the *Joker* arrived we went aboard and the gunner there was Harold Olsen. The *Hunter* and that crowd went to the ice. We worked away there and then we had a kinda unfortunate incident – we lost our gunner.

He was knocked over the side. The *Joker* had an enclosed wheelhouse below the bridge which was not used because of poor visibility among the ice and at night. We were chasing fin whales and when the gunner fired we watched the harpoon and when we looked back, the gun was spinning. We did not realise anything had happened until we saw a bit of commotion on deck and then we realised that the gunner had been knocked over the side. So there was obviously panic stations and things did not just work out right and unfortunately he was lost.

They launched the lifeboat but all we picked up was his cap. Being a young fellow it certainly shook me up and obviously the rest of the boys, Alex included, because he had been with him the season before. They made the mate up to gunner, a man with the name of Sigurd Erassmuson, and we went out again and seemed to find more whales than we had ever found before. However he just did not have what it took to make a gunner. He did about a week or a fortnight and then a man off the buoy boat the *Southern Star*, Jacobsen by name, took over. He was there until the end of the season.

The following year when I came down I was on the the *Sobkra*, an older boat, and that gunner was a fine enough fellow but he liked the ale too much and things did not pan out very well and so we finished up bottom catcher by a long piece – nearly 100 whales behind the top boat. So that did not work out well financially. Among all that carry on, one of my jobs was to clean the gunner's cabin and make his bed and so on but he never lay in the bed, he just lay on a seat and he just threw all his bits and pieces in the bunk. One rough day I went to clean the toilet and the thing had not been flushed. I was just about to flush it when he shouted to me, "No, do not touch that, it's choked."

We were heading in for Leith Harbour to get bunkers and go to the pictures or the kino as it was better known to us. We came alongside the bunker pier and tied up. This gang came on board. There was a hose on the pier and instead of putting the hose where you would have thought they would have put it, they stuck it in one of the scuppers at the side and opened it up and there was quite a bang and then there was you know what sticking everywhere and the old gunner shot out of his cabin with his hand over his nose saying there was dreet everywhere. He took it all in good part and called up the *Southern Guider* and the gunner aboard there by the name of Kjellstrom looked on it as a good fun.

The unfortunate thing with the *Sobkra* was that there was just too much drink. There was a still aboard and they made too much use of it. Doing the season at the island, you were away nine months compared to the seven at the ice so the boys at the ice were doing a shorter stint and making more money so I went to the ice in a catcher called the *Southern Rover* with the *Venturer* expedition. The gunner there they called him the Bishop, Arne Olsen, a very peerie man but he did not drink or smoke and he was a very good man to sail with.

The following year I got made up to go on deck, Whaler group 8, which was the normal procedure and the next catcher I was on and was there for 5 seasons was the *Southern Main*. She was a buoy boat and our main job was to pick up the flagged whales from the top guns, the fishing boats, and tow them to the factory. On the *Main* I got up to AB and that is as far as you normally went unless you had any qualifications which I did not have.

The gunner there was Ivar Jensen, a very ill-tricked guy. He used to work all devilment on me. One night we were picking up whales and it was blowing hard and very cold. He made a cup of coffee and came with a sandwich and said it was a german sausage which we called weiner pulser. They were not a very great taste - a bit of a niff with them. He had put it in between slices of loaf and he said that it was a hot dog but I was a bit suspicious. He looked and said, "What is wrong with you, there is mustard in it, don't you want it?"

I looked at them very closely and realised that the sausage was made of rubber. He said, "Don't tell any of the boys about this. You know the steward, go and speak to him tonight and see if he will make sausages for tea." This was so that he could plant this dummy in among the rest. The steward made this and onions and the trimmings. I had had my grub before and was sitting in the mess room wondering who was going to get caught out. The old fireman happened to take it on his plate and he was eating away. I realised he had got it because the fork would not penetrate it and it bounced off the plate on to the table and he fetched another jab at it and he shoved it in his mouth. He realised that he had been tricked and he said, "Fawn!" I was sitting across from him and he just turned around and hit me right between the eyes with it. The gunner and the steward were looking through the hatchway and they laughed until the tears ran down their faces. It was good for morale to have funs like that. It kept you going until the end of the season when you got back to Leith Harbour again.

Of course we always liked to have music. I could not have the fiddle aboard the catcher because there was no way you could get a chance to play. It was on board the factory and Alan Tulloch from Whalsay kept it and when we were along for the last bunker he would send it down in the basket. When we got back to Leith Harbour I would make my way to the *Southern Archer* where Victor Inkster was an AB aboard and was a crack hand on the box, and

I used to have a tune and Scottie Christie from Burra would vamp on the guitar. We certainly had some great times among it all.

One other thing that comes to mind was when we took part in one of the longest tows on record, 11,000 miles. The *Southern Broom* broke down off Enderby Land. We towed her alongside the factory ship from there to Cape Town, Cape Town to Dakar and Dakar to Middlesborough. It took six weeks and was a long haul. When we came to Middlesborough all the press was down meeting us.

GORDON WALTERSON

I first went down to the whaling in 1946. I joined the *Saluta* in Leith on 19 August 1946 and I paid off in South Georgia on 2 October 1946. I was junior ordinary seaman and I was going to the whaling to join a catcher. The same day that I signed off in South Georgia from the *Saluta*, I joined the *Southern Wilcox*, that was on 2 October and I was there until 15 November when I joined the *Unitas* on 16 November. I had been deckboy and then I was upped to Junior Ordinary Seaman.

I left her on the 4 December, the reason being that my contract was for the *Sondra* but that whale boat was still in South Africa being refitted after the war and never did come down for that season. The gunner we had was Hafton Amundsen and he asked the manager of Leith Harbour if I could come with him down to the ice. The manager said "No, he has to stay here because his contract is for the *Sondra* and there is another boy coming down on the factory and that will be the chap who goes to the ice."

They went away on the *Simbra* and that boat was lost. I think everybody on board was lost except one fellow, a John Leask from Burwick in Scalloway. From December onwards, I was on the island and, as I said the *Sondra* never came down in 1946 and I could not get to the ice so I was still in catchers up to 4 December on *Unitas 4*. After that I worked on the island where I was up to 25 February, which was more than a couple of months.

We did just any general job. There were two or three of us young ones who were supposed to be on the catchers but as the catchers were not there, we did any general work around the station. I mind working up in the bone loft for a week or so helping and hauling around there. There was one fellow off sick for a week and I worked with bogies shoving stuff on this peerie tram lines that they had around the island and then we worked a good while in the guano shed. That was where the meat meal came to and was put through the dryers when it was emptied out of the kettles and the bone meal and so on came in there, went through the dryers and it was bagged.

It was a great big shed with a concrete floor and an elevator. The bags would come down and be filled from a chute and we would run it through a machine to sew the top of it. We had peerie wooden barrows with iron wheels and we would haul the bag back over, tip it out on the end of a conveyor belt which would carry it away up to be stacked. Some of it was far too hot. They were in too big a rush with it and eventually it took fire and the shed burned down and a great lot of the guano was lost. They recycled some of it but most was burned to a cinder and was completely destroyed. The roof of the shed was destroyed.

After the *Simbra* was lost, they fitted out the *Sabra*, an old boat which used to be around Leith Harbour. When she was ready we left on 25 February 1947 and we were down at the ice until 16 March. We came back to Leith Harbour and I went on to the *Bouvet 1* on 17 March and went back to the ice and worked there until 17 April. They had got an extension of the season for two weeks from the Ministry of Food to get more whale oil and stuff back to Britain at that time. The gunner aboard the *Bouvet 1* was a man called Asbjorn Andersen and he had just started out as a gunner. There were three of us young ones, ordinary seamen, and one Norwegian chap who was a fully qualified AB. However, with Asbjorn we still managed, even with the old boat and inexperienced crew and all the rest, to get quite a few whales so we did not so bad. We came back up to Leith Harbour on 17 April and I transferred to the *Southern Harvester* and came to Liverpool on her. Some of us stayed and worked by and then went around and paid off in South Shields in June. So that was my first experience of whaling.

I was back at the whaling again on the *Southern Raven*, that was in 1948. We joined her in Liverpool and we came back to Glasgow and again paid off sometime in June. That was carrying whale meat. She took fresh meat from the factory ships and it was taken across by a catcher and they used to hoist it aboard and it was cut up and frozen and stowed away. I think she did one more year although I was not with her after that and then they gave up the whale meat thing, it was not a success.

I was not back again at the whaling until 1952. By this time, I had joined the *Southern Atlantic* as Third Mate. We were in Newcastle in 1952 and I joined her again on 13 September 1952 and went away to the whaling and was away until 3 July 1953. I was in various other Salvesens' ships back and fore. The next time I was down at the whaling was in the *Southern Collins* in 1954/55 and also 1955/56. I went across with the *Southern Harvester* in 1956 to Tonsberg and then went down on the *Southern Opal* for the 56/57 season. I was on the *Southern Garden* in 58/59 and again in 59/60. That was my last time at the whaling.

That time we left from Tilbury. In the lower forehold we loaded a whole lot of bond and drink to take down to Leith Harbour. We had called at Caripito for fuel oil and were away down further south when one morning we were sitting in the saloon and we saw one of the fellows, an Assistant Steward, in the pantry and he seemed to be full of drink. After that Capt Ross and I went to look around. We found a fellow in the alleyway and he had drink in him. Further along we met someone carrying a holdall and this fellow ran off. We ran after him, got the holdall and took it up into the Captain's Room, opened it up and it was full of drink, bottles and bottles of whisky.

Apparently some of the crew had managed to get down into the forehold and take out a lot of drink. It came to mind that when we were loading at Tilbury I was watching the hatch and they were covering up the hold and the dockers on the crane landed a weight fairly heavily and broke a hatch. I remember them asking me if it should be exchanged and I said, "No, I think it is alright to leave it." But apparently this hatch was broken for the purpose of getting through to look for the drink. This had been an organised thing.

So Capt Ross just made an entry in the log book. He did not make any fines but left the case open so when we came back to Tilbury the first that came aboard was a Detective Inspector and two Detective Sergeants. They wanted to see the crew members who had been named so they took them up and questioned them and then let them go. These fellows thought that this was fine but the detectives came back the next day and they questioned them and again let them go. They came back the third day and, during the questioning, (one had been asking the questions and the other one writing down), they said to these fellows, "Now look, we have listened to what you said on Monday and Tuesday, this is Wednesday and it is all totally different. You had better tell us the right story." So they did. They told them about working their way through the hold, taking up the drink and all the rest of it. The crew came from all different places and those involved were taken up to Grays Court. I, as Ship's Officer, was in the Court and listened to the whole case - the charges being read out and the sentences being given. The sentence was that they would be fined all the money they had coming to them for their season's work and they would be left only their train fare home.

ANGUS RIDLAND

I signed on the *Southern Opal* in Middlesborough on the 12th November 1947, as Senior Ordinary Seaman. There were twelve of us going to South Georgia to overwinter. On the way we were employed as tank gang, we cleaned and chipped the tanks that were empty. After putting fuel oil on board the factory ship at the ice, we cleaned the newly emptied tanks and picked up whale oil from her then headed for South Georgia and signed off.

My first job ashore was in the station gang. Herbert Johnson was the bosun. Anything that needed doing around the station was our job from shifting harpoons to fuel tanks, sand and shingle from the beach, discharging ships and snow clearing. The sand and shingle was used for floors and founds. There was a bit of paint work on the billets, outside and in.

Near the end of the winter I was told to help a motorman, Jens Jensen, on a boat on the slip, being overhauled, ready for the start of the fishing season. Looking back, it was the best move I ever made. Jens was married in Aberdeenshire therefore he spoke English well so we hit it off right away. We stripped down, overhauled and re-assembled the engine so I got to know it well. When we launched the boat I was told to stay on board as assistant boatman.

During the fishing season the boats worked a 12 hour shift. The main jobs were towing whales from a buoy to the plan where they were worked up, towing barges to load and unload any ship in harbour. We also had to carry stores to the catchers as they came in – harpoons, oil, etc. Near the end of this season the work got to be too much for one boat and I was told to use the other boat so they had two boats during the day shift.

Near the end of the season the factory ships arrived from the ice where they had been fishing; along with them came all their catchers. This was a very hard time for the motor boats – barges towed to and from the factories, men and their gear to shift, some ashore for the winter, others to the ships they were going home on. The catcher crews had to moor up their own boats for the winter before they left and as it required a motorboat to run the rope ashore and to the buoy astern, we were lucky to get time to eat. For us that were overwintering, it was a relief when the last ship had gone.

Stromness was an old whaling station that had been made into a repair depot. There was a machine shop, plater's shop and blacksmith's, so they could handle anything required in the overhaul and repair of ships. There was a floating dock moored at the end of a pier. All the whale boats were docked for any hull repairs, painting and stern tube and propeller overhaul. My job was to tow the boats into the dock from a buoy and tow them out again when they were finished and the next one in. During the winter it was an eight hour day with overtime, over and above.

Workwise the Stromness job was fairly easy after the season in Leith Harbour but the hours were long. I would start the boat at seven in the morning and didn't finish until about ten at night. Between trips to Leith Harbour and back carrying men, stores, machine parts, etc I had to stand by in case of any accidents so that I could take the casualties to the doctor in Leith Harbour. It did happen occasionally. After tea I would stand by as long as there was men working. Last run to return the catcher men who had been working on the boat on the dock, that was about eight thirty to nine. They were billeted in Leith. On getting back I could lay up the boat, take on fuel and make her ready for next day. You occasionally had a rough passage with wind, snow and heavy swell.

When the winter ended I shifted back to Leith Harbour and Kaare Iversen took over Stromness. During my time on the boat I had very fine fellows with me, Sammy Johnson from Quarff, Teddy Sandison from Nesting, Harry Paton from Whalsay and George Wiseman from Lerwick. George was made up to boatman later.

SAMMY JOHNSON

I first went to the whaling in 1947, after meeting Willie Moncrieff who put my name down for it. I went down to Leith where I passed the Doctor and then on to South Georgia on the *Polar Chief*. I was classed as AB because I had been sailing before and was put on the station gang in Leith Harbour, discharging and loading ships. We worked 12 hours a day, mainly carrying bags of whale meat meal weighing a hundred weight and a quarter.

From there we went to any shore work that had to be done. Willie Laurenson from Gorie in Bressay was bosun and Willie Gordon from Bressay was with us too. We were painting roofs at the time but as Willie Gordon didn't like heights we told him he could stay down and hand up the paint to us when we needed it. This worked all right until Willie Laurenson came along and asked him what he was doing. When told, he said there was no need for that and put him to paint the roof of the henhouse. So he <u>had</u> to go up and ended up 'painting himself in'. We felt it was not right for the bosun to do this to an older man and later, when speaking to Willie Gordon I said, "Willie Laurenson would be all right if he could speak." (He had a very bad stammer) and Willie Gordon replied, "Oh, no, he would be a thousand times worse."

The winter was fine as it was spent cleaning and painting the catchers, getting them ready for the next season. Freddie Johnson and I worked together on that job, which I enjoyed. After the winter we were back at our usual job again – discharging and loading ships.

The *Southern Opal* came in with a load of fuel oil and we were put on board to clean her tanks. We worked at that for 3-4 weeks, maybe more – some of the time working night and day. There were eight of us – Willie Mail from Walls, Johnnie Smith from Levenwick (Bosun), Lowrie Inkster and Peter Inkster, both from Burra, but I can't remember the rest. It was not a bad job, but it was long hours. Then she had to go to the factory to take on board a load of whale oil.

The second winter I did was on one of the motor boats, towing in whales from the buoys till the season finished. There were three boats. I was on one and Tommy Fullerton and Joe Laurenson, both Burra were on the other two. I did that winter along with Graham Clark from Yell and Teddy Sandison from Nesting. We were in a room together above the wash place.

At that time they got sheep from the Falklands and, along with Jamie Nicolson from Quarff, we salted a ewe but the salt never melted. It was just like it had been in a freezer. We used to have 'boil-ups' at the weekend and that was very good.

Sometimes we were called out at night to put folk to Stromness. You were on the boat on your own and you had to put them there and then go back to Leith Harbour. Sometimes it was snowing and that made it very awkward as you could not see very well and had to steer by the compass all the time. Sometimes we had to go to the Norwegian station at Busen with the Managers when they were having a night out and we would have to wait and take them back again but they always took us up to the mess room and gave us a meal. Then we could close up the boat and have a lie down with the engine running so it wasn't too cold while we waited.

There was one time we went up Coronda Peak. There were three of us - John Robert Jamieson from Burra, Bobby Peterson and myself. It took us a good while to go up as we were up to our knees in snow. On the way down again we just heaved ourselves on our backs and slid. After a bit we stopped and looked back and Bobby was not there! He was scared to come down again so we each took an arm and set off again. We had some good fun among it all.

The first year I was down at South Georgia, there was no fridge. The meat was either salt or tinned and about the time we finished the winter season we were getting pretty fed up with the grub. However, they built a 'fridge' the next year so the grub was better after that.

Then we got pigs down so we got pork at Christmas, New Year and on special occasions. In the winter we got a nip of rum every fortnight. Geordie Smith from Lerwick was 'hen-man' so we used to give him our tots of rum and he gave us eggs for a 'fry-up' at nights. We thought it was a fair exchange as the fresh eggs were good. The Norwegians liked meat balls, fish balls and that kind of things. They sun dried a lot of their fish. Baccaloa was good. It was about the best we got and everybody liked it. I don't know how they made it but have always wondered. I think there were black peppers, sun-dried fish, tatties and olive oil in it, but I'm not sure. It would be good to get the recipe.

Some of the salt beef and pork we got had gone mouldy but it was scrubbed off and we got it to eat, but it never seemed to hurt anybody. Makes one wonder where all the viruses come from nowadays!

NORMAN JAMIESON

I went to the whaling when I was 16. My older brother, Hamish, had been down there for two winters and a few seasons before I went. After peat cutting all summer and saving a bit of money, I decided to go and Hamish gave me another £20 to take me to Leith. My old man had been at the whaling and he said I was to take any job but not on a whale catcher. When I got to Leith I was offered a job on a whale catcher so I took it. I phoned home the next night and spoke to my old man and told him I'd got a job. "Oh, that's good. The best of luck. I hope it is up on top." "No," I said, "it's on a whale catcher." He had been a passenger ship man as well as being at the whaling and said, "Ah, well. Good luck again."

We left Shields and I enjoyed the trip down. I was among a lot of Shetlanders and served the tables there as a mess boy. On the way down we were asked whether we were willing to overwinter or not and I thought well if Hamish can do it, I can. But Hamish said, "No you'd better wait until you see what the island is like." But I put my name in.

We arrived at South Georgia and Hamish said, "Come here and look at this." And here was all the whale catchers. "My God," I said, "they're just like skerries." They were like a rock, the sea was just washing out and in over the deck. He said, "That is going to be your home for the next four months." Well I started to have my doubts. We moored up and the gangway went out and the first to come up the gangway was this two men with beards nearly to their waists and long hair. They looked like something out of the bible to me. This was John Thompson and Alan Laurenson. They were known as the Arab and the Beast.

I was mess boy on the *Southern Wheeler* and we left early because we were going to scout for whales. It was all very foreign to me and we set off heading southward to the ice. It was bad weather the whole trip down and I was very sick. For 7 days I did not know if I was going to live or die. I slept with my seabag in the back of the bunk to steady me. The biggest problem was trying to get my trousers on when I got out of bed in the morning because every time I lifted my leg I fell over. So I had to sit on the floor to get my trousers on and then I had to negotiate my way to the galley and dodge the big waves that were crashing over the deck. When the factory came down to the ice we went alongside for bunkers. My brother said, "Are you going to stick it?" and I said, "Yes, I think I'll manage." So I started to unpack the bag then.

The gunner on this catcher was Joe Ferguson, the only British gunner ever, a very small man from Glasgow. He was the man who showed Alan Ladd how to handle a harpoon gun in the film ‘Hell below Zero’. Alan Ladd did not like the idea of wearing a fur hat but Ferguson said, “A gunner does not wear a peaked cap and an open-necked shirt.” Alan Ladd was never at the whaling, his parts of the film were all done in a studio in London.

One day the steward sent me aft to get some peas and I came back with green peas and he wanted split peas. They were all in bags standing on the floor of the storeroom. I put them back in the bag I thought I had taken them out of. But a few days later, at breakfast time when I was waiting at the table in the saloon, the gunner started tapping something out on the side of his plate and it was a green pea and I thought I know where that one came from. Then the engineer dug one out of his porridge and said, “Mess, look what I have found in my porridge.” I said, “What is it?” “It’s a green pea.” “Oh, I didn’t know you got peas out of porridge.” “So,” he says, “You’ll have to report it to the steward.” I did so and there were a lot of other guys who found them in their porridge too. The old steward knew what had happened but he covered up for me, he said that it was something that must have happened on the factory.

We used to get whale meat aboard in big lumps and hang it up on the rail aft and for a couple of mornings I used to use it as a punch bag as I went aft. This morning I went aft to get stores and I took a swipe at this meat but by then it was frozen hard so my hand was in a bad state by the time I got back to the galley. The steward said, “What’s happened?” Well I couldn’t very well say I was knocking hell out of his lump of whale meat so I just had to say I slipped. That is maybe why I have arthritis in it now.

When the season finished I got a job for the winter in the big mess room. I enjoyed being ashore because I was in fine company. We learned to ski and we got pictures two or three times a week. But I ran into a big problem in the messroom. When I had cleaned up my tables and set everything up, someone was pinching my clean stuff – butter dishes, sugar bowls, etc - and putting their dirty stuff in its place when I was not there. So I thought I would set a trap for this fellow and I put bread in the sugar bowl and as the old saying goes when the fly shit in the sugar bowl, that remains to be seen.

I came in a couple of hours later and saw that my sugar bowl, etc had been shifted so I looked around until I found the sugar bowl with the bread in it. The boy responsible for the table came in. He was from Glasgow and was none too pleased that I had found him out so he said, “I think we’ll have to go and settle this outside.” But I did not wait for the outside bit, we had a set to there and then in the messroom and things got knocked over and broken. Another day he challenged me in the pantry and that was more than the mess man could stand and he said, "There's a problem here with you fellows and we'll have to sort it out." I got shifted to the cook's messroom and everything was splendid after that. I enjoyed my winter and did some skiing in the afternoons.

I was back on the whale catcher again the next season as deck boy. The following season I was on the *Sondra*. We were a buoy boat and I was along with an old AB called Jake Nisbet, a lovely fellow. He showed me all the ropes. He had been on trawlers out of Granton and had spent a number of years at the whaling as well. He was a good watchmate and full of tricks. One night he crept up to the bridge, it was all open bridges there and it was a very lonely place at night where you could do all your thinking about spending your money and things like that. This night he just threw his duffle coat in over the bridge at me and gave me a hell of a fright. One day we were on watch together and I said to Jake I was going to the toilet. We were in thick fog and cruising along at maybe 5 or 6 knots. He said, "OK. Check the radar before you go." I did this and like a silly beggar I just checked what was in front of us. I had just finished my business in the toilet when I heard the telegraph going and felt her coming astern. When I came back to the bridge I found out why. One of the other catchers had just crossed our bows and we should have given way. Old Jake was not happy but we got over that and remained pals.

One afternoon when I was doing my hour in the barrel looking for whales I saw a pink albatross coming towards me. "Now," I said, "what's this? Have I been too long in the Antarctic, or is this real?" No one would believe my watchmate and I about this but we persuaded the gunner to tell the factory ship and, yes, there was an answer. Bird watchers in the Falkland Islands had sprayed some albatross to see if they could find out how far they were travelling in search of food.

Another year one of the top catchers broke down and had to be towed back to the island. Her gunner, Gunnar Christensen, came on board our catcher and we were a full catcher for the remainder of the season. That was a great experience. He was one of the top gunners and he managed to keep his place. One year I was on a catcher which we called the "Southern Submarine", she was the *Sigfra*. We fished going east all the time and ended up 4000 miles east of South Georgia. That was a long steam back. We had a second mate, Danny Morrison from Leith, a well known fellow at the whaling and an excellent skiier. He won second prize at the cross country skiing which was a great achievement as there were guys from Norway there who had won gold medals. So Danny was among the top ones. It was a poor season and we were away at Enderby Land when it finished.

We had heard lots of stories about big seas and rough storms but this was the storm to crown all. We drifted that old boat which was a thing we should not have done in 120 miles an hour wind. The factory ship, *Southern Harvester*, had look outs placed fore and aft but she could not get her head up to the wind and they drifted her all night with that look out. In the morning the Captain said to the 2nd mate, a fellow from Poland, Fryzndorf, "Were you scared last night?" "No," he said, "not at all." "Well," he said, "you're a bigger damned fool than I thought you were."

That season ended with us having to steam 4000 miles back to South Georgia. It was a rough ride. I remember Willie Watt from Lerwick coming on the air one night singing 'A life on the ocean wave' and it certainly was that. The catcher was just burying herself and in the mornings you could pick the krill off the bridge. We had a young mess boy on board, Geordie Robertson from Bigton. This catcher had a for'ard mess room and there was a bit of a misunderstanding one night when he tried to run the deck without telling me what he was doing. I had said to him, "In this bad weather when you're taking the mess room gear to the men in the fo's'cle, flash the deck lights and I'll know you're coming and I'll slow her down." Geordie thought he would make it this night and we hit a big sea and I heard the rattle of the soup and meat kits he was carrying. I jumped to the wing of the bridge and looked out over the dodger and there was Geordie hanging on to the railings aft. I really thought he had gone but I went down and got a hold on him and we both got up on the boat deck together and the only thing he could say was, "I've lost half of the kits." And I said, "To hell with the kits so long as you have not lost your life. Go away up for'ard and get changed."

When I arrived home after my first trip, Mother said to me, "Well, what did you think of it?" I said, "There were times when I wished I was back at school." And she said, "Boy, it must have been bad." Seeing my girlfriend on the evening before I left and knowing it was going to be two years before I got back was kinda hard to say the least. We both felt it a lot. An old pal of mine gave me a loan of his motor bike to go and see her that night.

The second winter I did I was on the whale catchers in what they called the dirty gang. Three of us had to clean all the springs that were in the bottom of the whale catchers. We used to take the sheaves and the big springs adrift and put tallow and oil back in them and see that they were all working properly for the next season. We used to get on our oily gear and lie in the bottom of the catchers all day. We would take the dirty gear off when we went to get our grub and put it on when we went back down again. At night we finished at half past four but got paid till nine o'clock as extra money for doing this dirty job. Workmates down there were fantastic. Most of the crew on the whale catchers were Norwegians but I never felt out of place. They were great shipmates and first class seamen. We made some great friends and we are still pally today after all these years. The homecomings from the whaling were great as you can imagine after being away for two years.

30 years after the whaling ended, I was working for OIL on a supply boat. We did the overhaul and maintenance on the Ministry of Defence buoys, one in Grytviken, one in Stromness and one in Leith Harbour. It was emotional and overpowering at times to go ashore and see the station and look at the barracks where we lived. It brought back a lot of happy memories. The deer is there all over the place, looking good and very friendly. And being an old whaler, I could tell the military people there all my old stories which I was very proud to do.

BILLY CRAIGIE

My seatime started in 1957. When I left school there was little work available in Shetland so I decided to go to the sea school. We did a 3 or 4 months course of nautical training aboard the old *Dolphin* at Leith. After I had gone through that we had to try and join up with shipping companies so we used to write letters to the various companies seeking employment and the first company I was with was the Corry Line. They had coal boats which went up and down the English Coast and I got a job on the *SS Corfield*. That was in July so I stayed on her for a peerie start but I got fed up with her coming into port every night and I was wanting to go to sea so I decided to pack that in and I came home and I got a job on the *St Ninian*. I did a few trips on her but it was not too much different and the Aberdeen Pool was not being very helpful so I said to my father, "Any chance of going to the whaling?" He said, "Well, yes. I'll write to Captain Smith and see if we can get you away." I got a reply from Capt Smith saying that he could not guarantee a job but if I came down to Leith, he would maybe get me squeezed in.

So I headed off down to Leith and got signed up with the *Southern Harvester* but on the way down I had picked up the Asian flu. I had to have a medical first. Dr Mac gave us our medical. We had to line up, take our shirts off and stand in front of this old fashioned x-ray machine with your chest stuck out and he discovered this great big black spot on my lung so he said to me, "Well I don't know about you. I don't think you're very well. Have you ever been ill?" "No," I said, "I've never been ill." He said, "Well, you're coughing and spluttering. I think it's the flu. Ach, away you go." So he just signed the sheet and that was me.

We went to Shields and joined the *Southern Harvester* there and we met in with the rest of the crew. We had a bit of fun in Shields going around the pubs, a young boy fifteen and a half years old and never had a drink in his life. We helped to get the rest of the stores aboard the ship and then headed over to Norway and picked up the Norwegian crew in Tonsberg. We were there for a day or two and then headed off to the West Indies. This was to Aruba for that was where we refuelled on the way south. To get to South Georgia usually took us a few weeks. Once we got there the crews all got split up, some of the boys went to the catchers, some ashore to Leith Harbour and to Stromness. I was one of the mess boys on the *Southern Harvester* so I just stayed there. You usually got a job as a mess boy and then you progressed from there and each season you went down you progressed up a group.

After a few days the *Southern Harvester* headed for the ice and that was us at sea for at least four months. Sometimes you went all around the Antarctic Continent. The *Southern Harvester* would maybe go around to the west and the *Southern Venturer* would head east and other times they swapped around. We would go around the South Shetlands, South Orkneys and Elephant Island and sometimes into the Weddell Sea or even around to the Ross Sea. And then you would process your whales. Of course at that time I was still a mess boy and then as I progressed, I eventually got on to the deck. Once I had done my first season and just towards the end of the season they used to come around and ask for volunteers to do the winter and I thought well, will I or will I not? I took the plunge and decided to do the winter. I was fortunate, I got a mess boy's job in the hospital and that was one of the best jobs I have ever had in my life.

We used to start at 6 o'clock in the morning and we would clean the cabins and tidy up the hospital and sort out the breakfast and dinner and then we would usually finish about dinner time and the rest of the day could be spent skiing or taking photographs and just having a ball of a time. One day one of the boys came into the hospital, he had dislocated his shoulder. Everybody had been out and there was nobody in the hospital and the doctor was nowhere to be seen. After a while we managed to contact the doctor and he came to the hospital. The boy was in agony so he gave him a few shots of morphine to kill pain and he came out and locked the door behind him and said, "Now whatever you do, do not let him out of this room." I thought, well what the heck is going on here. He said, "Just keep this door locked and don't let him out."

After about ten or fifteen minutes I heard the room being all smashed up. The tables and chairs and everything were crashing up along the walls and me, being just a mess boy, I did not know what was going on. After a little while the doctor came back and we got the boy out of the room and on to the table in the operating room and laid him out there. I'll never forget it, the doctor just took his big boot and stuck it in the boy's side and just pulled his arm and put it back into place. So that got him sorted out. We put him to bed and he was all right after that. So that was what was done, medical care was very basic. It was the same on the dental system, if you had a toothache or anything like that you just went up to the assistant doctor and he pulled it out there and then whether the tooth was good or bad.

But I enjoyed it. I had a bit of a hobby there. I took up developing photographs because with being in the hospital we had the use of the dark room. We used to tint up photographs for the boys and we used to give them half a dozen to a dozen photographs for a couple of hundred cigarettes. We just worked this sort of barter system. And at night time when we were relaxing we used to go up to each other's cabins. Some of the boys made mats out of the bits of old nylon foregoer left over from the whaling season. It was amazing what the boys would do. Some used to carve whales' teeth and others would paint whales' eardrums and penguins' eggs. Some would develop photographs on home made developers. They used to make wooden boxes and put a glass plate on top. We then put the negative in and put the photographic paper on the top of it and put the light on for about four seconds and then develop it. It was all very basic. We had movies at the cinema and you could play table tennis or you just created your own fun and that was it.

Once you had done your winter the *Southern Harvester* or the *Southern Venturer*, depending on which ship you were designated, came back down again and picked you up from South Georgia and then you started the season all over again. I was back on the *Southern Harvester* and did my normal season and there was not much that happened that particular year. I got a job in the local fish factory for the summer. The following season, 1959/60, I was back down again and by this time I had become a whaler so I was on deck that year and I got interested in cutting up the whales. We got various different jobs to do when we were not cutting up whales. I got a job in the tank gang for a while. I was down there scraping tanks with the old bucket and the scraper and the wire brush. You got a peerie bit extra money for doing that kind of work. Later that year we headed off down to South Georgia again. I was still on the *Southern Harvester* but this time I got a job on deck as boiler screwer and I did some flensing as well.

I mind one particular time we were just standing yarning and I felt this piece of cold steel running along the side of my hand and the next thing I knew the blood was just pouring out. The flensing knife had just sliced right through the side of my hand and my peerie finger was just hanging on. I thought Oh God, what the hell do I do here? We were on the night shift and I thought the Doctor will never be up at this time of night. So anyway I made my way up to the Doctor's cabin. He said, "What's happened to you, Willie?" I said, "I have just nearly sliced off my finger." He said, "Oh come on then we'll get you sorted out. I'll go and get my clothes on." He came back and said, "Well, Willie, unfortunately I cannot get into the cabin for any anaesthetic so I'll have to stitch it up as it is here and now. If you feel sick then just stick your head between your legs."

He just took the needle and stuck it in my finger and sewed me up. You would never get away with that in the modern hospitals. He just patched me up and looking at my hand to this day, there is hardly a scar there, he made a beautiful job of it. It was amazing what the doctors could do, they could turn their hands to anything that was needed. It was just the way of life down there. There were no hospitals or medical wards in those days. You had the cabin which was used as a hospital and that was it and that was how the doctor used to work. I'm sure there are lots of boys who could tell you similar stories to that situation.

On the last couple of seasons we were not doing so well for whales. They were starting to thin out and I think Salvesen themselves were starting to realise that the whaling was coming to an end. That was coming up to 61 and I thought that there was no point in staying in a job that was not going to be there in a couple of years time so I decided to leave. I thought I would come away home and try something else, either go back deep sea or something like that.

I really enjoyed the whaling, I enjoyed it immensely. Some did not like it, they missed their families, they felt lonely but I enjoyed all my time at the whaling. I enjoyed the comradeship and the boys we went to sea with and we used to have some great times. We went ashore together and when we came home at the end of the season we used to have our whalers' ball and our dances and things like that which have all gone now. Occasionally we might have a reunion every couple of years or so. If the whaling came back tomorrow I think I would be off again.

GEORDIE ROBERTSON

After I left the school I was at the herring fishing on the *Sunshine* and when that finished I got a temporary job on a farm in Orkney taking in the hairst. While I was there I telephoned Salvesens in Leith and asked for a job at the whaling. We were working away when my mother contacted me and told me that word had come from Salvesens that I was to report to Leith. My boss in Orkney, John Johnston from Wyre, took me to Kirkwall in his peerie boat and saw me on board the *St Ninian* and paid my fare for me. It was very good of him. At Salvesen's office I met Jerry Smith who came from Whiteness. I had my medicals and then went down to South Shields to join the *Southern Venturer*.

When I got to South Georgia I was put on the whale catcher, *Sigfra*, at the island with Norman Jamieson from Yell. She was a buoy boat. We had some good laughs aboard there and Norman is still a very good friend of mine. One day we were in very thick fog and we could hardly see the gun at the bow of the catcher. I went up to the bridge with a cup of coffee for Norman just as we almost ran into a huge iceberg. Thank heavens we avoided that or we would not have been here today.

The mess room on the *Sigfra* was for'ard and I had been feeding the men and had to take everything back to midships for cleaning. We had metal pots that fitted together and a handle to carry them with. I put the plates in the pots, fitted them together and went to the top of the hatch. I had to wait for a signal from the bridge. The man on the wheel was Norman Jamieson. He lifted his hand up to me which I thought was the signal so I shot out of the hatch and made for midships. At that moment she shipped a lump of water. I was washed along with the lump of water and lost all my pans overboard. I was nearly a goner but the quick thinking of the man on the wheel saved me. I had to be taken to the factory as my arm was badly cut. I had to get it stitched so I was kept on the factory for a few days. It was awful. The stink was terrible, enough to put you off your food and the food on the factory was not as good as the food on the catchers so I was glad to get back on board the *Sigfra*.

The following season we left Glasgow on the *Southern Garden* and went to Caripito in Venezuela for a cargo of fuel oil. While we were loading the oil some of the tanks overflowed and the alleyway down the port side of the ship was running with bunker oil. It was some mess.

I did the winter in 59/60 and enjoyed it. It was a hard life but we did all the repairs to the catchers in all sorts of weather. Some did not manage so well. One young Norwegian mess boy had been ashore saying goodbye to his friends and had missed the factory ship. When he realised that he would not be able to get home he hanged himself.

Once or twice during the winter a ship would come in to Grytviken and she would have mail on board for Salvesen's men. We would take a catcher to pick up the mail. Sometimes there was a trip up to the Falklands to pick up sheep and lambs and they were taken to South Georgia and slaughtered. One time the butcher took badly and had to go into hospital. The Chief Steward for the winter was the same steward that we had had on the whale catcher. He asked me if I would work in the butcher shop so I told him I knew all about killing sheep and he took my word for it. We managed no bother at all. We had some good feeds every night for supper in the room I shared with Ellis Sales, Jimmy Burnett and Billy Ramsay.

One day we had to repair a big hawser that had broken. It was at a place called Jericho where a lot of the catchers were moored for the winter. The mountain sloped right down to the beach with a lot of loose rock among it. After a hard struggle we got the shackle unearthed and the new hawser put on. We were on our way along the beach to get back on board the boat when there was a rumble and the hole we had dug just caved in. If we had been there another two minutes we would all have been killed. There were nights when we thought we would never get back off the catchers again when a sudden gale of wind came up and you were stuck out on them. They were all tied together and the gangways between them would start breaking up.

I mind one good day we had we got 7 blue whales. The gunner was so pleased that he told Victor Inkster from Burra to go down to his cabin and get the men a drink. So Victor went down and took every single bottle out of his cabin and headed for'ard to give everybody a drink. There was some shouting from the bridge when the gunner saw him going with all the bottles.

There were lots of ups and downs at the whaling but you always had to look out for number one and that was yourself. There was a chap from Mallaig, Peter Gillies, who was coming out of the barrel. I think there was ice on the rigging and he lost his footing on the long step between the rigging and the ladder that led up to the barrel. He fell on to the deck and was seriously injured but lucky that he was not killed outright or fell into the sea where he might have lived for two minutes. The whale catchers were the hardest life but we were far better in a way because every man knew his job and you worked as a team. I mind going in among the ice floes and we shot seals and skinned them. The gunners took the skins home with them. I came home with a catcher one time and the hold was full of seal skins. Boy, the stink of it coming through the tropics was unbelievable, it nearly took your breath away. What they did with them I don't know but they must have been rotten by the time they got to Norway.

On the whale catchers at Christmas time you got a dram from the gunner. Drink was never allowed at the whaling except for a tot of rum every week if you wanted but we settled instead for a bottle of whisky or rum when the season finished. When I went ashore for the winter I had four bottles. I managed to get the steward's ones as well and he did not really know that he had lost them. I managed to get a tin of yeast off the whale catcher for making home brew during the winter so we had plenty of yeast for a long while and when we ran out of yeast we used tattie skins. Charlie Nicolson from Scalloway and Geordie Gray from Lerwick were the main stillers that winter. They had it set up underneath a building called Trehus and they had to crawl on their bellies to get in. But they always had to sample it so if you had two bottles of still coming off, you were lucky if you got one. They kept the other one to themselves as samples. A sort of quality control, I suppose.

There was never really any trouble amongst the crews at all. Everybody got on well together and any problems were soon sorted out. The Police came around from the Point one time and searched all the cabins for cookers. You were not supposed to have that because it was a fire hazard as the insides of the buildings were all made of wood. I mind one young fellow who was caught with something and his punishment was to dig the snow out of the entrances to the buildings. He was quite happy as the digging kept him warm but the poor bugger of a Policeman was frozen standing watching him. We were annoyed as he would waken us at 6 o'clock in the morning because he would sing as he was digging so we threw snowballs at him. That went on for a week and then it was stopped. Tonk was the name of the Policeman. He came from the Falklands and was a very fine fellow. He had his job to do and that was it.

I mind one time we were very low on bunkers and we were lying in the lee of an iceberg which was about 20 miles long. The factory was coming towards us as we did not want to go out into the open sea, being so light. I was up on the bridge when all of a sudden a sperm whale blew along side us. Victor Inkster shouted down the voice pipe to the gunner that there was a sperm whale alongside. He was in his bunk and thought Victor was joking and he told him to shoot it if that was the case. Victor went to the gun and did just that and the whale rolled over dead in the water. When we heaved it alongside we saw it had been shot before and it was towing nylon foregoer and a long piece of whale line. So there we had a fender to go alongside the factory ship. Just after the gun went off the gunner appeared on the bridge in his long johns and vest and could not believe what had happened. That gunner was Willem Johansen. He was a young fellow but sadly he developed cancer and died at the Falklands a year or so later. He was very good with his crew and kept the same crew all the time. The only ones who changed were the mess boys.

I thought the whaling was fantastic. It was a hard life but you made your own entertainment. You played crib or dominoes and on the factory ship there were film shows. The winter was harder because of the weather. Sometimes you could hardly see your hand in front of you. One minute it was flat calm and sunshine and the next it was a howling gale and you could not see for snow. It is fine to meet up with the old whalers again and relive some of the old times. There is a strong bond among us and I enjoy the reunions. If the whaling was going yet I would still be there.

ROBERT WISEMAN

I went away to Army Cadet Camp outside Edinburgh and while I was there I got one of the other boys to show me how to get to Bernard Street. We went by in the bus and he pointed it out. So I went and spoke to George Adamson. As soon as I came in there he said, "You're a boy of John Reid Wiseman," and I had never seen the man before in my life. I came home on the Wednesday night after the camp and I got a telegram the following day, the Thursday, to go away as a mess boy. So I went with the rest of the whalers and just followed them. I had to go to the famous Jerome's for my photo and all that carry on and medical and then that was it.

We went down to Leith Harbour and my first sightings of Leith Harbour was, I don't know how to explain it. As Robbie Strachan from Bressay said, "My boy, yon is where dy home will be for the next six months." And there it was. I did three seasons as mess boy and then I got outside as I was always wanting to get outside with the rest. I was hooking on the rosedown and then I decided I would volunteer to do a winter which put me into this famous boiler scalers or soot gang as they were better known. That was quite an experience but you were younger then and it did not matter, it was your job and you were quite pleased with it. I mind we were with this peerie Leith fireman, he had been a fireman on the Ben Boats and he was my partner. There were eight altogether and you worked in twos, and of course him being an old experienced fireman and me never been at that before, we went aboard this catcher which had Scotch boilers as they called it and he said, "Well, I'll go up here and I knock out this dogs and you'll go down there ready to get this tubes punched." So I said, "All right." So I went below and the door swung out and I got covered in soot. Of course, he roared and laughed. He knew what was going to happen and I did not have a clue. But I thought well that's fine, Jackie, you caught me this time but you'll not do it again. I'll be ready the next time. But it was all done in fun.

I think it was the final year I was mess boy that we had a misfortune with the pigs. We had a young Norwegian mess boy who came down with us and when we were in Las Palmas or somewhere he bought a peerie slug gun. He was not the cleanest of mess boys, as you might say so they put him to the piggery to work along with the pigman. One day, when the pigman came back from his dinner, the pigs were in an awful state, a distress and grunting and what an oncarry and when he came in this peerie mess boy had taken the slug gun and was shooting at the pigs and driving them nuts.

So he gave the boy a slap around the lugs and chased him and then the boy thought he would have to get his own back. So he went to number one store and got some cannisters of rat poison and signed for them and went back to the piggery. He slipped the poison in among their feed when the pigman was not looking. It was all stirred up together and fed to all the pigs. It wiped out most of them. It killed over one hundred pigs. I mind them working all night killing them because they were in an awful state. They put them on the bogies on the rails and took them down to the barges and the motor boat took them out to the Black Rocks and dumped them. There was an undercurrent there and anything that was dumped was never seen again.

At that time there was a great murderer in Britain called Peter Manuel so of course that boy got nicknamed Manuel. When he came into the messroom a great cheer would go right up through the place, everyone would say "Hurray, it's Manuel." But then he could not be sent home, he had to stay until the season finished. When we were coming home in the *Southern Opal*, somebody said in the messroom, "Where's that Manuel? What became of Manuel?" They said, "Oh, he's in the galley." And that just caused an uproar. Get him out of there immediately because that was where they had given him a job, as galley boy on the way home. So he got a short shift out of there. It was comical in one way but could have been serious.

In the winter I did there were six of us in the cabin and the snow was piled so high that we had to use the lights all the time. We were in the bottom half of the hut and the other boys were in the top half and the snow was half way up their windows as well. We had a still on the go, we had a spare cabin next door to us with nothing in it so we just kept the heating on there and we put all our drums of home brew in it and when they had done their thing we would take them out ready for stilling. I can mind going down to the mess room on a Friday night and the usual thing if you were trying to signal to someone that there was anything doing you would sing "Still the night" and then you knew you could go up there and get a tot.

The plumber had to get his share because he had plumbed in the steam from the radiator for us. The baker had to get his, he got the first bottle off because he was the guy who had given us the yeast. If you tried to give him the second or third bottle, he knew and was not pleased. So you had your contacts to get the necessary ingredients. After a few bottles, we would test the quality and would pour some in a spoon and hold a match to it and if it went with a lovely blue flame, it was good, we would keep it going but if it started to spit and splutter we knew it was coming to the end of it and it was time to get it dismantled and washed out.

We had a hole in the cabin floor – it must have looked like Colditz or something really because we had sawed out a big piece of the floor and nailed it together and then the still went down there. We hid it down there and then put the piece of wood and put the carpet over it and then the table in the middle of the floor so if there was any searches made it was quite alright. I mind one Saturday afternoon, a whole lot of the officials came around and they made a search and they looked in our cabin. The bottom bunk had a curtain along it, and we had no time to get the still in the usual place so we set it in the bunk and drew the curtain. They looked in every locker but they never drew back that curtain. If they had hauled it back, they would have found the still. It was the only place they did not look.

Ginger Ling, from Southampton, had his still in a big acid jar. He had put the acid jar in and built two lockers together to hide it and he used the metal thing you got with the spool for a camera on a string for sampling. He would take it now and again for a peerie taste. Of course they went into the locker and he had no time to get it moved. They asked him, "What do you do with this?" He said, "I wash my feet in it." "How did you get it in?" "Oh," he said, "I built it in." "So", they said, "We'll get two mess boys up here to take that away as evidence." They were going to charge him with making illegal alcohol, which they could do. Somehow or other they dropped the jar at the top of the stairs so the evidence was kaput and that was the end of that. When I met Barry Strachan recently, we recalled this incident.

There was never any trouble when you did have a dram, you just more or less stayed in your cabin, you did not go wandering around with it. But you could always tell when the Highland men were on it. You could hear them at Hillside, you could hear the screeches of them and they would start singing and then there was all this Gaelic things and you knew they were at it straight away because it was a kinda mournful sound.

One year on the way down we went into Carapito. We got our sub and they allowed us to go into town. Normally we were allowed no further than the canteen. This year I mind ones coming back and trying to get through the gate with a bottle but the Police would not allow that, they would take the drink off you. There was one who persisted, I will mention no names, he tried several different ways of getting it in but got stopped every time. The last time he tried the policeman at the gate said, "One more time and you are going to be here a very long time." He was going to lock him up. He went back outside again and drank and shared the bottle with others. So I suppose he got the bottle in eventually but not in the way he wanted.

After that you were not allowed up to the town. When you got your sub you just went to the canteen at the side of the river. To get to it you had to use the catwalk above the mud on the river bank. This mud was inhabited by millions of small crabs and each had one huge claw which they would wave at you. More than one whaler fell over the side of the catwalk, in among the crabs, on the way back to the ship. Inside the canteen, there was a row of cages along one side. Some held monkeys and others parrots. One Norwegian tried to open the door of the parrots' cage but the owners got a bit upset at that. There was also a big billiards table. By the end of the night, it would be covered in beer cans and maybe somebody sleeping in the middle of it. There would be a juke box blaring all the time until somebody put a chair through it. When nature called you went out on the steps at the back of the canteen, just on the edge of the jungle, where there was the biggest pile of beer cans that I have ever seen in my life and you just did what was necessary out there. You knew that was going to be your last spree before the season began.

When we called at Las Palmas, homeward bound again, we did not get subs or get ashore. On the *Southern Opal* we had Capt Baikie. He was a kinda fierce man and strong on discipline. He ran his ship very much by Board of Trade standards and I don't think he cared an awful lot for whalers. A mess boy's job became available on the *Southern Guider* and I went to try to get on her. I went to the office to ask about it and was told to go aboard and see the mate but an Orkney boy, Willie Work, had got there before me and he got the job so I never got on the catchers but I worked on them for the winter along with Jackie Haines from Leith.

The following season we had very good fishing. Everything was flat out, 'full cook' for days on end. They kept coming in with the whales and I mind when they emptied kettles with the bones they were just put into bogies and taken out and dumped in a great pile because they just could not cope with it. And then when things quietened down again they took it all back in and processed it. I mind the winter I did I went down to the catchers that I was going to be working on and I stood aft. It was just a dreech black wintry day and I watched the *Southern Opal* going out past the Black Rocks and I thought, "Now what has du done? Whatever bloody possessed dee to do this? Well, it is just too late now." Then I went down below to have a look at what I might be doing. I did not really have a clue. I knew we were working on the boilers but did not know how to get started until this Leith guy came on. The boilers kept their heat for a few days but after that it was bitterly cold. I mind us getting a guy to make us a tank which held gas oil and we got a peerie sputnik, as we called it, rigged up and we used to sit huddled around this sputnik with a cup of tea.

In this gang, called the soot gang, we had a separate table in the messroom because we were in such a mess that they more or less kept us segregated from the rest. When we had got all the tubes cleaned, there was a fellow who came aboard after us with a handful of ball bearings and he used to go up to the top of the boiler where you had punched the tubes from the top right through to the bottom ones. He had a handful of ball bearings and he would drop a number of ball bearings down the tubes and then go the bottom of the boiler and if he did not pick up the same amount of ball bearings that went in at the top, he made you do the whole lot over again. Luckily enough, we did what we were meant to do so we never had to go back over them again but that happened sometimes. It was a bit of a mesmerising job with all the tubes you had to punch and clean out but we surely did it right. It was quite easy to bypass one or two because you were working in a peerie cramped space. You were nearly round like a tyre, bent and trying to punch this tubes down and there was no right lights or anything.

When I was on the rosedown on the plan, you sometimes had big build ups of meat and stuff lying around for days. Sometimes the catchers would bring in a whale which had been lost for a while and it was literally falling to pieces. Sometimes it was so rotten that it was just like custard. You could not hook it to the boilers, it had to be pushed in with squeegees so you can imagine the smell that was coming off that. Even when you put your clothes to the laundry and got them back, the smell was still there. When you had worked with that for a while you never noticed the smell but when you came into the mess room to eat with others who were working at different jobs, they did not want to sit near us. You felt as though you had been put to Coventry because they could not bear the stink. We would say, "What is wrong with you? It is the smell of us making your bonus. What are you greetin' about?" But it was all in good humour.

I mind that heavy season when we were out and started at six in the morning until six at night and I think we got half an hour or twenty minutes for dinner and no smokos. If it eased up slightly, we could get a smoko and have a fag. The Norwegian foreman would rattle a bit of wood on the corrugated iron and say, "More, more, faster, faster" to keep the machines going. We thought that we would slow this bugger down. To do that, we would get a grenade, push it in with your foot, and it went up with the bucket and as soon as it hit the knives, it would shatter the blades and he would have to stop and take off the damaged blades and put on new ones so that gave us plenty of time for a smoke and then he would shout again, "Come on, get going again. You must watch for the grenades." And we would say, "Yes, fine, fine." But we did it quite often. Then if there were no whales coming in, and it was getting towards the end of the season, they would start shipping the guano out of the guano sheds. You might be in the shed or on the barge stowing the bags and you would tow it around to the side of whichever ship was taking it on board. If there was no whales then a great thing was they would say, "Right, you gang, you stay back today, you are washing the plan down," and the rest would get designated other areas until more whales came in and then you went back to your normal job.

It was a good life and I liked the grub and all, I never saw anything wrong with it. I did care not for the buccaloa at all but I did not mind the whale meat, I liked it. But all the rest, the salt junk and that was all right. I never ate a penguin's egg, maybe I was a finicky bugger but I did mind seeing them in the boxes but I can never mind getting them to eat but obviously must have done. Wednesdays and Saturdays we got tabnabs. You could go up and each man got a fancy cake of some description and you always tried to get a couple extra for yourself. If you broke a cup you had to go to the Chief Steward and tell him what had happened. It was like going through an inquisition to get a replacement.

The first time I went aboard the *Southern Opal* I was told to go down to the store room and the man there would give me a mattress and I had to sign for it. I also got a galvanised bucket, not a new one but it was not dirty, you could see that it had been used. He also gave me a tablet of Sunlight soap and a sweat rag and said to me "Sign here." So I signed the bit of paper. He said, "If you don't take the bucket back at the end of the season, we'll charge you for it. So mind I want the bucket back." I said, "What about the soap and the rag?" and he said, "You cheeky little bugger." Which I probably was but I thought it was kinda humorous.

Above:
Scott Christie, Burra Isle.
Photo: T Thomson.

Right:
Flenser begins work on 98ft blue whale on board ***Southern Venturer****.*
Photo: S Williamson.

Above:
Aft plan deck, ***Southern Venturer****. At top left can be seen the big steam winches for hauling the whales up on deck. 2 men at right are working on the lids for the cookers.*
Photo: N Thomson.

Right:
L to R Angus Ridland, Lerwick; Kaare Iversen, Scalloway.
Photo: A Ridland.

L to R Norman Jamieson, Yell; Peter Gillies, Mallaig. Front, Jimmy Johnson, Lerwick. Peter Gillies later fell from the barrel of the ***Southern Archer*** *and was badly hurt, but survived. Photo: J Johnson.*

L to R Victor Inkster, Joe Laurenson and Tommy Fullerton, all from Burra Isle enjoying a tune. Photo: M Mowat.

The most famous whaler of them all, John Thomson of Yell, known affectionately by everyone as 'The Arab'. Photo: N Thomson.

Jimmy Nicolson, Quarff, cutting the lower jaw off a fin whale at Leith Harbour. Photo: A Ridland.

Andrew Anderson, Yell, carrying a harpoon on board the factory ship, ***Svend Foyn****, 1940.*
Photo: A Anderson

Ill-fated whale catcher, ***Simbra****, delivering whales to the factory ship. John Leask gives graphic account of her loss in his story.*
Photo: A Anderson.

*Above: Snow clearing, South Georgia style.
Photo: A Williamson.*

*Right: L to R Dr Mac, well known to all Shetland's whalers; a whale catcher engineer.
Photo: G Thompson.*

WILBERT HOSEASON

My first season was 1954 and I went down with the *Southern Venturer*. I would have been 16 in November and it was October I went to South Georgia. I left the school and ended up on the *St Clair* the same night. It took us about a month. They did not go too fast or they would not have enough fuel left. I was in South Georgia for two or three days and then we set sail for the whaling grounds. We fished for about three or four weeks for sperm whale. There was no quota on sperm, you could take as much as you liked and they were all male. The fishing came poorer and poorer as the years went on. In 1955 I went down on the *Southern Garden* and we had to wait on the island for about six weeks before I went on a catcher. That was the *Southern Archer*.

In 1956 I went down to South Georgia on the *Southern Broom* and joined the *Southern Angler* and then I finished up on the island. I put in a season there. I did two winters, season-winter-season. It was very a good life, nobody seemed to bother you. The first winter I did I was on the catcher teams. The catchers were lying alongside and we had to chip and paint them. We were all in gangs and I was on the painting gang. At the same time the engineers were working on the engines. When everything was ready, they would get steam up on the catchers and take them out for trials. The second winter I did I was in the station gang doing all sorts of work around the place. I think there was only three of us, a Western Isles man and a Norwegian and myself. We had the time of our lives, just the three of us.

I never set a brew during the winters I did but I had a few glasses of it. Some of it was right good stuff. There was an old Norwegian called Willem, he had done a lot of winters, he had a still set in an empty cabin. The doors were locked but he went out and in the windows. He piped into the steam heating and we watched him going in and then there was this cloud of steam which came out. They had to get a plumber to shut the steam off.

I nearly broke my neck skiing one Sunday. I was coming down by the hospital and one foot twisted one way and one the other way. I was not going very fast but I could not go anywhere for weeks after it. I don't think it was ever right again. At that time I was working on the catcher teams. I would go off in the mornings and just stay on board and the boys would bring grub back to me. It would have been lonely on your own with nobody in sick bay through the day.

I won a bottle of rum and six tins of beer in a lifeboat raffle one night. I did not go to pick it up as I did not believe the boys when they told me. When we got it up to the cabin I had a lot of friends that night. It was surprising what a little of drink could do. We had more of that than we could cope with but we never let it get out of hand.

Some days when we were painting the catchers it was warmer than it would have been here. You got a lot of days when the sea was lying like glass. The snow seemed very much the same as here. It often snowed at night. We got quite a deepness of it in the winter time and we had a tractor and shovel that we used to clear the snow and that was a great help.

I was in Lerwick and saw the *Southern Actor* lying alongside Victoria Pier, something I thought I would never see. Tammie Robertson took me down to Lerwick.

I thought on the whole that the grub at the whaling was very good. The bread and tatties were usually not very great but I would not complain about the grub at all. I liked the baccaloa. Baccaloa and lobscouse.

When you were in the station gang you sometimes had to work on the catchers as well. You might be there one day and working in the big freezers the next, just any place. The Norwegians had a Union but we had none. They tried to do us out of overtime and one of the Norwegians helped us to get it sorted out. We had a lot of overtime in the winter, 3 or 4 hours per night. If you worked one hour you got paid for 3. If you happened to work five minutes over the hour then you got paid for another hour.

There was a transport ship that came down to Grytviken. We went there with the *Bouvet*, an old catcher just used for harbour work, to fetch stores. The skipper got drunk and fell asleep at the wheel. We hit a lump of ice, bounced off and hit it again before the man woke up. He was knocked on his backside and the *Bouvet* was holed. There was no Board of Trade man down there. The Skipper told me to steer and kept giving me orders. The Highland man who was along with us kept giving me orders too.

But yes it was a good way of life.

JOHN INKSTER

I went down to the whaling in 1958. I just did two seasons at the whaling as a mess boy. I asked my uncle to write to Salvesen and see if there were any jobs going and I got back word that I was to go for a chest x-ray at the old Montfield Hospital and when we passed that we were bound for South Shields. I always mind the first night when we went away in the old *St Clair*. It was a very rough night and I just went straight to my bunk and I never got up again until we landed in Aberdeen. As soon as my feet hit the pier in Aberdeen I spewed and I mind all the old men saying, "Boy, du'll never make a whaler." But I was never sick again and now all that old whalers, most of them are all dead but they were very good to us. They took us with them and showed us all the ropes. I mind Bunty Leask and Geordie Hunter and Donnie Tait and Sandy Wiseman and Eddie Hutcheson, they fairly looked after us. And nobody was better with us than Henry More from North Roe, he was very good.

We got to South Shields and of course they had to visit all the old haunts there and we tagged along too. It was an education. We set off to Tonsberg, picked up all the Norwegians and then we headed across to Aruba. That was a great time. That was the first time that I think I ever had rum and coke so I was not very well the next day but I thought it had been worthwhile. Then we headed for South Georgia. That was some sight when you saw it for the first time. If you thought Shetland was bleak, by God South Georgia was something different. It was really wild but it was very interesting with all the different kinds of bird life. And when you saw Leith Harbour it put me in mind of the klondyke up in Alaska.

We spent a day or two in Leith Harbour putting all the gear on board the catchers and getting ready and when that was done we headed off for the ice. When we started fishing we were on 12 hour shifts, that's when our work really started. That first season I was in what they called the big mess, that was just the ordinary whalers' mess and to the ordinary whaler grub was a very important thing and you fairly learned to do things fast because they did not like to have to wait for their grub. Unless you were smart and got in fast with the kits, they did not think much of you and you had to be very wily with the rest of the mess boys.

There was a lot of jostling and maybe a left hook or a right cross thrown but it was fairly good humoured. The big day of course was the big scrub out day. That was the day that you had to use caustic and most of us boys from

Shetland had rubber boots with us but some of the boys from down south did not have any and it burned the soles off their shoes and they were just white. It was a great day that and you had to watch because the caustic fairly scalded things but by jove the mess room was fine and clean after it.

We had some great fun when we were on the shifts. There was a lot of water being thrown around. You would go to your bunk and the first thing you would know was a bucket of water thrown over you. That would end it, you never had dry clothes for days. Then another great thing was when we were finished at night we would go around with the HP sauce bottle. You would end up getting doused all over with HP sauce or boot polish and all things like that. It was all done in good fun. There were films, the kino it was called. It was good. They used to have the same film several times over but we always went to see it. We could nearly say every line to end up with.

During the season there was an awful mess on deck. There was blood and meat and a horrible smell. It was all over the ship. And I mind things used to get very dirty and then there was a power of scrubbing that had to be done. In the bad weather instead of going aft along the plan deck with all the mess and the ship rolling, we would go through the factory and that was just as bad. The smell of the meal and the heat and striding over hot pipes and things you were just fit to be scalded. I mind one season we were down there, there was a big Norwegian mess boy, I just can't mind that boy's name now. He was a most powerful fellow and he suddenly took ill and he died and I can mind that yet, it was a very sad occasion because he was buried at sea. That day sticks out in my mind. It was nearly flat calm with a mist and it was really a very eerie kind of experience that. That same year Eddie Hutcheson died and he was buried at sea as well.

Well we carried on and then the season started to come to a close and we headed back for the island. That was a fine time because we knew we were then starting on the way home again and watching all the catchers coming back in and tying up and scrubbing out as you might say. It was worthwhile and of course we got a run ashore on the island. There was always maybe a football match or a night at the cinema in Leith Harbour. Then we headed north again and it was coming through the Forties you always had a bit of a tirl-up and and then into the tropics and you tried to get the bronzie for coming ashore in Lerwick. Of course it was a great time when you were coming in to Liverpool then everybody had what they called "the channels". You wandered around aimlessly for days just longing to get home. Then of course the great day came and you tied up. It was usually in Gladstone Dock and some of us maybe had to stand by for a few days but you always got ashore at night and you had a good time.

I mind Ertie Thomason and myself working by and we had a great time. When we finished we came up together right to Aberdeen. We maybe stopped off at Leith on the way up. Then of course it was the coming home to Lerwick that was the highlight of your time away. Stepping ashore at the Steamers' Pier in Lerwick was a great time and then you started to look forward to going back the next season.

There was no doubt about it, the whaling was a good life for us young fellows at that time. Now there is plenty of work in Shetland and at least it gives the poor old whale a chance to survive and that's certainly a good thing. I think most ex-whalers would say that they would go to the whaling again if they did not have to shoot the whales and I think that is probably true. Of course when you came home you did have maybe a bit more money than anyone working at home and you always managed to get yourself a motor bike or some kind of transport. It was a bit harum scarum in the summer when you all met at dances. But we certainly had a good time and we always looked forward to going back the following year and seeing mostly all of the same old faces. It was fine to see them again and we certainly enjoyed our time at the whaling.

JOHNNIE DALZIEL

I think that the best memories of the whaling that I have is from the first trip that I did. Just before I left school a man came to the school and said he was looking for apprentices to go to John Browns Yard in Glasgow and work on the QEII and I was supposed to be one of them. But nothing ever came of it and my father said one day that there might be a job going at the whaling if I was interested. And I said I certainly was. We had to go for an x-ray in Lerwick and then after a few weeks we got a date to be at the Office at Leith. We picked up the x-rays the day that we left and the first thing we had to do when we got to Leith was to go and get our photographs taken at Jerome's in Leith Walk. I still had this x-ray in my pocket and, after going all the way up to Jerome's and back down to Bernard Street, my father said, "Boy, does du hae yon x-ray?" I looked in my pocket and it was gone. So we had to about ship and we walked and walked and walked and then by God we found it lying in the gutter. So that was a relief.

We then had to go and get all the necessary documents signed and then we set off on the train to South Shields. A little bit past Berwick, somebody looked out the train window and said, "Boy, there she is." And you could see this massive ship with the red, white and blue funnels. We changed trains at Newcastle Station for South Shields. Then we arrived at this monster of a black ship, the *Southern Harvester*. We got on board and my father knew most of the men that were there. One of them was the mate, Magnie Scott from Papa Stour. Another one was Doctor Robertson who wrote the book, 'Of Whales and Men'. There was everything coming aboard from tatties to grices. I got a job as a mess boy.

About a week later we set off for Norway. One day I looked over the side and I saw three battens going by and to anybody like myself who went about the banks it seemed like madness not to stop and pick them up. Little did I know that when we got to Norway thousands of them would come aboard. There were all kinds of stores and harpoons and rope and just everything coming on board. At that time 1957, it cost £1.5 million to rig out a factory ship. After about a week we left for Aruba where we called to pick up fuel oil. As we went south it got hotter and we were sweating all the time. We were very relieved when we got into the cooler weather and through the Roaring Forties. We got fine weather all the way down that year.

When we got to Leith Harbour that was another experience altogether. It was a lot colder then and we had to put on more clothes. A lot of the timber went ashore, there were tons and tons of it. We also put ashore stores and mail and all the catchers had to get everything put on board – harpoons, ropes, flags, stores, etc. We eventually set off for the south ice and were steaming southwest one day when I saw this great white lump and that was my first sighting of an iceberg. The wind was about a force 8 or 9 and it was not too far from us. I was supposed to be on the factory for the season but a mess boy fell sick on the *Sondra* and I was asked to go aboard her and I said yes as I was keen to get on a catcher. So one morning between 3 and 4 o'clock I was swinging in a basket on my way down to the deck of the *Sondra*. The basket landed on its side and I crawled out on all fours. It was a different kind of life altogether aboard there. She was a buoy boat, not a full catcher.

On the factory you worked a 12 hour shift but on board the *Sondra* we started at 6 o'clock in the morning and finished at 9 at night. There was always a lot of noise when they were in delivering whales to the factory. The bunkering always took place in the middle of the night. You had to get out of your warm bunk and hump all the stores from for'ard to aft. Our job was to tow whales back to the factory and I was very lucky for the first three weeks as we had very fine weather so I was never sick. One morning I was woken up with a helluva bang. I thought we had hit an iceberg so I got out of the bunk in my drawers and went up the ladder and discovered we had shot a whale. When I heard the whistle of the rope going out, I thought the best place for me was in the bed. It was not a very good morning, a lot of spray going about and it was very cold.

My second trip I was on another buoy boat with a British crew. Among them were Jake Nisbet from St Abbs, Danny Morrison from Leith and Norman MacDonald from Stornoway. The following year I was on a full catcher, the *Southern Runner*. I went to South Georgia that year on the *Southern Venturer*. Our gunner that year had been the top gunner with the Hector Whaling Company on the Baleana expedition. He reckoned we would have 800 whales more than anybody else. Every time we saw a whale he went to the gun and just stood there for hours at a time and must have been frozen. We were not bottom boat that year but we certainly were not top as he had promised.

The last year I was at the whaling I went down on the *Southern Garden*. She was 64 years old and was just a proper old rust bucket. There was a droll crew aboard her from all over, Yell to Ireland. We hit a bit of bad weather off the Azores and they were beginning to think she might sink. She took a lot of water and washed the lifebelt off the side of the bridge. That same night we were up in the galley having a cup of coffee about 9 o'clock. The doors were standing open and the 3rd cook had taken the bread out of the oven when a big wave came in one door and took the bread out the other one. Everybody was sitting on the table with their feet up so that they did not get them wet.

There was a lot of fun on that trip. One night Colin Johnson decided he was needing a haircut and there was a queue for the barber in the alleyway. Christie Ratter and I said we could clip hair. Colin, being a first tripper, believed us. We started off trying to do a good job and then we began to work nonsense. There were bald bits and tufts all over his head and then we decided we could not do any more for him. Colin swore at us and pleaded with us but we put the clippers away and he had to go out into the alleyway among all the men and wait his turn for the barber. All the barber could do was take off all his hair. I don't know if Colin has forgiven us for that yet.

That year we went to Caripito for fuel oil. Old Dr Mac got drunk and thought he saw alligators in the swamp. When we finished loading the oil they had to turn the ship around to go back down river and while she was turning the branches of the trees were catching in the after housing and the rails around the stern. She had a kind of primitive ventilation system and we would sit and clip up papers into little bits, push it into the ventilator and it would come out like snow in the cabins further along. That season I was on the *Southern Soldier*. I was on watch with Jimmy Cormack from Eyemouth and Tammy Nicolson from Aith was on watch with Norman MacDonald from Stornoway. Anker Moller was the gunner that season and one day we were chasing whales when nobody else was chasing, it was just a flying gale. The whales ran before the sea for a while. We saw them on the starboard side. I pushed the telegraph to 'full ahead' and it broke. At this time she buried her gun platform in the face of a wave and when she cleared the gunner was about 12 feet up the forestay, hanging on with one hand. We got one whale after 8 hours' chasing. It was about a week before we got our telegraph repaired so during that time all the signals for the engine room had to be made by voice pipe.

One very fine day we were towing whales to the factory. I was on the wheel and my mind was hardly on what I was doing and I could see the factory. All of a sudden this huge blue whale blew right in front of us. I went down and shook the gunner awake and said, "There's a blue whale at the bow." I went back up to the wheel and when I looked around there were blue whales all over the place. The gunner alerted the factory as we were towing whales and doing only about 5 or 6 knots. As it was fine weather we were towing the whales with tail strops rather than the chains. Very soon all the full catchers in the area arrived on the scene and by night time they had caught 68 blue and 8 fin. The biggest whale I ever saw was 96 feet long, that was on the *Southern Harvester*. I think the biggest one ever caught was 114 feet long.

When the season was over I came home on the *Southern Venturer*. There were 10 of us in the cabin, in what had been the slop chest during the season. We were just alongside the mess room and opposite the galley. They were a lightsome crowd, the youngest 17 and the oldest 21. The switch to control the light in the cabin was right alongside one of the bunks and the person in that bunk always wanted to read his book at night. When we said, "Pit the light oot," and he refused we would throw our boots and shoes at the light and put it out that way.

On the voyage it was the 2nd cook's birthday. The bakers had made him a bonny cake and it was set on a piece of plywood. I happened to come past the galley door and saw him going out the door on the other side so I nipped in and took the cake to the boys in the cabin and said, "Come on, boys, eat up." It was sliced so everybody grabbed a piece and scoffed it. We had to break up the wood and throw it out the porthole. We had just got this done when the cook came in and said, "Right, boys, where's the cake?" Of course we knew nothing about any cake.

I did five seasons at the whaling. It was a good life and if it was still going I would still be there. But it all came to a sudden end.

GIBBIE FRASER

We arrived at South Georgia aboard the *Southern Garden* in early November 1958 and tied up at Stromness where Salvesen had 2 floating docks for servicing the catchers. There was also plater's shops, lathes and all the tools needed for repairing them. Next morning an old catcher, *Sabra*, came and took a lot of us deck boys around to Leith Harbour to join our respective catchers. The one I was to go on was lying at anchor just off Leith Harbour, she was the *Southern Broom* and had been a corvette on convoy duty during the war.

There were only a few engineers and firemen on board and very little grub. I found a tin of sardines in the galley and that did me till next morning when the floating factory *Southern Venturer* arrived. We went alongside early and began to take on board everything we needed. All our cooking utensils, etc. came on board in a big box and we had to wash and stow it all and take our stores to the storeroom aft and make food ready as well. When time came to turn in I felt I had walked miles. Next day we finished getting everything on board – harpoons, rope, flags, beacons – the amount of gear seemed endless.

We sailed for the ice around midnight. I awoke about 2am and the catcher was rolling and pitching, it seemed like a rough night. At 6am an AB wakened us for our duty and the Norwegian deckboy I shared the cabin with and I went along to the galley to help get breakfast ready. I remember it was fish balls and meat balls, both of which I got to like, but not that morning. With the smell of new paint, the cooking and the motion of the boat, we both turned very seasick. The cook, who was also the steward, gave us each a slice of dry bread and told us to go up on the boat deck and eat that as you could never go along the main deck of a catcher at sea, it was always awash. His strategy for curing sea sickness did not work and we both made for the comfort of our bunks again and stayed there until next morning when we got up and turned to and we never felt bad again.

The first few weeks we spent fishing for sperm whales, they were slow moving and could dive and stay down for about 20 minutes. Some of them seemed to know how to beat us as, just when they were coming within range, they would lift their tails out of the water and dive straight down. It was as if they were waving at us.

It was into December when the baleen whale season began and we were to take fin, sei and blue whales and there was a very short 4 day season for humpback whales. We, the deck boys had quite a busy time. We had to help in the galley as needed and serve up the food to the crew. I was in the Officer's messroom as the Norwegian deck boy was a group higher than me and had been to sea for a while. He was a bit older too, about 19 I think. When the meals were over we would wash up and then we had to clean cabins and alleyways, toilets, etc. When we caught a whale the Norwegian boy was needed on deck to help on the gun platform.

The catcher hunted whales at about 12 knots but if we found some or if another catcher in our area saw some and reported them on the radio, we went up to full speed to get to them, about 18 knots. When whales were seen or reported, the gunner would ring the telegraph from its position at full ahead to full astern then back to full ahead to full astern and then to full ahead again. When you heard the four rings you knew that you were on to something and the adrenalin began to pump. At full speed the whale boat shook and trembled, pans and plates rattled as she cut through the water. On a fine day the bow wave would ride up the flare and only begin to break when it fell back towards the sea. It was a fine sight, a catcher at full speed.

As we drew closer to the whales the tension grew and the gunner would be watching intently trying to see if any had calves as he would not take them but looked for the biggest in the group to give the most oil and meat. At about 300 yards the asdic man would begin to search for them using the same type of asdic which had proved so effective against the U boats. He would watch a roll of paper slowly unfold with little smudges on it here and there which tied in with the echoes he was picking up on his headphones. At the same time he turned a dial which sent out a signal probing in the direction of the whales. As the range shortened, the time between the echoes lessened and everybody's heart beat a little faster with the expectation of a kill and the bonus it would bring. The asdic man's running commentary on the whale's distance and bearing from the catcher was relayed to the bridge, gun platform, barrel and engine room by loudspeaker. At about 120 yards, the gunner would go to the gun and free up the brake and cock the gun ready for firing. A whale harpoon gun loaded and ready to use is so finely balanced, a baby could move it. Down below the engineer would be standing by the steam valve listening to the commentary and getting ready to shut down the engine when the gun went off as the shock and sound could be heard all over the ship.

Below in the fo'c'sle the 2 AB's off watch would be aware, by the vibration, that we were chasing and they would also hear the asdic man's voice on the loudspeaker, "Port 15,100 yards, port 10,100 yards, port 10,90 yards." As we got nearer, his voice would get higher and he would talk faster and the thrill of the chase was on.

The man in the barrel had a birdseye view of the proceedings and would be able to see the whales underwater. When they are being chased at full speed they blow the air out of their lungs before breaking the surface and the trail of bubbles could clearly be seen from the barrel. He would shout, "Coming up! Coming up!" when a whale was in position to shoot. When the whale came within range the gunner would take aim for what seemed an eternity and then pull the trigger. With a tremendous explosion the harpoon would fly from the gun taking the foregoer in a high arc behind it and you would think that it was going to go over the whale's back and miss but in the last instant it would drop and bury itself into the living flesh. The engineer would stop the engine and the catcher would glide on until we saw if the whale was dead. If it wasn't we would have to follow it and try to heave it closer to the ship in order to put in a killer harpoon.

By this time the chief engineer would be at the winch, 2nd mate would be at the winch brake, mate and deck boy going to the gun platform and the radio operator would begin to get a radio beacon ready. The man at the wheel would keep his eye on the gunner to see which way he wanted him to steer, there was a telegraph on the platform so the gunner could command the ship from there.

In the engine room the air compressor would be started up. This led to a hose on the platform with a metal pipe like a large hypodermic needle which would be fitted to a long wooden handle and the two held together by a length of rope which was payed out at the same time as the handle. The needle was plunged in to the whale and the handle taken back on board and stowed leaving the rope attached to the needle. The rope was heaved on to retrieve the needle when there was enough air in the carcase to enable it to float.

The fireman in the stokehold had his work cut out at this time. From going full speed and making as much steam as he possibly could, he had to shut down fires and stop the steam pressure going over the safety limit but he also had to be ready to build up steam again very quickly when it was needed. He would be informed by the engineer ringing a buzzer a certain number of rings when the order was for slow, half or full speed so he could adjust his fires accordingly.

Two bamboo poles about 18 feet long would be made ready by the radio operator. One would have a big red flag with the catcher's number on it – in our case No 3 – and a battery powered light and small canvas flag with a three digit number on it. This was the number allocated to that whale so a record could be kept of its size, sex and how much oil, etc it produced. This enabled our bonus to be worked out and it also provided evidence of how many whales were caught for the whole season and ensured that the expedition kept within the guidelines laid down by the International Whaling Commission. The second pole had a radio beacon attached and the operator would check the frequency and relay the information to the factory and they in turn could direct a buoy boat, always an older and slower catcher, to pick it up. On the lower ends of the poles were metal lances about 4 feet long which would be plunged into the carcase and this kept the poles upright. Along with the radio beacon there would be a radar reflector.

The AB's on deck would use a rope of hard nylon with two lead balls in the middle about 20 feet apart to throw over the tail, one end would be made fast to a heavy bit of sisal or manilla rope and passed around the tail and the end would be tied around itself and then a few turns would be taken on the capstan and the rope tightened around the base of the whale's tail. On the end of this rope, which was about 30 feet long, were 2 cork floats each with the catcher's number on them. This rope was used by the buoy boat to retrieve the whale.

If the whale was not dead it would be shot again with a killer harpoon. This was just like a length of pipe with 2 small fins on either side just behind the threaded portion at the front where the explosive grenade point would be screwed on. This harpoon was a lot lighter than the full harpoon and did not need such a big charge to fire it as the whale was always just at the bow of the boat when it was used. When it was fired there was a 3 second delay before the grenade exploded deep within the animal, you could see its body shudder when the grenade went off. The flag and beacon would be put in the carcase and the nylon foregoer cut near the harpoon, the end hauled on board and it would be spliced on to another one. The deckboy and mate would have reloaded the gun with the harpoon which led to the other side of the winch.

If a whale took out a lot of line, the 2nd Mate would try to slow it down by heaving on a rope tackle which led from a long arm on the winch brake. He would also have to keep his eye on a block up the mast as there was a series of coiled flat springs in a portion of the hold attached to a wire rope which went up through the deck and through a block attached to the mast. On the end of this wire was the block through which the foregoer led from the winch to the platform. It was just like using a fishing rod that didn't bend, the springs below put on tension instead.

A whale taking out a lot of line meant a wet and dangerous job for the AB's. They would have to go into one of the big, wood lined wells or bins on either side of the hold and coil the rope in as it came back on board, always being ready to jump out quickly if the whale suddenly fought back and took out more line. There have been instances where someone did not get out of the way in time and lost a leg or arm. It happened on a catcher many years earlier when they did not carry so big a crew. The radio operator was having to coil the rope when the whale took a run and he got caught in the rope. It took off his leg below the knee. The cook came along with a bag of flour and stopped the bleeding by sticking his leg in that and then they had to carry him up to the radio room so that he could tell the factory what had happened and alert the doctor.

Once the whale had been cut adrift the catcher moved away. The man in the barrel would be pointing in the direction of the rest of the whales and we would work up to full speed again. And so it went on until it became dark and we lost the whales due to poor visibility. In the middle of the Antartic summer there is no night and you were on the go all around the clock if there were whales about.

Every now and then the catcher would have to go to the factory ship to refuel. The number of days could vary depending on how much fuel had been used chasing or if the weather was bad we would spend time lying in the lee of an iceberg and not use so much. If the catcher had been getting whales they would pick up maybe 3 or 4 and tow them to the factory and deliver them all bar one which would be kept alongside for a fender. The catcher would go in on the starboard side of the factory and a heavy reinforced oil pipe would be lowered down and the fuel oil turned on. The harpoons which had been taken out of the whales we had caught had been straightened by the blacksmith on the factory ship and were returned along with the flags, beacons, etc.

We also took on stores, fresh bread and sometimes a big lump of whale meat which would be hung on the rails of the boat deck for a few days before we used it. There was a shop on the factory ship called a slop chest and if we put in an order for clothes, chocolate, cigarettes, toiletries – in fact anything you could need – it would be put on board next time we bunkered. When everything was on board we would let go and deliver the whale to the stern of the factory, then it was off hunting again.

A great life – pity it all had to end!

JIMMY SMITH

The whale catcher *Southern Harper*, built by Smiths Dock & Engineering Co of Middlesborough in 1951 as Newbuilding No 1221, was the second last catcher built for Salvesens, her sister-ship *Southern Hunter* No 1222 being the last. The *Harper* was 149 feet long overall with a beam of 28 feet and a depth of 16 feet. She was powered by an open-crankcase Triple Expansion steam engine of 1800hp giving her a top speed in the region of 17 knots.

How did it come about that I signed on the *Southern Harper* at Leith Harbour, South Georgia on the 27 November 1961? The story starts a couple of years earlier when I commenced studies at the Radio Department of Leith Nautical College. Initially I stayed aboard the Training Ship, *Dolphin*, moored in the West Old Dock but later moved to student accommodation at Leith Sailors Home. While staying there I regularly saw Salvesen's whaling crews passing through on their way to and from the Antarctic. Among the whaling crews were three young fellows of about my own age, Johnny Dalziel, Billy Morrison and Gibbie Fraser, (who has compiled this book). I had long conversations with all three about life in the Antarctic and it was they who gave me the idea of trying out the job myself.

In late 1960 I came through the PMG Examinations with a 2nd Class Certificate and the writtens of a 1st Class. The writtens were valid for 12 months only and, rather than lose them by default which could easily have happened if I had gone deep-sea, I found a job with Messrs Redifon Ltd of St Andrews Dock, Hull as a Trawler Radio Officer. Hull was booming at that time with a fleet of around 120 side trawlers doing 3 week trips to the Arctic.

I liked the job and the pay was good so I hung on as long as possible, only returning to Leith with a few weeks to spare before the Autumn PMG exams.

I passed the second part of the 1st Class ticket and, while in Leith, contacted Salvesens regarding a job in the whaling fleet. The industry was drawing to a close and this was probably the only opportunity I would have of seeing the Antarctic.

There was a vacancy for a whalecatcher Radio Officer in the *Southern Venturer* expedition. I got the job and shortly afterwards, on 9th October 1961, signed on the *Southern Venturer* at South Shields. We left the Tyne a couple of days later, crossing the North Sea to Tonsberg to load whaling supplies and take on the remainder of the Norwegian crewmen, then sailed for Aruba in the Dutch West Indies for bunkers.

After leaving Tonsberg, I was put on day-work along with Finn Haakonsen the Radio Officer of the *Southern Broom*. During the passage to Aruba and then on to South Georgia we were to overhaul and refurbish all the *Venturer's* radio aerials, over forty of them and then overhaul and paint catcher numbers on the fleet's whale beacons, around a hundred and fifty units. These were battery powered radio beacons used to re-locate whales at sea after they had been buoyed and flagged.

Once at sea on the way south the *Venturer* became a huge floating workshop as her own crew and the catcher crews travelling to South Georgia were deployed on dozens of tasks, preparing the ship and her equipment for work on the Antarctic whaling grounds.

When I was offered the job at Leith, I was advised to learn some Norwegian and in this respect was very lucky to be put to work along with Finn Haakonsen as he spoke excellent English and was pleased to teach me the basics of his native tongue. When the Slop Chest opened I purchased a 'Teach Yourself' book and a pocket dictionary and started a crash course in basic Norsk.

During the crossing to Aruba, while moving whale beacons from the lower hold to our deck work-area, I twisted by back badly. I saw the ship's doctor, had a couple of days off work and made a quick recovery, or so I thought. Unfortunately it came back to haunt me the following summer and caused me no end of physical and mental anguish over the next seven or eight years. Eventually I found a Chiropractor who helped a great deal and put me on the road to recovery but it still bothers me to the present day.

Once across Biscay and into warmer weather there were regular film shows on deck and also a weekly concert. The films were usually in English with Norwegian sub-titles or vice-versa. I found this a handy way of picking up phrases and also Norwegian spelling. The ship's concerts, compered by John Gilbert from Edinburgh, universally known in Salvesens as Romeo, were very good. There was a surprising variety of talent on board. At the start of a concert, voting cards were handed out to a selection of the audience to award points for the best acts. At the end the points were counted and every time the winners were Johnny Dalziel, Sand, on fiddle and Bobby Sinclair, Tingon, on accordion. They were a delight to listen to and played many an encore.

When there wasn't a film or concert we played a great deal of 500 in the evenings. Robert Strachan from Bressay, Philip Johnson, Burra, and Nicol Thomson, Burravoe, shared a four-man cabin which became a favourite meeting place for Harry Johnson, Bixter, Tommy Robertson, West Yell, and myself for a game of 500. Out of the six there were usually four available to play, and we passed many a lightsome night at the card table. I never was much of a card player but enjoyed the company and the banter.

After leaving Aruba on 6th November with a full load of bunkers, we crossed the line at around Longitude 43degrees West en route for Leith Harbour. For 'Crossing the Line Day' we had the afternoon off, a programme of Deck Sports was arranged and we were issued two bottles of beer a man. There were a wide variety of events, deck races, long jump, high jump, triple jump, pillow fight, putt the shot, toss the fender, etc. A league table of points was kept and the overall Ship's Champion was Geordie Sales, Lerwick who scored high in all events. Captain Virik presented the awards and Geordie's was a Parker fountain pen. Later on the Ship's Welfare Office drew their raffle which had been eagerly awaited. First prize was a Kurer Combi, a portable shortwave radio with built-in record player. This was won by Jimmy Balfour, Sullom and at night the 'Crossing the Line' concert was won, as usual, by Johnny Dalziel and Bobby Sinclair, so on the whole the Shetland contingent had a very successful day. After crossing the line it was back to work as usual and a couple of weeks later we were in the Roaring Forties. By this time most of the outside preparations were finished and soon we sighted our first icebergs.

On 27th November we arrived at Leith Harbour, six weeks out from South Shields. The Shetlanders who signed off the *Southern Venturer* and on to their catchers were as follows:-

Willie Watt	Lerwick	*Southern Harper*
Geordie Sales	Lerwick	*Southern Harper*
Jimmy Smith	Cunningsburgh	*Southern Harper*
Colin Johnson	Dale, Voe	*Southern Actor*
Jimmy Balfour	Sullom	*Southern Archer*
Tom Johnston	West Burrafirth	*Southern Broom*
Ellis Sales	Lerwick	*Southern Runner*
Ronnie Couper	Skeld	*Southern Runner*
Johnny Dalziel	Sand	*Southern Soldier*
Tammy Nicolson	Aith	*Southern Soldier*
Billy Morrison	Yell	*Southern Archer*

Our Gunner was Kaare Lie, he had travelled south on the *Venturer* while the first Mate, Olav Morsund, had just completed a winter at Leith Harbour, as had the galley boy, Douglas Ritchie from Eyemouth. We moved our gear on to the *Harper*, got the winter moorings cleared and then berthed alongside the *Venturer* to take bunkers and load supplies and whaling equipment.

Amongst the rest of the work I checked out the radio room and radio batteries and located a suitable AC supply for the tape recorder I had bought while we were in Tonsberg. This was installed on a spare corner of the chart table, the *Harper* having a combined Chartroom and Radioroom amidships and was to provide background music for the boys and myself when we were out of range of radio broadcasts as was often the case down at the south ice.

Once everything was aboard, the Gunner decided to go seaward for engine and steering trials. When we cleared the harbour entrance he rang down for 'Go on' speed, this was chasing speed, everything she could muster. At this speed there was serious vibration around the bridge and superstructure and in the radioroom I soon found out what the drawer full of wooden wedges was for. After steering gear trials which involved flinging her round the ocean at 'Go on' speed, he eased back to 10 knots and set course for Leith Harbour again. On the way back I called the *Venturer* for tests of the radio equipment, direction finder, distance measuring equipment, etc. and found everything in order. Outside the harbour entrance we stopped near some kelp beds and put the fishing lines over the side. We soon caught about two dozen of what looked like a plucker or a Norway Haddock, some sort of ocean perch I suppose they could be termed. We gutted, finned and skinned them on the way in and the steward fried them on the bone for supper. After supper I fetched a batch of whale-lamp batteries from the hold and put them on charge in the charger box provided in the radioroom then rigged some whale-lamps and radio beacons on to poles, hoping they would soon be required.

Next morning we were off, one of the first to leave, set course ESE and started scouting ahead for whales. The rest of the catchers followed in ones and twos, and finally the *Venturer* herself. We had been issued with concise instructions regarding radio frequencies and procedures to use on the whaling grounds, when to use radio telephone and when to use telegraphy, the use of the radio scrambler gear, ciphers, etc. There were scheduled transmissions to and from the factory ship every 4 hours from 0400 to 2000 with an extension to 2100 or 2200 if conditions required. At these times each catcher took a radio bearing of the factory's beacon and did a D.M. (Distance measurement) in relation to the factory. Once on the whaling grounds the factory became the centre of your universe. There was rarely any land to bother about, only ice which was probably on the move anyway, so everything was judged and plotted relative to the factory ship.

We ran off ESE for several days, passing through the South Sandwich Islands which looked even more inhospitable than South Georgia. Sailing close by Nightingale Island, an active volcano, I wondered if it had been named after a navigator called Nightingale as it did not look like it would have found favour with the feathered variety. Nightingale was the last land we would see for over three months, although we did not realise it at the time.

Off to the east of South Sandwich we got our first whales, and also the first of the season for the *Venturer*. We sighted a factory ship alone on the horizon so the Gunner decided to close her and see if she had any whales. She turned out to be the *Kosmos* of Sandefjord, no whales and not a catcher in sight. As we rounded her stern, Willie Watt who was in the barrel shouted down, "Hvalblast" (blowing whales ahead) and there they were, half a dozen low bushy spouts of sperm whales less than half a mile away. The *Kosmos* had obviously been shadowing them, waiting for one of her own catchers hurrying back from scouting. Within a minute the Gunner was on the gun with the Mate standing by, the Chief Engineer and the 2nd Mate on the winch and everyone tense as we crept up on them.

There was a gale of wind and a heavy swell running which probably helped to mask the noise of our approach so we were virtually on top of them before the Gunner shot the first. In no time it was alongside, the tail strop was on and the air-pump running. The radio beacon, lamp and flag were fixed and we backed away while the Mate and the galleyboy loaded the gun for another shot. This was not the high-speed chase I had expected but I soon found out that hunting sperm whales is a case of stalking whereas baleen whales are usually hunted at high speed.

In this case the whales had not gone far before they resumed their leisurely cruise along the surface so we got another two before they sounded and went deep. Once they sounded we started to circle slowly, with all eyes peeled, snatching a mug of coffee and a smoke while we waited for them to re-appear. Eventually they came up less than a mile away, so we closed in again and got two more but the sixth sounded and was not seen again. All this time the *Kosmos* was nearby watching us. We took a circle and passed close along their port side, our crew waving and cheering. The Tonsbergers were shooting whale while the Sandefjorders could only stand and watch as their catchers were 50 to 60 miles away. One up for Tonsberg!

We called the factory and reported no more whales in sight. They told us to pick up what we had and tow back to meet them. This was all new to me, just as the first part of the operation had been and I realised how lucky I was to be on the boat with Willie and Geordie. They had been on whalecatchers since leaving School, were fluent in Norwegian and knew every move. While running off from South Georgia they had pointed out what various things were for and told me what to look out for. I had rehearsed it all in my head many times but, as usual, rehearsals are conducted in a flat calm. When it happens for real in a gale of wind and heavy swell it is not quite the same. However, things went smoothly, we got all five whales secured, three on one side, two on the other, took a bearing and distance to the factory and off we went feeling that we would never be poor again!

Delivering whales at the stern of the factory for the first time, in the dark and with a heavy swell running, was a slightly hairy experience. You had to come close to the factory's quarter, catch their heaving line, bring across the messenger, shackle it to the tail strop and then drop the whale. This was repeated for each whale, but the main problem was that you could not go astern for fear of breaking the tails of those you had alongside. Broken tails made whales very difficult to handle or haul up the ramp, something which did not go down well with the Bosun and ABs on the factory. When delivering, the only engine movements possible were slow ahead and stop. Our Gunner always went to the wheel for this job and he was excellent. On the gun platform he often blew his top and raged when things did not go according to plan, but alone on the bridge under the factory's stern, even in the foulest of weather, he was as cool as ice and never put a foot wrong.

We worked our way northeastwards towards Bouvet, an isolated volcanic peak poking out of the ocean at 54 degrees South and 2 degrees east of Greenwich. We never sighted it but according to the Antarctic Pilot it has no harbours and the only landing is on exposed boulder beaches. Someone misguidedly planted the Norwegian flag on it about a century ago, so it is officially Norwegian territory, but I doubt if it has yielded any revenue to the Crown so far. From Bouvet we worked into the southeast towards the Antarctic continent and finally reached the pack ice at about 30 degrees East, off Queen Maud Land.

One of the Norwegian factories, the *Pelagos* of Tonsberg was further east, off Enderby Land when she became trapped in the pack, struck heavier ice when trying to break out and was badly damaged forward. Her catchers towed her free and the collision bulkhead held although it had to be shored up. With the fo'c'sle head awash, the pressure on the bulkhead was such that they had to tow her stern-first. They made slow progress all the way to Cape Town, the nearest port, where she was discharged and ended up sold for scrapping. The catchers steamed home to Norway. Without a factory ship it was the end of the line.

The *Pelagos* was an old passenger ship with a counter stern that had been converted by having a ramp built on under the counter. We had passed her several times between Bouvet and the ice. She had been whaling from pre-war and had had a good run for her money. At this stage her quota was probably worth more than the ship herself.

During our passage towards the ice we had experienced a variety of weather, fine clear whaling days, scruffly awkward whaling days, days of severe weather when you had to knock off and heave-to, days of fog or falling snow when you couldn't fish because nothing could be seen. You might even hear whales blowing in the fog but couldn't chase or catch them. There were always a variety of bergs around, small, medium or large. Some of them were many miles long, huge sections of the Antarctic ice-shelf which had broken off and were drifting northwards to melt in warmer waters.

To most ships, icebergs are something to be avoided but to whalecatcher crews they were a welcome sight, especially with night approaching if you planned to remain on the same ground for the following day. If you were staying-put in a particular area, normal procedure would be to stop at nightfall and lie beam-on, rolling heavily all night. If there was a big berg about you made a bee-line for it as darkness came down and got tucked in on its lee side. Then, with one man on watch on the bridge and one in the engine room, the rest of the crew enjoyed a good night's sleep.

Christmas was celebrated at sea with no bergs around for shelter, just lay beam-on for supper and a dram, then turned and eased away before the swell till daylight. At the New Year the weather was the same with a worsening forecast. We stopped beam-on for supper in a heavy swell and rising wind. During supper the steward went aft for extra bread and on returning chose the saloon door to come back in. As he opened the door, she dipped her rail and rose under a breaking lump of sea. The poor man was washed in the door but managed to throw the bag of bread on the table as he came, so it remained dry. The wave slammed the door behind him leaving a lot of itself washing around inside. Luckily, most of us had kept our seaboots on so we had dry feet.

There was a drain in the galley floor which the galleyboy and messboy whipped open and with a squeegee and fire shovel soon had the water away. By the time we finished supper it was a flying gale and snowing heavily so the Gunner decided to put her head-to-wind and lie hove-to. In those conditions you couldn't run as you might be running into the weather side of a berg, with no warning and no chance of escape. Lying hove to, you would be aware of approaching bergs by the presence of a drift of broken bits coming off them and by the wind and sea easing in their lee. If they were big enough you could stay in the lee, otherwise you could avoid them and let them pass.

There were no bergs that New Year, just a shrieking hurricane and driving snow. Those not on watch wedged themselves in their bunks and tried for a few hours' sleep. The wind eased a little as the daylight came in. I got up, checked the radioroom, then on going outside met Willie who was on the 2 to 8 coming off the bridge. "Mornin' Jeemy," he said, "Coorse nicht, shu's taen a treshin dastreen." On looking forward I saw what he meant. She had certainly taken a thrashing. The harpoon gun was about the only thing forward which was still in place. The gun platform rails were flattened and the forward engineroom telegraph was gone, nothing left but the pedestal bolts. The rope-tunnel lids were lying askew with buckled hinges, the foregoers had been washed out of their boxes below the gun and were parcelled round the winch, the spare harpoons, weighing 160 lbs each, were out of their racks and scattered round the deck like matchsticks. The Gunner ordered me to call the factory, get a bearing and distance and request repairs.

We had breakfast and tidied up as we steamed towards the *Venturer*. On arrival about 10.30am, we picked up a fender whale and went alongside. There was a heavy swell running and it was snowing again. Down came the basket with Douglas Brown from Yell who was Repairer on the *Venturer* along with his assistant, a young Norwegian whose name I forget. Douglas surveyed the scene, took a few measurements, collected remnants of the telegraph which we had found wedged under the winch and they went back up in the basket. Later they returned with a replacement telegraph which they had made up from the remains of ours and various other bits and pieces, a bag of bolts, nuts and other parts and a box of tools. They set to work in appalling conditions. The factory had taken the wind on the port bow to give us a lee but spray from her forefoot was coming across the gun platform where they were working and there was no means of rigging a windbreak. We were ranging alongside in the swell and it was still snowing. That day I had my eyes opened and saw what was possible at sea in severe conditions if you had people with the skill to do the job and the determination to carry it out.

By mid afternoon the replacement telegraph was fitted, chains and linkages joined up and working like new, stanchions and rails straightened and everything shipshape. We hauled out and recoiled the foregoers, checked and restowed the harpoons and by nightfall were clear of the factory and ready for action. Douglas Brown and his young asistant had done a magnificent job in extreme conditions but they did not think it exceptional, to them it was all in a day's work.

We worked along the edge of the Antarctic ice, sometimes among the pack and sometimes well seaward of it. Hunting among the pack was a slow process. We got some good fin whale there. They seemed to be feeding on krill deep below the ice and were well fed and sluggish. They would come up in a patch of clear water and blow for a while before diving again. It was rare that you were in the patch they chose to surface in. Usually they would come up some distance away and off you went, crashing through ice floes, trying to reach them before they dived. It was very hard on the ABs as their accommodation was forward, so in their free watch there was a constant bumping and grinding of ice floes a foot or two from their bunks. In addition they had to come on deck every time the gun went off whether you hit a whale or not. They never complained but after a spell in the pack they were glad to get back to the roll and heave of the open ocean again.

By late February/early March we were crossing the Weddell Sea. The southern winter was starting to bite, we had a good deal of fog, sometimes freezing fog. This meant lying drifting, especially if there were whales in the vicinity. Drifting in fog gave you time to check and overhaul various bits and pieces. After everything had been checked and double checked we usually resorted to jigging for fish or playing 500 in the messroom. I had obtained an old cabinet loudspeaker from the Chief Radio Officer on the factory and fitted it in the messroom. We ran a cable down from the extension socket of the tape recorder in the radioroom and had a little background music as well. On the way south on the *Venturer* I had been able to copy of number of tapes from the big recorder in the ship's welfare office and these came in handy at the ice where you went for long spells with no reliable broadcasts available.

Aboard the *Harper* it was Fem Hundre we played, not Five Hundred. Geordie Sales and Dougie Ritchie both played to Norwegian rules and in the language as all the rest of the players were Norwegian. I just learned the variations to the rules and followed suit. We often played cards at night when towing in whales or waiting our turn to go alongside for bunkers. If the game was short-handed, sometimes a man going up to the wheel would leave his hand for the man coming off, and having poured a mug of coffee and rolled a cigarette, the new man would pick up and carry on the game.

In early March we passed close to the south of the South Orkneys, the first land we had seen since South Sandwich at the end of November. We were steaming west, searching all the time but not seeing much. A couple of days later we sighted Bridgeman Island, an active volcanic cone at the north end of the Bransfield Strait, near Graham Land. Bridgeman Island rises from the sea like a factory chimney, smoking at the top. It reminded me of the high chimneys you see around Immingham and Killingholme when approaching the River Humber. The coast there is so flat that you barely see the land, just smoking chimneys rising from the sea.

Passing into the Bransfield Strait we fell in with whales again and spent the rest of the season in the Strait or among the South Shetland Islands which lie on its west side. I can still remember most of them, Clarence and Elephant Island to the north, King George Island with Penguin Island on its east side. Penguin Island is baking hot all the time, snow never lies on it, just melts as it falls. Livingstone Island, Low and Snow Island, two pinnacles called Hells Gates and Smith Island at the south end, a massive sliver of rock sticking out of the sea, several thousand feet high, many miles long but perhaps only a mile or so wide. When approached from the northwest it looks like a stack, not an island at all. Finally there was Deception Island lying in the Strait, the rim of a dormant volcano, a huge ring of rock with a harbour inside about seven miles long and three miles wide. It was called Deception on account of the entrance which is very narrow and almost hidden with a steep cliff on one side and a boulder beach on the other. The wreck of our sister ship, the *Southern Hunter*, was lying half submerged on that beach. She had gone too close on the shallow side, caught and buckled her propeller, grounded and could not be salvaged. In the middle of Deception Harbour the water is 90 fathoms deep. You have to go many miles offshore from Deception before you find 90 fathoms again. The 90 fathom hole is the throat of the dormant volcano. Ashore there are hot mudholes and sulphur springs along the beach but as far as I know the main part has not erupted in modern times.

While we were fishing in the Bransfield Strait the weather grew steadily colder, winter was closing in. At night, in calm weather, the sea would freeze. Little patches of ice the size of a fifty pence piece would appear then they would amalgamate to about the size of a pancake, hence the term 'pancake ice', and would continue to grow. When stopping for the night warnings were laid on the watch to be vigilant and call the Mates immediately if ice started to build up. It did not seem possible that ice could build up to danger point in a matter of hours but Willie assured me that some years earlier they had been further south at the end of the season, in similar conditions. One night the man on watch fell asleep and didn't call his relief. The relief woke eventually by himself, went up to investigate and found ice level with the after deck. They were able to get way on her and break out but it was a close shave.

Finally when we were back north near Elephant Island, the season finished. "Stopp Fangst" was the message from the factory. Immediately a course was plotted for South Georgia and we were on our way. About this time it was announced that there would be just a skeleton crew at Leith Harbour for the winter and all catchers including spare catchers from South Georgia would be steamed home to Norway. Crews were being made up for the spare catchers and we were to lose Willie Watt and his watchmate Kaare Jensen who were to go on the *Southern Star*. Rocky Kibble, our Asdicman, and myself would be acting-AB for the voyage home. That suited both of us fine. We would have plenty to do and would be working normal whaleboat watches, four-on four-off during the day and six-on six-off at night. This meant four hours overtime per weekday, eight hours Saturday and twelve hours Sunday.

Once back at Leith Harbour, we cleared away our whaling gear and made ready for the voyage home. One night some of us went ashore for the final film show in the Kino, Leith Harbour Cinema. The film was, appropriately enough, The Vikings starring Kirk Douglas. I thought the whole thing a bit far fetched and didn't stay till the end. With female company I'm sure I would have enjoyed it, but sitting there with Dougie Ritchie and Kaare Jensen, there was something missing. They felt the same so we went to the clearance sale at the Leith Harbour Slop Chest instead.

The *Harper* was nominated to spend a couple of days fishing for penguin food before leaving for home. Boxes were put aboard and extra hands armed with handlines and rippers came from the *Venturer* to assist us. Most of them were Norwegians whom I did not know but among them was Bill Mouatt from Scalloway whom I knew well. "Aalwis laekit a day at da haandline" was how Bill put it. We fished outside along a kelpfield till the wind took up and we drifted too fast, then dropped a grapple over a lump of kelp, heaved it aboard and made fast to it. This worked well till the wind increased again and the kelp tore away. After that we moved into the bays and on the afternoon of the second day we had caught our 'quota'.

Salvesens ships had, for many years, taken home penguins for Edinburgh Zoo and this was to be the final consignment. We delivered the fish and the extra hands back to the *Venturer*, tied up alongside, had some of our catch for supper, then cast off and started for home. Rocky had been allocated to go on Geordie's watch and I went on with Geordie's former watch-mate, Trygve Torskangerpoll. Trygve and I had the eight to two that night and the scene coming out of Leith Harbour will stay with me all my life. The bay was flat calm, the moon was crystal clear above the snowy peaks while the high cliffs and the waters below were inky black. There was no sound save the swish from our bow and the gasp and sob of the steam engine at half speed. You wished the moment would last forever. Almost everyone was on deck and some of the old hands had a tear in their eye. This was the final farewell to a place that some of them had known for most of their working lives. Soon the dream was shattered, we cleared the entrance and met a fresh northwester and a sharp swell. It was oilskin time, hoods up and mittens on, homeward bound at last.

The voyage home was fairly peaceful. After a few days the Roaring Forties ran out of breath, the sea calmed, beards came off, haircuts all round, and the fine weather gear got an airing. We rigged an awning over the open bridge to give ourselves some shade at the wheel and started cleaning, painting and acquiring a suntan to take home.

We proceeded at 'most economical speed' all the way to the Line. The *Venturer* had sailed several days after us so we jogged along until she caught up. By the time she arrived we were low on bunkers but arrangements had been made for us to bunker under way. There were no fender whales now and anyway the factory did not intend stopping. Bunkering on the end of a spring on the 'wrong' side of the factory was not as satisfactory as the way it was done at the ice but we did it twice, once at the Line and a second time off the Portuguese coast. That time the heavy luggage belonging to the UK personnel was put aboard the factory as she was bound for Liverpool. We were to fly home from Norway so one holdall per man was our allocation. On completing the second bunker, we put on speed and left the Venturer behind. The *Southern Actor* and us kept company for the rest of the voyage.

An interesting thing happened in the English Channel. Off Dungeness we found ourselves closing a cable laying operation and had to make a sharp course alteration. The Gunner picked up the bridge microphone which was connected to the Marconi Seamew R/T in the radioroom and made several calls to the *Actor* which was about 2 miles astern but got no response. He assumed that something was wrong at our end, took the wheel and asked me to go down and call them on the Transarctic, our main transmitter.

After a while we got a reply. He had answered on the Seamew but we hadn't heard him so he had had to start up his Transarctic as well. It was amazing, we knew the Seamew was low powered but in the clear air of the

Antarctic we could normally communicate eighty to a hundred miles, sometimes more. Such was the electronic pollution around the coasts of Northern Europe that two miles was out of range.

On the morning of 11th May 1962 we sighted Southern Norway and soon were sailing towards Oslofjord. We branched off into Tonsberg fjord and, following a thundery downpour off Tjome, tied up in bright sunshine at the village of Melsomvik, just south of Tonsberg, 42 days from Leith Harbour. The trees were bright green along the shore, birds were singing and many of our shipmates' friends and family were on the quay to welcome them. The 2nd Mate, Arne Nilsen, belonged to Onsoy on the east side of Oslofjord. His two brothers had come across in the family fishing boats, a pair of fortyfooters called the *Trygve* and *Bolinda* to meet him and take him home. A bus arrived on the quay to take the UK personnel to overnight accommodation. All that remained was to shake hands with departing shipmates and say, "Takk for sesongen" and "Har det bra, du." We were signing off, 7 months and 2 days from joining the *Southern Venturer* at South Shields.

We said goodbye to the little ship that had been our home and had carried us safely over many thousands of miles. It was to be almost 30 years before we saw her again. In 1990 she docked at Lerwick as the purse seiner *Karahav*, owned and operated by a family from Havoysund, near Norway's North Cape. She was back again in 1995 and finally met her end in 1998 when she grounded during a blizzard in the Northern fjords. The crew were rescued and a salvage arranged. When she was towed off she rolled over and sank in deep water. No further salvage was possible. She had fished whales in the Antarctic for the first 10 years of her life, then converted from steam to diesel, she had fished capelin and herring in the Arctic and North Atlantic for over 30 years and been very successful at both jobs. They built sturdy little ships in Middlesborough!

TOM JOHNSTON

On leaving school at 15, the whaling seemed attractive as two of the local young men from West Burrafirth, Gibbie Fraser and John Laurenson, were already there.

I wrote to Salvesen and got a reply saying that owing to the fact that the whaling was nearly finishing they were sorry but there were no vacancies. Seeing my disappointment, my father contacted Addie Manson from Brae who had been Bosun on the *Southern Harvester*. He invited us to visit him and have a talk. He had finished with the whaling but he was willing to enquire on my behalf. I later got a letter from Salvesen to say a position was available on the whale catcher *Southern Broom*. I was very excited. This was the catcher Gibbie had done several seasons on, although he was not going that year. He came along with a photograph of the vessel and explained things to me for which I was very grateful.

When it was time to leave I travelled down to South Shields with whaler Tammie Nicolson from Aith, to join the factory ship the *Southern Venturer*. My first position was Deck/messboy. After a month's travelling we arrived at Leith Harbour, South Georgia. I joined the *Southern Broom*, a catcher for the *Southern Venturer*. She had already been painted and overhauled by the men who had stayed down during the winter.

The cook, the other mess boy and myself had to unpack all the galley and messroom equipment and stores. The night before we were due to sail the gunner lost part of his thumb in a door and was taken to the factory ship for medical attention. We sailed next day without him. The Chief Mate was to act as gunner but he found this difficult so the catcher's position was changed to temporary buoy boat towing whales to the factory ship from other catchers.

When the gunner Asbjorn Andersen returned to the *Southern Broom* we went back to being a full catcher again. He proved to be one of the top men at his job. Half way through the season the *Southern Gambler*, which had previously been on hire to a firm in Southern Peru, joined the fleet. I was then transferred to this catcher which was to act as buoy boat but to me it wasn't as exciting as being on an active catcher. This wasn't such a good vessel either, it was full of cockroaches. I remained on her till the end of the season.

When the season finished all the catchers stocked up. Their crews stayed aboard and took them back to Norway to be overhauled. That year the

Southern Venturer was sold and we flew home from Norway.

Later on during the year I was surprised to get a letter from Salvesen offering me a position on the catcher the *Southern Harper*, a buoy boat to the factory ship, the *Southern Harvester*. I joined her in Norway along with two other Shetlanders, Andrew Arthur and Billy Ramsay. We set out for South Georgia. Halfway through the season the ex-corvette, the *Southern Lotus* was chasing a whale. An error was made by the junior engineer. Instead of stopping the engine before going Full Astern, he went from Full Ahead to Full Astern and the crankshaft was sheered off. The catcher, out of action, had to be towed to Leith Harbour.

The next best catcher was the one I was on, the *Harper*, as she still had her asdic in working order for tracking whales underwater. We returned to Leith Harbour as well to hand over our vessel to the *Lotus* crew. We transferred to an older catcher, the *Southern Foster*, where I spent the remainder of the season.

Coming back to Leith Harbour once again, we were told we would be joining the *Lotus* to be towed by the factory ship back to Norway. A lot of preparation was made to get chains and heavy wires for the tow. The chain was in the middle of the wires to weigh it down in the water to prevent it pulling tight between the catcher and factory ship during the tow. We set out trusting the men had done a good job, it was a long journey ahead. Approximately a day out of harbour we hit horrific weather. Owing to the weight of the wires and chains the catcher couldn't get her bow up over the waves so we were pulled through the middle of them. This caused considerable damage to the vessel, bursting doors, flooding the galley and messroom taking some of the cooking equipment with it and smashing our dishes. As a 17 year old it was a very frightening experience for me, as everyone was concerned that if the tow lines parted we were at the mercy of the sea with no engine. Owing to the rough seas I was feeling very ill and home seemed a long way away. No food could be cooked but with the conditions no one felt like eating.

After a few days the storm died down and it was a case of mopping and tidying up what was left. The remainder of the journey was successful and we arrived safely in Norway proving the men had done a good job on the tow lines.

That was the end of Salvesen's whaling times. I enjoyed my time spent there and found it all memorable. I stayed with Salvesen and joined their Merchant fleet for several more years.

GLOSSARY

a steer...a mess
almark ....renegade sheep
bonxies..arctic skuas
barder ....baleen from whale's mouth
braw ....good
caa...to drive sheep
clewed up..finished
clined ....spread
crappin ....dish made with fish livers
cru ....enclosure for sheep
doose ....fall with a thud
dreech..dreary
fit eatch ....adze
gawpen..handful
geo ....sea inlet
grices...pigs
hairst ....autumn
kye ....cattle
moorit...natural brown
peerie ....small
pirls ....animal droppings
plantie crub ....small drystone enclosure
reeslin...struggling
skerries...offshore rocks
spewings ....vomit
sprootin' tatties ....taking sprouts off potatoes

Gibbie Fraser was born in 1942 and left school at fifteen. With not much work available in Shetland at that time and an undying interest in boats, he wrote to Salvesen in Leith for a job at the whaling and was rewarded with a position on one of their top whale catchers, *Southern Broom*. Life on a whale boat could be uncomfortable but it was also exciting, challenging and at times dangerous but it was a great way of life for a young man.